16.95
-15%

D1077732

)n 6/98

Intro

for E

Introductory Statistics for Environmentalists

Paul Moore
and
John Cobby

 Prentice Hall Europe

London   New York   Toronto   Sydney   Tokyo   Singapore
Madrid   Mexico City   Munich   Paris

First published 1998 by
Prentice Hall Europe
Campus 400, Maylands Avenue
Hemel Hempstead
Hertfordshire, HP2 7EZ
A division of
Simon & Schuster International Group

Typeset in 10/12pt Garamond
by Alden Bookset, Oxford

Printed and bound in Great Britain by
TJ International Ltd

Library of Congress Cataloging-in-Publication Data

Moore, Paul.
    Introductory statistics for environmentalists / Paul Moore and
  John Cobby
      p. cm.
  Includes bibliographical references and index.
  ISBN 0–13–121807–7
  1. Statistics. I. Cobby, John. II. Title.
QA276.12.M664 1997
519.5′024′333—dc21   97-41465
                                                       CIP

British Library Cataloguing in Publication Data

A catalogue record for this book is available from the British Library

ISBN 0-13-121807-7

1 2 3 4 5   02 01 00 99 98

Contents

Preface

This book grew out of our experiences in teaching introductory statistics courses to first-year students at the University of the West of England. Students on courses such as the BSc Environmental Quality and Resource Management, the BSc Environmental Science and the BSc Geography and Environmental Management degrees, wanted a companion text to help reinforce the material covered in their first-year statistics courses. Although a number of excellent introductory statistics textbooks exist, we found none that introduced statistical concepts by considering environmental examples. The best we could suggest to students tended to be either general texts with examples from a range of fields, or books aimed at geographers or biologists. We firmly believe that students pick up statistical ideas more clearly if they see these ideas related to problems which they will meet at university and in their subsequent careers. We hope that this book will better meet the needs of students who wish to understand the uses of statistics in relation to the environment.

The majority of the examples and exercises in this text relate to real-life data. This we believe is important if the reader is to appreciate the true power of statistical methods in the environmental sciences. We are indebted to the MINITAB corporation for allowing the use of many interesting datasets, and also to the controller of Her Majesty's Stationery Office for permission to use data taken from *The UK Environment*.

Coverage and text organization

Our experiences suggest that many introductory courses in statistics throughout the country are increasingly focusing on the appreciation of analysis techniques and the interpretation of results. The coverage and content of this text is consistent with this trend. Although students are led through the necessary numerical calculations, great emphasis is put on the subsequent interpretation of the results. We have also recognized that statistics is increasingly taught in conjunction with suitable software packages. Throughout the text, references have been made to the role that spreadsheet packages such as EXCEL (version 5 for Windows) and statistical packages such as MINITAB (version 10 Xtra for Windows) can play in the analysis of data.

This text contains twelve chapters, which could form the basis of an introductory statistics course lasting between one semester and one year, depending on the detail of the coverage.

Chapter 1 is short and should be read by all readers as it summarizes the role that statistics plays to all scientists interested in the environment.

Chapter 2 is necessary only for students who are interested to learn of the possibilities that EXCEL and MINITAB offer for data analysis. If you do not intend to use a software package, or are already familiar with a suitable software package, this chapter may be omitted.

The first section of Chapter 3 should be read before any of Chapters 4 to 10, as it outlines the forms of data encountered. The remainder of the chapter is in our opinion best considered early, but the material may be left until a little later in some courses.

We would recommend that Chapters 4 to 8 be studied sequentially, as the material of each chapter builds empirically upon the material from previous chapters. The remainder of the text could be considered in a variety of sequences to suit the particular needs of the student.

Paul Moore and John Cobby
Summer 1996

1 Introduction: Statistics and the environment

1.1 Good intentions/poor scientific method: an example

The environment affects every one of us, and every one of us is responsible for ensuring that the environment we leave behind us is fit for our sons and daughters. Difficult decisions will have to be made to ensure a sustainable future. These decisions cannot be based upon political expediency, nor upon the prophesies of non-scientific doomsday environmentalists. Instead, these decisions must be reached through consideration of improved environmental data and research. Good intentions are an important start, but the environmentalist who wants to play his or her part in ensuring a sustainable future **must** gain an appreciation of the fundamentals of scientific research, including the statistical analysis of data.

1.1 Good intentions/poor scientific method: an example

The authors of this book regularly help students with the analysis of data relating to dissertations that they produce in their final year. One student carried out a survey relating to public attitudes towards the environment. One finding quoted in a draft chapter was that:

> *this study shows that 70% of the public would be willing to pay more VAT on petrol to help reduce exhaust emissions.*

This finding looked very interesting so I probed the student for more information. Firstly, I asked how large the sample size was. **Thirty** was the reply. At this juncture I pointed out that the 70% should really be quoted with a margin of error, in this case the population estimate could reasonably be within 16% either side of the 70% estimate, i.e. $70 \pm 16\%$, and only then if the sample was truly random. When I enquired as to the likely randomness of the sample I found that nearly all of his sample came from colleagues at the university, most of them from an environmental degree course. I pointed out that students on an environmental degree course were hardly representative of the British population when it came to their views on environmental matters.

To his credit, the student concerned took on board my comments, and through a 'crash course' in estimation from samples, managed to produce a very creditable dissertation.

This student later told me that this was the first time statistics had made sense to him, and seemed useful, because the problem he was dealing with was 'real and of direct interest'.

The authors of this text have endeavoured to make the examples in this book 'real and of direct interest' to the reader. We hope that this text will help the reader to work for a better environment by gaining an understanding of a number of statistical methodologies, and an appreciation of the power, and limitations, of statistics.

2 Computational aids: Calculators and software packages

2.1 Introduction
2.2 A primer in EXCEL 5.0 for Windows
2.3 A primer in MINITAB 10 Xtra for Windows

2.1 Introduction

In this text a wide variety of analysis techniques are considered. The required calculations can at times become laborious, particularly if large datasets are being dealt with. It is beneficial to let modern technology help with the 'number crunching' side of things so that the researcher can concentrate more effort on the practical interpretation of the results. The reader, of course, should realize that software packages will usually produce an answer to a calculation, or carry out a hypothesis test, even if the calculation or test being carried out is totally inappropriate, given the nature of the data.

The computational aids that the reader is most likely to use are calculators, spreadsheet packages, and statistical software packages.

1. **Calculators**

   Students embarking on a course of study would be well advised to purchase a reasonable calculator. The authors would suggest that a calculator with a standard deviation mode (sometimes called a Stats mode by some manufacturers) would be a wise investment. These start at around £5.00. For a few pounds more a calculator with a linear regression mode can be purchased. This is very useful when studying Chapter 10 of this text. The authors believe that, for most students, this would be the best compromise between calculator functionality, ease of use, and price.

   More sophisticated calculators with graphics capabilities can be useful at times, but only purchase one of these if you have the time and inclination to find out exactly how it works. Many students we teach have the best calculators on the market, but cannot carry out simple tasks with them because of their complexity.

2. **Spreadsheet packages**

   A spreadsheet is a computerized version of the ledger book, which has been used by generations of accountants. For a number of years these packages have been very useful for drawing graphs and for the calculation of basic summary statistics. In recent years a number of spreadsheet packages have introduced the ability to carry out a wide range of statistical procedures which were previously only available with specialized statistical software packages.

   Some of the most common spreadsheet packages that the reader is likely to meet include EXCEL, LOTUS 1-2-3, SUPERCALC and QUATTRO PRO. In this text a number of references will be made to EXCEL 5.0 for Windows.

3. **Statistical software packages**

   A number of statistical software packages exist, most of which would allow the reader to carry out any of the methods discussed in this text, and usually much more besides. Any environmentalist who wishes to carry out statistical analysis of their data would be well advised to become competent with at least one statistical software package. Some of the packages that are used most frequently include MINITAB, SPSS and SAS. In this text a number of references will be made to MINITAB 10 Xtra for Windows.

In the sections that follow brief overviews of EXCEL 5.0 and MINITAB 10 Xtra are provided. Both packages are very user friendly if the user is accustomed to using Windows-based software.

2.2 A primer in EXCEL 5.0 for Windows

Exhibit 2.1 shows a typical EXCEL 5.0 screen display. The key features of the screen display are as follows:

1. **The worksheet window**

   This displays the area where data is entered into the spreadsheet. There are many more rows and columns than can be shown in the screen at once. In order to view other areas of the worksheet you can click with a mouse on the **scroll bars**. In Exhibit 2.1 the user has typed in data relating to the levels of the pesticide DDT found in 27 Falcons in a field study.

2. **The menu bar**

   The majority of operations to the spreadsheet are carried out by selecting one of the nine options from the menu bar. For example to open, save, or print a spreadsheet, the relevant menu is obtained by selecting the **File** option from the menu bar.

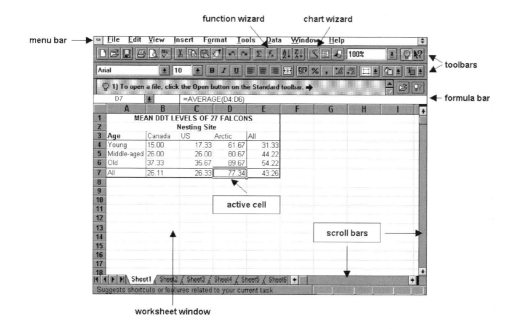

Exhibit 2.1 A typical EXCEL screen

Readers of this text will be particularly interested in the range of statistical procedures that EXCEL 5.0 can carry out. These statistical procedures can be viewed and chosen by selecting the **Tools** option, followed by **Data Analysis**. The resulting menu is shown in Exhibit 2.2.

3. **The formula bar**
This bar displays the current cell address of the active cell, as well as the contents of this cell.

4. **Toolbars**
Many of the facilities provided with EXCEL can be accessed quickly with these toolbar icons. Two of the tools that are the most useful in terms of this text are the **function wizard** and the **chart wizard**.

EXCEL has many statistical functions which the **function wizard** makes easy to use. For example there are functions to do the following:
(a) Find the mean, standard deviation, minimum, and maximum of a set of data.
(b) Functions to carry out a chi-squared significance test.
(c) Functions to carry out a *t*-test.

The **chart wizard** allows the user to create handsome graphs and charts by following a simple step-by-step procedure.

5

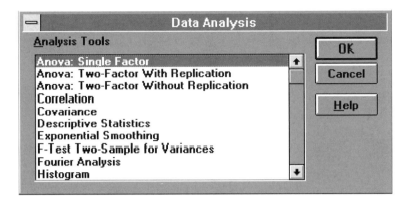

Exhibit 2.2 The **Data Analysis** option

For a thorough introduction to EXCEL we suggest that you consult a text specifically devoted to this subject. One excellent text to consider is:

> Murphy, J. (1995) *Using Microsoft EXCEL 5.0 for Windows*. Houghton Mifflin.

2.3 A primer in MINITAB 10 Xtra for Windows

MINITAB for Windows provides an excellent balance between ease of use and power. Virtually every analysis technique covered in this text can be carried out with this package, yet it is still easy to use.

Exhibit 2.3 shows a typical MINITAB screen layout. The key features of the screen display are as follows:

1. **The data window**
    This is the place where data can be manually entered and edited. In Exhibit 2.3 data relating to the global concentrations of CFC-12 and the thickness of the ozone column has been entered into the data window.

2. **The menu bar**
    As with EXCEL, the operations you wish to carry out on your data can all be found through menus relating to nine menu categories. For example, if you wish to save, print or retrieve a file, the relevant menu is obtained by selecting the **File** option from the menu bar.

    The statistical procedures and tests are available through menus obtained by selecting the **Stat** option from the menu bar. The **Graph** option will produce a menu showing the range of graphs that MINITAB can produce.

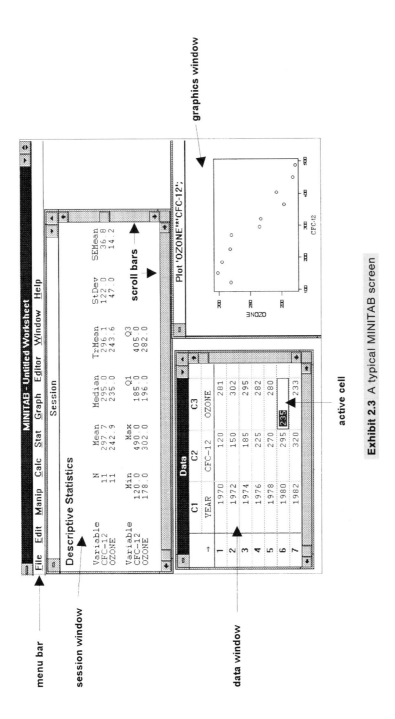

Exhibit 2.3 A typical MINITAB screen

The remaining menu bar options allow you to edit your data, transform your data and copy data or graphs into another application.

3. **The session window**

   Once you have carried out any analysis (other than graphs), the results are shown in the session window. These results can easily be browsed, saved or printed (using the **File** option).

4. **Graphics windows**

   If you produce any graphs, these are shown in another window called a graphics window. Once again, the contents of a graphics window can also be easily saved or printed.

For a thorough introduction to MINITAB for Windows we suggest that you consult a text specifically devoted to this subject. One very worthwhile text is:

Pelosi, M.R. (1995) *Doing Statistics with MINITAB for Windows Release 10*. John Wiley.

3

Obtaining environmental data:
Surveys and experiments

3.1   Introduction

Over the following chapters a whole host of powerful statistical ideas will be covered which will prove invaluable to us as environmentalists. Each technique is reliant upon the data used; so if the data is biased, so too will be any analysis based upon it. For this reason the key concepts behind effective data collection are to be covered **before** any methods of statistical analysis are considered.

3.1.1 Surveys and experiments, primary and secondary data

Suppose that an environmentalist is interested in the maximum amount of cadmium pollution allowable to sustain healthy salmon stocks. The environmentalist might decide to estimate the salmon stocks, and measure the cadmium levels in a number of waters to answer the question. This approach of taking nature as she stands is a **survey**. An alternative approach would be to purposefully contaminate some waters with predetermined levels of cadmium pollution and record the results on salmon life. When factors are artificially set like this by mankind, the approach is said to be an **experiment**. (In this case an experiment of dubious morality!)

In both cases the environmentalist has obtained the data personally, and this is then known as **primary data**. It is possible that if he or she had contacted the National Rivers Authority (NRA), similar data may already exist. When data is taken 'second hand' for such surveys it is known as **secondary data**. In general, secondary data is not usually in exactly the preferred form, but of course it is a lot less time consuming and less expensive to collect than primary data.

In this chapter we will firstly consider the types of data that are encountered (Section 3.2). We will then consider sources of secondary data (Section 3.3), survey methods (Section 3.4) and methods of experimental design (Section 3.5).

3.2 Forms of data

The science of statistics is concerned largely with extracting information from data. Table 3.1 shows a typical small dataset. The table shows a set of three measurements (tutorial groups, test marks and revision time) for four final-year environmental science students.

In statistical terminology we say that there are three **variables**, namely the tutorial group, test marks and revision time. The term *variable* reflects the fact that each measurement varies from one student to the next, and cannot be precisely predicted. The items upon which the variables are measured, in this case the students, are known as **observational units**.

3.2.1 Types of variable

The variables that are measured on an observational unit may be either **qualitative** (categorical) or **quantitative** in nature.

Qualitative variables reflect non-numeric attributes that an observational unit possesses. For example the tutorial group variable in Table 3.1 is a qualitative variable. Other examples include blood groups (A, B, AB, O) and sex (male or female). Sometimes the distinction is made between **ordinal** and **non-ordinal** qualitative variables, the difference being that ordinal qualitative variables have a meaningful rank order, for example, degree classifications are ordinal in nature (1st, 2(i), 2(ii), 3rd, Pass, Fail).

Quantitative variables are numeric measurements. Sometimes these measurements are made on a **discrete** scale where the variable can take only one of a certain

Table 3.1 The revision time and resulting scores of four environmental science students

Name	Tutorial group (A, B or C)	Test mark (out of 10)	Revision time
Jason Banks	A	8	180
Sue Curry	B	10	350
Ron Hill	C	7	210
Jill Smith	A	4	45

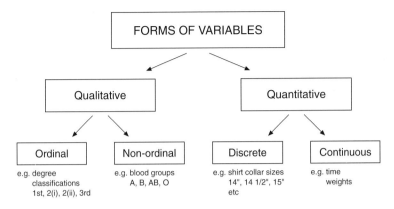

Figure 3.1 The different forms of data encountered.

number of definite and separate values. The test mark variable in Table 3.1 is an example of a discrete variable as students must score either 0 or 1 or 2... up to a maximum of 10 marks. (There is no necessity, however, for a discrete variable to have a fixed upper limit.)

Other quantitative variables are **continuous** in nature. This means that they are measured on continuous scales where the variable can take absolutely any value at all (although the range of possible values may be limited). An example of a continuous variable is the revision time variable from Table 3.1. Other examples of quantitative variables include the following:

- *discrete examples*
  - number of foxes in a litter
  - shirt collar sizes (this example shows that discrete variables are not always integers, shirt collar sizes go up in half inches)
- *continuous examples*
  - heights
  - weights

3.3   Sources of secondary data

You may be fortunate enough to find some data already in existence which meet your requirements. It is always worth thinking whether any agency, environmental organization or government department might hold the sort of data you are looking for. For example, if you require data relating to water quality in England and Wales, it would be sensible to contact the National Rivers Authority (NRA) to see if they have any relevant data they may give you access to, before embarking upon a costly study of your own. A great deal of data is published by the Office of National Statistics

(ONS) in the UK, and by commercial organizations world wide. These are held in most city libraries and libraries of educational establishments, and you can ask your librarian for the relevant indexes. Some particularly useful publications include the following:

Environmental Data Report (United Nations Environmental Programme)
State of the World (Earthscan Publications)
The UK Environment (HMSO)
Social Trends (HMSO)
Annual Abstracts (HMSO)
Monthly Digest (HMSO)

In recent years a number of computer databases have been introduced giving us access to a wealth of data, and one such database is the 'Harvest' database which has a commercial slant. New databases are being compiled all the time, so again, ask your local librarian if there is a database that might cover your needs. You may also find data by carrying out a search on the World Wide Web.

Despite your best efforts at data searching, the data you want may not actually exist. If this is the case don't be disheartened, look on the bright side, it may mean that your study is breaking new ground. The following sections will help you to collect your data effectively.

3.4   Survey methods

Much of statistics is concerned with making **inferences** about a **population** by considering a **sample** from the population. For example, if we want to determine the average age of Canadian spruce trees in a forest we would not carry out ageing tests on all the trees in the forest. Instead we might take a sample of 100 trees, estimate the average age of these trees, and hope that our results are representative of the forest as a whole.

In statistical terminology, the population is the group of items about which we wish to make inferences, and in this case all the Canadian spruce trees in the forest constitute the population. The sample is the group of items in the population that were selected to make measurements upon, and in this case the sample consists of 100 trees. Finally, the items in the population upon which the measurements are made are known by statisticians as **observational units**, and in this example the experimental units were trees.

When carrying out a survey (or as we shall see later, an experiment), the general aim is to select a number of **observational units** from the population to form a **sample**. This sample needs to be representative of the population as a whole, but also needs to be chosen such that the cost in terms of finances, time and environmental damage are reasonable. A number of well-used sampling methodologies are outlined in the next few pages.

3.4.1 Categories of sampling methods

Sampling methods can be grouped into two classes: **probabilistic sampling methods** and **non-probabilistic sampling methods**.

If a list of all the members of a population can be compiled, then it is possible to find the probability of any member of the population being included in the sample. Methods where this is possible are known as **probabilistic sampling methods**; the list is known as the **sampling frame.** As an example, if we take a probabilistic sample of voters and use the electoral register as the sampling frame, the probability of, say, Jim Smith being included in the sample could be calculated.

Other sampling strategies do not use a sampling frame. As an example, if a sample of North Sea cod was required in order to test the fish for fungal disease, the sample would be **non-probabilistic.** We have no list of all the cod in the sea and the chance of a particular fish being selected cannot be precisely calculated!

We shall discuss some of the more important sampling methods, as shown below, in the following section.

- *Probabilistic methods*
  Simple random samples
  Stratified random samples
  Multi-stage samples

- *Non-probabilistic methods*
  Quota samples
  Systematic samples
  Judgemental samples

3.4.2 Simple random samples

The idea of a random sample is *the* most important concept in sampling theory. It simply means that each member of the population has an equal chance of being selected for the sample, and that the inclusion or exclusion of one member of the population has no effect upon whether other members of the population are included in the sample or not.

As an example, consider the first two columns of Table 3.2, which shows the final year examination marks of ten final year Environmental Studies students. If we wanted a random sample of four examination scripts for the external moderator to look at, we could simply write the ten names on pieces of paper, put them into a hat, and pull out four names. This would constitute a random sample.

If the population to be sampled was very large then this procedure could be time wasting, and a large hat would be needed! Instead we would use **random numbers** to dictate the sample. The method here would be to allocate a number to denote each student. Numbers are then selected at random and the appropriate students from the randomly selected numbers form the sample.

Table 3.2   The final year marks of 10 final year environmental science students

Student	Mark	Allocated digits
Bill	62	0
Sue	52	1
Gary	46	2
Gina	59	3
Shireen	67	4
Neil	51	5
Geoff	48	6
Natasha	40	7
Ahmed	62	8
Emma	58	9

As an example, we could allocate the digit 0 to Bill, 1 to Sue, etc., as shown in the final column of Table 3.2. We then choose digits from 0 to 9 at random. This **does not** mean think of a number off the top of your head; truly random numbers should be obtained from a set such as those shown in Table B9 in Appendix B. If we use the first few digits on the first row of Table B9 we obtain the following sample:

	6 2 8 2 5
Digit	*Student*
6	Geoff
2	Gary
8	Ahmed
2	Gary (already selected, ignore)
5	Neil

So our sample consists of Geoff, Gary, Ahmed and Neil.

Note: *Do not get into the habit of always starting to use the random number tables from the first digit; it was only done this way here for the ease of the reader.*

Electronic sources of random digits

Tables of random digits are no longer used as often as they were, because random digits can now be obtained from most good scientific calculators, spreadsheet packages and statistical software packages. For example, random digits can be obtained by using the **RAND( )** function in EXCEL, or the menu sequence **Calc, Random Data, Uniform** in MINITAB for Windows.

3.4.3 The stratified random sample

You may have noticed that the random sample we took from Table 3.2 consisted of all male students, even though the population included half female and half male.

This is a drawback with the random sample; sometimes, by a fluke, particular groups are underrepresented or overrepresented when a proportional mix might be preferred. The **stratified random sample** overcomes this problem by ensuring that various sub-groups within a population are represented in the correct proportions within the sample. So, again referring to Table 3.2, we might decide to select four students at random, but choose them such that two must be male and two female. A typical selection procedure, using the second set of 5 random digits from Table B9 would be as follows:

Random number	Student
6	Geoff
5	Neil
1	Sue
2	Ahmed (Ignore, we have two males)
9	Emma

So the stratified sample consists of

Males:	Geoff, Neil
Females	Sue, Emma

This form of sampling has two advantages over random sampling. Firstly, the overall accuracy obtained from the sample is improved and, secondly, information is found from subgroups on the population as well as the population as a whole. This could be useful if the external moderator wanted to check for any evidence of 'gender bias' in the examination marks.

3.4.4 The multi-stage sample

Supposing you want to visit and question 200 sixth-form students to ascertain their knowledge of the greenhouse effect. You could:

- write to all educational authority in the country to obtain lists of schools and then write to each school for a list of students and hence compile a list of all sixth-form students;
- randomly select 200 of the students;
- visit each of the 200 students.

This procedure would be time consuming and costly. You might well end up with one student in Aberdeen, another in Penzance, one in Aberystwyth, and so on. An alternative approach would be to select the sample as follows.

1. Randomly select five educational authorities.
2. From each educational authority select four schools.
3. From each school select 10 students.

15

The students selected in this **multi-stage** sample would be a lot easier to visit, being from just 20 schools from just five areas of the UK.

The information obtained from such a multi-stage sample would not be quite as precise as estimates obtained from a random sample, but the loss of accuracy would be fairly small in comparison to the gain in practicality.

3.4.5 Quota samples

If you have ever been stopped in the street to answer questions on which washing powder you buy, or which radio station you listen to, you were probably selected for a **quota sample**.

The general idea of quota sampling is similar to that employed in taking a stratified sample. For instance, if a sample of 100 people is to be taken to determine radio-listening habits, approximate proportions of the sample are predetermined to come from different subgroups of society. Such a sample might consist of the following:

Grouping	Number needed
Males aged 15–19	10
Males aged 20–39	18
Males aged 40 or over	22
Females aged 15–19	10
Females aged 20–39	18
Females aged 40 or over	22
	100

Quota sampling differs from stratified sampling in that the sample is not selected in a truly random fashion. Typically, as part of the sample, an interviewer will take the first ten males they encounter aged between 15 and 19 years, so any males in this age range who pass by later in the day will not be considered for selection.

Interview bias can be a serious problem with these samples. For example, how many interviewers would select a youth in the 15–19 age bracket who was obviously drunk!

Despite these limitations, quota samples are still widely used by major research companies, particularly where a great deal of accuracy is not paramount, due to the ease of carrying them out. (In fairness, it should be pointed out that most reputable market research companies train their interviewers to reduce the risk of bias mentioned earlier becoming too serious.)

3.4.6 Systematic samples

With the systematic sample every kth item is selected to form the sample, where k is chosen so as to provide a suitably sized sample. As an example, supposing a sample of 100 users of a multi-storey car park is required to answer questions relating to traffic congestion in a large city. A suitable procedure might be to establish the typical daily usage of the car park (for the sake of argument we will assume 1000 vehicles per day). A systematic sample could now be found by selecting the driver of every 10th car leaving the exit gate.

In general, k can be chosen from the formula

$k = N/n$

> (with k rounded down to the nearest whole number if the result is a fraction)

where n = required sample size

N = population size.

The benefit of the **systematic sample** over the random sample is that a sampling frame is not needed. In the previous example a random sample would have required a list of all the car drivers using the car park (or at least a list of the cars driven by them) from which a random sample could be selected. This would be a messy business with cars constantly entering and leaving the car park. The downside to the systematic sample is that the procedure is **not random** and sometimes great care must be taken to avoid bias.

Bias can creep in when the items being sampled exhibit some kind of predictability. For example, if exhaust pipes from a production line were to be tested for legality it is possible that a systematic sample of every 10th exhaust pipe might well produce pipes all welded by one welder because of the nature of the mass production process.

Systematic samples of course can be used when a sampling frame is available, by selecting every 10th item from a list, but as such a sample is not truly random it is really preferable to use a truly random sample if such a sampling frame does exist.

3.4.7 Judgemental samples

Occasionally, expert knowledge and judgement has to take a leading role in selecting samples. For example, if an estimated count of dolphins around the British coast is required, there would be little point in trying to estimate the population at randomly selected areas around the coast of Britain. Such a sample might well indicate a population of zero dolphins. Instead, some expert knowledge must be used so that the count is carried out in areas where dolphins are likely to be found, such as the Cardiganshire coast in West Wales. Samples carried out in such a way are known as **judgemental samples**.

General notes regarding survey methods

1. In general use a probabilistic sampling method wherever possible. This allows the likely accuracy of sample results to be expressed mathematically (see Chapter 7).

17

2. Take care to estimate any possible bias in your sample.
3. Many techniques in this text, and much of statistical theory, assumes that data comes from random samples, so if you are still not sure what a random sample is, read this section again.

3.4.8 Computer-generated random samples

Many spreadsheet packages and statistical software packages provide facilities which help to select samples. For example, MINITAB for Windows can select a **simple random sample**. The required menu selections are:

Calc, Random Data, Sample From Columns

The EXCEL spreadsheet package can select **simple random samples** and **systematic samples**. The sampling facility is accessed by selecting

Options, Data Analysis, followed by **Sampling**

3.5 The design of experiments

Supposing a local council has decided that all its vehicles must have a catalytic converter fitted so as to reduce the amount of greenhouse gases emitted into the atmosphere. There are two possible suppliers of catalytic converters: they could use converters produced by either 'Cleanair Pipes' or 'Nonox Emissions'. How should the council determine the best system to purchase?

A simple (flawed) possibility

A simple approach would be to fit a 'Cleanair Pipe' system to one vehicle, a 'Nonox Emissions' system to another vehicle and then to check the best system by measuring the emissions from the two vehicles. However, this approach is seriously flawed. In fact it is **impossible** to test whether one system performs significantly better than another from a single measurement of each system.

3.5.1 A completely randomized design

The simplest experimental design is the completely randomized design. This could be used to assist with the council's problem regarding the choice of catalytic converter to use. The approach would be as follows.

Take a truly random sample of all the council vehicles and fit the selected vehicles with catalytic converters made by 'Cleanair Pipes'; similarly, take a truly random sample of the remaining vehicles and fit them with converters made by 'Nonox Emissions'. (*Note*: Often the number of vehicles fitted with each form of converter would be equal, but this is not essential.)

If we had five converters of each type available for the experiment, the result of CO_2 emissions per hour might look like the following:

Cleanair Pipes	Nonox Emissions
1.3	0.8
1.4	1.6
1.1	2.2
0.8	1.3
2.1	5.2

In statistical terminology the two forms of catalytic converters are known as the two **treatments**, with each treatment having five **replicates**. In Chapters 8 and 9 the analysis of data collected from completely randomized experiments such as this will be considered. Of course the same design principle can be extended to cater for experiments concerning more than two treatments, and the analysis of data of this format is discussed in Chapter 10.

3.5.2 The randomized block design

We might have been unlucky with the complex random experiment used earlier. It is possible that by a fluke of randomization, the 'Cleanair Pipes' product was used four times on large dustcarts whereas the 'Nonox Emissions' product was not used on such vehicles. Clearly the results of such an experiment could be misleading as the effectiveness of the catalytic converters is bound to vary from one type of vehicle to another. A better experimental design would ensure that each of the catalytic converters was used on similar vehicles. In this way the two converters could be compared on a fair basis. For example, we could test each converter on dustcarts and on road maintenance vehicles, lightweight vans, saloon cars and estate cars. As with the completely randomized experiment, the vehicles from each category are selected using a true randomization technique. The collected data for such an experiment might look like that shown in Table 3.3.

Table 3.3 CO_2 emissions (per hour)		
Vehicle	Cleanair Pipes	Nonox Emissions
Dustcart	1.3	1.3
Transit van	1.1	1.1
Ford Sierra estate	0.8	0.7
Ford Sierra saloon	0.7	0.8
Mercedes van	1.2	1.8

As with the completely randomized design we again have two treatments, each with five replicates. The vehicles used are known by statisticians as **blocks**. This is a throwback to the earlier days of experimental design where blocks were usually blocks of land used in agricultural experiments.

The idea of blocking can, of course, be extended to experiments with more than two treatments.

The analysis of data from randomized block experiments is covered in Chapters 8, 9 and 10.

Exercises 3

Exercise 3.1

Briefly define the following terms (refer back to the chapter if any of the definitions are not yet clear to you):

(a) Population
(b) Sample
(c) Observational units
(d) Random sampling
(e) Stratified random sampling
(f) Systematic sampling
(g) Multi-stage sampling
(h) Judgemental sampling
(i) Quota sampling
(j) Completely randomized experiments
(k) Randomized block experiments

Exercise 3.2

Give an example of each of the following:

(a) A continuous quantitative variable
(b) A discrete quantitative variable
(c) An ordinal qualitative variable
(d) A non-ordinal qualitative variable

Exercise 3.3

An environmental analysis research establishment has won a prestigious contract which will necessitate 10 members of staff working in Florida for 12 months. Twenty equally suitable members of staff have volunteered to go to Florida, and a sample of 10 of these employees is to be taken to determine who is to work on the Florida contract. The following list shows brief details regarding the 20 volunteers:

Name	Sex	Job grade	Years of service
Abrahams, C.	Female	Senior scientific officer	20
Barnes, N.	Male	Higher scientific officer	5
Cornwall, K.	Female	Scientific officer	10

Davies, J.	Female	Higher scientific officer	4
Dixon, K.	Male	Senior scientific officer	15
Gallier, P.	Male	Scientific officer	4
Hughes, D.	Female	Scientific officer	6
Khimji, A.	Male	Senior scientific officer	10
Lawes, A.	Female	Senior scientific officer	12
Moore, P.	Male	Higher scientific officer	4
Oliver, R.	Female	Scientific officer	2
Patel, I.	Female	Higher scientific officer	10
Rhodes, M.	Male	Scientific officer	1
Storey, M.	Male	Higher scientific officer	2
Thomas, K.	Female	Scientific officer	3
Tovey, T.	Female	Higher scientific officer	8
Underwood, R.	Male	Higher scientific officer	7
Wakefield, R.	Female	Scientific officer	8
Wiseman, K.	Female	Scientific officer	11
Younis, E.	Female	Higher scientific officer	14

(a) Use the following random numbers to obtain a **simple random sample** of 10 employees from the list of 20 volunteers:

34, 20, 18, 06, 98, 11, 14, 60, 12, 11, 76, 05, 50, 08, 10, 41, 13, 88, 01, 03

(b) Select a **systematic sample** of 10 employees from the list
(c) The employees are a mixture of males and females, and are also employed on a range of job grades. Taking the workforce of the research establishment as a whole, the breakdown of employees according to their sex and job grade can be summarized as follows:

	Male	Female
Scientific officer	10%	30%
Higher scientific officer	20%	20%
Senior scientific officer	10%	10%

(i) Explain the benefits of selecting a stratified sample of employees to send to Florida.
(ii) Explain how you would choose a suitable stratified sample of 10 employees. You should state exactly how many employees of each stratum should be selected.

Exercise 3.4

Many software packages will select random samples of data very easily. If you have access to MINITAB, EXCEL, or another suitable package, investigate how this package could select a random sample of the employees from Exercise 3.3.

Exercises 3.5 to 3.9 are discussion type questions. As is the case with most real-life problems there is not necessarily a definitive correct solution to each problem, different approaches have merits and drawbacks according to the resources available and the necessary level of accuracy required from the data obtained. These exercises are best used as discussion questions for small groups of students.

Exercise 3.5

Consideration is being made to upgrade a small airport to a major international airport. A survey is to be carried out to obtain the opinions of people who are likely to be affected (say people who live within 15 miles of the airport). How would you obtain a sample of 800 respondents?

Exercise 3.6

100 mud specimens are required from the beach at a West country holiday resort, in order to assess the levels of harmful substances. How would you choose your sample?

Exercise 3.7

A sample of the audience at a local theatre is required in order to gauge their views regarding ticket prices. How would you obtain a sample of 200 members of a particular audience?

Exercise 3.8

An environmental awareness group is going to carry out a survey to determine the level of support that the group holds among undergraduates. How could a sample of 2,000 students in higher education be selected?

Exercise 3.9

As part of a study of energy conservation, it was decided to measure the heat loss from houses with (i) single-glazed windows and (ii) double-glazed windows. Houses on a 1980s housing estate were chosen for the experiment as a number of nearly identical houses could be easily identified, some of which had the original single-glazed windows, others of which had replacement double-glazed windows. It is also known that some of the houses in the area have loft insulation, while others do not.

Explain how you would collect the experimental data. (In terms of the experimental design, technical explanations of how the heat loss is measured are not required.)

4

Data presentation techniques

4.1 Introduction

Environmental experiments and field studies often produce reams of raw data. It is usually impossible to make much sense of this data merely by scanning it. However, if a little time is invested in presenting the data through appropriate tables or diagrams, the key features of the data often stand out.

In this chapter a number of data presentation techniques will be introduced. These methods are simple yet invaluable, as they enable the environmentalist to effectively present information to an audience, and they also provide clues as to what further analysis of the data is most appropriate.

4.2 The tabular presentation of data

A list of raw data conveys very little information. For example, the data below relates to a field exercise in Somerset, where the number of sparrows' nests per hectare were counted for each of 36 hectares.

1	0	0	2	1	1
1	0	1	1	2	0
0	1	4	2	1	0
1	1	0	1	0	1
3	0	1	1	2	1
0	1	2	3	1	1

Table 4.1   **A frequency distribution table for the number of sparrows' nests per hectare**

Number of sparrows' nests	Tally	Number of hectares
0	++++ ++++	10
1	++++ ++++ ++++ ///	18
2	++++	5
3	//	2
4	/	1

Data such as this conveys little to the reader. A carefully constructed table is invariably far more informative. In this section the appropriate forms of data tabulation for qualitative and quantitative data will be presented.

4.2.1 *The frequency distribution*

The data introduced above, concerning the number of sparrows' nests in each of 36 hectares, is far more digestible when presented in the form of a **frequency distribution**, as shown in Table 4.1.

The frequency distribution was formed by working through the raw data, systematically, and keeping a tally of the number of fields containing a given number of nests. It shows at a glance the number of one-hectare areas containing no nests, one nest, two nests and so on. Clearly, the most common scenario is for a one-hectare area to contain one nest, plenty of one hectare areas contain no nests at all, and relatively few hectares contain more than one nest. This is as we might expect, given the territorial nature of sparrows.

In statistical language the number of sparrows' nests per hectare is the **variable**, and the number of fields containing the given number of nests is the **frequency** of the variable taking a particular value. In this example the variable is a **discrete variable**, the only possibilities for the number of nests per hectare were 0, 1, 2, 3 . . . .

In our example all the possible values of a variable were listed, with the frequencies written alongside. In general, this is only possible for discrete variables, and categorical variables; frequency distributions such as this are often known as **ungrouped frequency distributions**. The reason for this terminology will become clear after considering the **grouped frequency distribution**.

It is worth while pointing out that if a graphical presentation of an ungrouped frequency distribution is required, the appropriate diagram is the **bar chart**, as discussed in Section 4.3.

4.2.2 *The grouped frequency distribution*

When dealing with continuous data it is impossible to list all the possible values that a variable might take, so the simple ungrouped frequency distribution cannot be used.

Instead we must form ranges of possible values of a variable, and count the frequencies of a variable taking a value within a particular range. The methods employed are best explained by consideration of an example.

Example 4.1

When considering the ecology of an estuarine environment, it is important to consider the nature of the sediment in the estuary. One important feature of the sediment is its size, as the particle size partly determines the speed at which erosion and deposition take place.

The following data relates to the particle sizes (µm) of 37 grains from a sample of sediment from the Severn estuary (by kind permission of Dr D. Case, University of the West of England).

8.2	6.3	6.8	6.4	8.1	6.3
5.3	7.0	6.8	7.2	7.2	7.1
5.2	5.3	5.4	6.3	5.5	6.0
5.5	5.1	4.5	4.2	4.3	5.1
4.3	5.8	4.3	5.7	4.4	4.1
4.2	4.8	3.8	3.8	4.1	4.0
4.0					

It would be useful to form a grouped frequency distribution for the particle sizes of the 37 grains, so as to 'get a feel' for the distribution of particle sizes.

Method

The smallest particle in the sample was 3.8 µm, and the largest 8.2 µm. We need to define convenient **classes** which cover all values between these extremes, and usually these are best chosen to be of equal width. Table 4.2 shows a frequency distribution for this data, where six classes, each with a **class interval** of 1.0 µm, have been used. Having defined the classes, the frequencies of particles with sizes within each class have been counted with the aid of a tally, as with the ungrouped frequency distribution example seen earlier.

Table 4.2 **Frequency distribution for the size of particles collected from the Severn estuary**

Particle size (µm)	Tally	Frequency
3.0 to under 4.0	//	2
4.0 to under 5.0	//// //// //	12
5.0 to under 6.0	//// ////	10
6.0 to under 7.0	//// //	7
7.0 to under 8.0	////	4
8.0 to under 9.0	//	2

This frequency distribution in Table 4.2 allows us to appreciate that the particles tend to lie between 4.0 and 6.0 µm, with few particles being smaller than this, and particles larger than 6.0 µm accounting for about a third of the particles.

In geological terminology, particles between 2 and 6 µm are defined as fine silt, with particles between 6 and 20 µm being defined as medium silt. So our sample could best be described as fine/medium silt.

4.2.3 Notes regarding the choice of class intervals, and the graphical presentation of a grouped frequency distribution

In Example 4.1 the classes were chosen to be of equal width. Usually this is the best scheme to adopt. There are, of course, times when unequal class widths are more sensible. For example, Table 4.4 shows the number of cases of meningitis in England and Wales during 1989. As this disease predominantly affects children, it makes sense to use more detailed class divisions for the younger members of the population. It is also preferable to keep the number of classes to a manageable level, more than a dozen classes are rarely necessary.

Finally, if a graphical representation of the information from a grouped frequency distribution is required, the appropriate chart is the **histogram**, which is discussed in Section 4.3.

4.2.4 Stem-and-leaf displays

One drawback with forming a grouped frequency distribution, as in Table 4.2, is that the original data values are not recorded and are hence lost to us. An alternative display of the data which is gaining popularity is the **stem-and-leaf display**.

To demonstrate how this display works we'll reconsider the data introduced in Example 4.2. You'll remember that this concerned the measurements of particles collected from the Severn estuary.

All data values from 3.0 to 3.9 have the same **stem** of 3. The first decimal point which varies from observation to observation is the **leaf**, so a value of 3.8 has a stem of 3, and a leaf of 0.8. The first two values in the list of data are 8.2 and 6.3, which would be shown on a stem-and-leaf display as follows:

Stem	Leaf
8.	2
6.	3

Using this procedure, the data is worked through systematically to create the following stem-and-leaf display:

3.	8 8
4.	5 2 3 3 3 4 1 2 8 1 0 0
5.	3 2 3 4 5 5 1 1 8 7
6.	3 8 4 3 8 3 0
7.	0 2 2 1
8.	2 1

You may notice that, apart from showing the actual data values, the stem-and-leaf display also shows the general shape of the distribution. These two properties make stem-and-leaf displays particularly useful when exploring data.

Useful extensions to the standard stem-and-leaf include showing the leaves in increasing order of magnitude, and showing two stem-and-leaf displays back to back. These ideas are shown in Example 4.2.

Example 4.2

As part of a recent pollution study, the levels of SO_2 (ppm) in the atmosphere were measured for two sites in the Bristol area. Readings, which were obtained for two sites over a 24 hour period, are shown below:

Site 1 (near city centre)						Site 2 (in the rural outskirts of Bristol)					
29	35	31	40	24	23	32	15	17	21	23	41
38	50	31	62	20	25	33	12	16	24	20	35
41	21	21	38	63	27	27	16	42	26	23	19
38	25	45	34	30	43	20	19	34	11	22	23

Use a suitable stem-and-leaf display to present this data effectively.

Method

By forming a **back-to-back** stem-and-leaf display the distribution of SO_2 for both sites can be viewed simultaneously. This allows us to immediately see that although there is a good deal of overlap in the SO_2 levels, the SO_2 levels recorded in the city centre site do tend to be a little higher than in the rural site.

Table 4.3   Distribution of hourly SO_2 levels for two sites in the Bristol area

City centre site		Rural outskirts site
	1	1 2 5 6 6 7 9 9
9 7 5 5 4 3 1 1 0	2	0 0 1 2 3 3 3 4 6 7
8 8 8 5 4 1 1 0	3	2 3 4 5
5 3 1 0	4	1 2
0	5	
3 2	6	

In this example the stems represent tens of units, and the leaves represent units. So a stem of 2 and a leaf of 1, represents the number 21. This example was chosen especially so that the reader realizes that stem-and-leaf displays can use any suitable units of measurement!

It is also worth while pointing out that Table 4.3 shows the leaves for both sites in ascending order of magnitude, with the smallest values shown closest to the stem. This is a good habit to get into, as it makes life easier when we study measures such as the **median** and **quartiles** in Chapter 5.

4.2.5 The cumulative frequency distribution

When dealing with the data shown in Table 4.4, it might be useful to be able to see at a glance how many cases of meningitis were recorded in the under 5's, or in the under 15's. This type of information is provided simply by constructing a **cumulative frequency distribution**.

Table 4.4   Cases of meningitis (all forms), in England and Wales (1989),
by age

Age	Number of cases
Under 1 year	673
1 to under 2 years	354
2 to under 3 years	193
3 to under 4 years	129
4 to under 5 years	79
5 to under 10 years	204
10 to under 15 years	144
15 to under 25 years	345
Over 25 years	552
	2,673

(Source: *Communicable Disease Statistics (1989)*, table 4, p. 24. HMSO.)

Looking at Table 4.4 we see that 673 cases were reported in children aged
under 1 year; 354 cases were reported in the 1 to under 2 years class, so in all
$354 + 673 = 1,027$ cases were recorded in children under 2 years of age. Similarly,
the total number of cases in the under 3's is found by adding 1,027 and 193, giving
a total of 1,220. Continuing this procedure produces the cumulative frequency distribution shown in Table 4.5.

As with many distributions obtained from published sources, the distribution
shown in Table 4.4 provides a problem in that the final age category is quoted as
>25, with no upper boundary being stated. When this occurs the best we can do is
use common sense along with a knowledge of the subject area to estimate an upper
boundary. In this case the age of 110 was chosen as very few people live beyond
this age; it is quite likely, however, that the real upper boundary would be quite a
few years younger than this.

It is commonplace for percentage cumulative frequencies to be used instead of the
cumulative frequencies, or sometimes both are shown, as they are in Table 4.5.

Percentage cumulative frequencies will be seen to be particularly useful when we
look at how data can be summarized in Chapter 5.

Table 4.5   Number of meningitis cases in England and Wales (1989) in people
younger than the stated age

Age	Cumulative frequency	Percentage cumulative frequency
1	673	25.18%
2	1,027	38.42%
3	1,220	45.64%
4	1,349	50.47%
5	1,428	53.42%
10	1,632	61.05%
15	1,776	66.44%
25	2,121	79.35%
110	2,673	100.00%

4.2.6 Tables

The frequency distributions covered so far are fine for presenting data relating to one measured variable. However, if two or more variables are measured on an observation it is often more revealing to consider more than one variable at a time. The following example illustrates the point.

Example 4.3

The following data was collected as part of a study carried out to investigate the effects of the pesticide DDT on falcons. Birds from three nesting areas (USA, Canada and the Arctic), and of three age categories (young, middle aged or old), were captured, and their DDT levels recorded.

Investigate the distribution of DDT levels in the birds, paying attention to whether birds of particular ages, from particular nesting areas, or from particular age/nesting area combinations, tend to have high levels of DDT.

Bird ref.	DDT level	Nesting area	Age
1	19	USA	Young
2	17	USA	Young
3	16	USA	Young
4	16	Canada	Young
5	13	Canada	Young
6	16	Canada	Young
7	74	Arctic	Young
8	69	Arctic	Young
9	72	Arctic	Young
10	25	USA	Middle aged
11	24	USA	Middle aged
12	29	USA	Middle aged
13	28	Canada	Middle aged
14	24	Canada	Middle aged
15	26	Canada	Middle aged
16	82	Arctic	Middle aged
17	80	Arctic	Middle aged
18	80	Arctic	Middle aged
19	34	USA	Old
20	37	USA	Old
21	36	USA	Old
22	36	Canada	Old
23	39	Canada	Old
24	37	Canada	Old
25	91	Arctic	Old
26	88	Arctic	Old
27	90	Arctic	Old

(*Source:* MINITAB example file Falcon.mtw.)

Method

A simple first step to investigate the DDT levels would be to form a frequency distribution as shown in Table 4.6.

Table 4.6   The DDT levels of 27 falcons in an experiment

DDT levels	Tally	Number of birds
Under 30	++++ ++++ //	12
30 to under 60	++++ /	6
60 to under 90	++++ //	7
Greater than 90	//	2

This frequency distribution seems to indicate that the most common situation is for a falcon to have a DDT level below 30. A number of birds have levels between 30 and 90, and only a small minority have DDT levels in excess of 90. This could be taken as suggesting that high DDT levels are unusual, and hence there is little to worry about.

If we now tabulate the data according to the DDT levels **and** the nesting area, a much more revealing pattern emerges. It is evident that **all** the birds nesting in the Arctic region had DDT levels in excess of 60, whereas **no** birds nesting from the US or Canadian nesting sites had DDT levels as high as 60. Hence, there can be seen to be a particular DDT problem with birds nesting in the Arctic region.

Table 4.7   DDT levels of falcons in a study by nesting area

DDT level	Arctic	Canada	USA	Total
		Nesting site		
Under 30	0	6	6	12
30 to under 60	0	3	3	6
60 to under 90	7	0	0	7
90 or greater	2	0	0	2
Total	9	9	9	27

As a final step we could go further and tabulate the data according to the nesting areas **and** the age of the birds, as shown in Table 4.8. This table again shows that birds nesting in the Arctic have high DDT levels; it also shows that older birds from any nesting area tend to have higher DDT levels than younger birds from the same nesting area. This is pretty much as we might expect as DDT levels build up over a bird's lifetime.

Table 4.8   DDT levels of 27 falcons in a study from three nesting areas (Arctic, Canada and USA) by age

DDT level	Arctic			Canada			USA			Total
	y	ma	o	y	ma	o	y	ma	o	
Under 30	0	0	0	3	3	0	3	3	0	12
30 to under 60	0	0	0	0	0	3	0	0	3	6
60 to under 90	3	3	1	0	0	0	0	0	0	7
90 or over	0	0	2	0	0	0	0	0	0	2
Total	3	3	3	3	3	3	3	3	3	27

Note: The codes 'y', 'ma', and 'o' refer to young, middle-aged and old birds respectively.

Example 4.3 highlights how effective a well thought out table can be. In order to create a useful table it is worth bearing the following points in mind:

1. Always ensure that the categories of the table cover every possible case.
2. Provide detailed totals and subtotals.
3. Label rows and columns clearly, and provide a clear and concise title for the table.
4. It is rarely possible to produce anything more complicated than a three-way table without confusing the reader!

4.3   The pictorial presentation of data

To many people, information presented by even the best frequency distribution or table is hard to grasp. Gaining a feel for the data presented in such a way often demands a level of numeracy or concentration which the intended audience may not be willing or able to give.

A pictorial representation of data, on the other hand, is capable of transmitting information quickly and effectively, while demanding little of the audience. This is why advertisements, newspaper articles, and television news bulletins usually present numeric data pictorially. It is important that environmentalists collect some of the tools of the trade so that they too can present data effectively, especially when the data is for public consumption.

4.3.1 Bar charts

One of the simplest statistical diagrams is the **bar chart**. This is typically used to present the data from an **ungrouped frequency distribution** (which you'll remember relates to the frequencies of a **discrete** or **categorical** variable).

When used in such a manner the horizontal axis (x axis) represents the possible values of the variable being considered. Bars are then drawn with the heights representing the frequency with which the variable took a particular value. An example would be to draw a bar chart to represent the sparrows' nests data tabulated earlier in Table 4.1. Figure 4.1 shows this bar chart.

An alternative presentation of the same data would be to draw lines to represent the frequencies rather than bars. This produces the chart shown in Figure 4.2.

Bar charts are very versatile diagrams, and can be used to display more than just the data from an ungrouped frequency distribution. For example consider the data shown in Table 4.9. We can represent this data as shown in Figure 4.3. With this representation the horizontal axis represents the period of time over which the rainfall was measured, and the heights of the bars show the rainfall over each period. Rather than draw separate bar charts for England and Wales, and Scotland, two sets of bars

Number of hectares containing the given number of Sparrows' nests

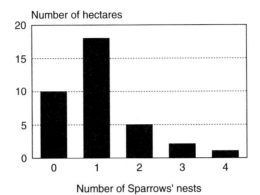

Figure 4.1 A bar chart representation of the frequency distribution shown in Table 4.1.

Number of hectares containing the given number of Sparrows' nests

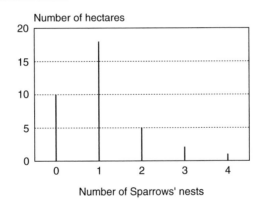

Figure 4.2 An alternative representation of the frequency distribution shown in Table 4.1.

Table 4.9   Total rainfall (mm), in England and Wales, and Scotland by quarter (1990)

		Rainfall	
Quarter	Period	England and Wales	Scotland
1	Jan.–March	298	791
2	April–June	135	278
3	July–Sept.	134	342
4	Oct.–Dec.	271	334

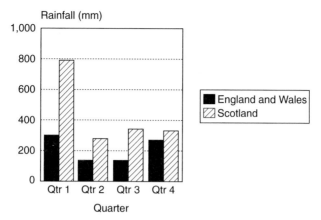

Figure 4.3 Total rainfall for England and Wales, and Scotland, by quarter (1990).

have been drawn on the same set of axes. This is an example of a **multiple bar chart**, which is a very useful presentation tool indeed.

An alternative method of showing the same data would be to form a **compound bar chart**, as shown in Figure 4.4.

With the compound bar chart, the bars for England and Wales and Scotland are drawn on top of each other rather than side by side. The height of the combined bars represents the total rainfall for England, Wales and Scotland for each quarter of 1990.

It should be pointed out that compound bar charts only make sense when the total height of the compound bars has a useful interpretation. In Figure 4.4 this was the case, as the total height of the compound bars represents the total rainfall

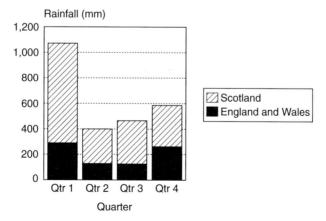

Figure 4.4 Total rainfall for the UK (excluding Northern Ireland), for the four quarters of 1990.

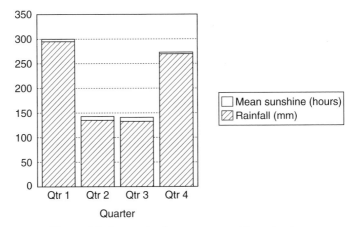

Figure 4.5 A meaningless compound bar chart.

over England, Wales and Scotland. On the other hand, Figure 4.5 shows a meaning-less example of a compound bar chart. The height of each bar relates to the sum of the rainfall in millimetres, and the average hours of sunshine for England and Wales.

4.3.2 Some golden rules relating to bar charts

When constructing a bar chart it is important to bear the following points in mind:

1. It is customary to leave spaces between each bar (or group of bars in the case of a multiple bar chart).
2. **Always** start the vertical axis at **zero**. Failure to do so can mislead the reader. In fact unscrupulous advertisers sometimes fail to do this to deliberately provide a false impression.

As an example of how a bar chart could be misleading, consider the two bar charts shown in Figure 4.6. It might seem from figure (a) that Burger's restaurants are rapidly moving towards recycled Burger cartons. However when the graph is plotted correctly in figure (b), the movement towards recycling doesn't seem nearly as impressive!

4.3.3 Histograms

Just as the bar chart can be used to present the information from an ungrouped frequency distribution, the histogram is used to present the information from a grouped frequency distribution. (You should remember that grouped frequency distributions relate to the frequencies of continuous variables.)

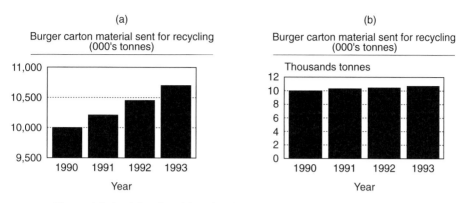

Figure 4.6 A misleading (a) and an honest (b) bar chart for the same data.

In Example 4.1 we produced a frequency distribution for the size of particles recovered from the Severn estuary. This distribution was as shown below:

Particle size (μm)	Frequency
3.0 to under 4.0	2
4.0 to under 5.0	12
5.0 to under 6.0	10
6.0 to under 7.0	7
7.0 to under 8.0	4
8.0 to under 9.0	2

The histogram shown in Figure 4.7 could be used to present the distribution of the particle sizes graphically. At first sight this histogram may look like some of the bar charts seen earlier, but in fact it is quite different.

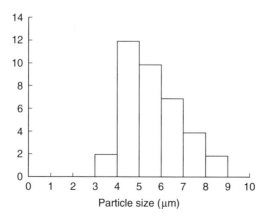

Figure 4.7 The distribution of the size of particles collected from the Severn estuary (microns).

The first thing you may notice is that the blocks are drawn adjoining each other with no spaces between them, which is always the case with histograms. In this example the data shown in Example 4.1 was recorded to one decimal place. Hence the class 3.0 to under 4.0 μm actually covers all particles measuring between 2.95 and 3.94999...μm. Similarly the 4.0 to under 5.0 μm class really covers all sizes from 3.95 to 4.94999...μm, and so on. So the classes cover a continuous range with no discontinuities between them. Likewise, the blocks representing each of these classes are drawn on a continuous horizontal axis, with no gaps between them. So, in this example the first block is drawn from 2.95 to 3.95, the second bar is drawn from 3.95 to 4.95, and so on.

In simple examples such as this, where all the group intervals are of equal widths, the histogram consists of blocks of equal width, with the heights being equal to the frequencies of observations lying within the intervals each block represents. However, **this is not** always the case.

Consider again the same set of data, but tabulated in a slightly different manner such that the last two categories, 7 to under 8 μm, and 8 to under 9 μm, are now merged into one category, 7 to under 9 μm. This gives rise to the following tabulation:

Particle size (μm)	Frequency
3.0 to under 4.0	2
4.0 to under 5.0	12
5.0 to under 6.0	10
6.0 to under 7.0	7
7.0 to under 9.0	6

If we were to draw a histogram for this data by making the height of each block equal to the frequencies, we would arrive at the graph shown in Figure 4.8. This histogram

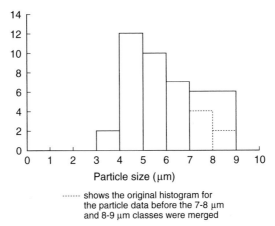

.... shows the original histogram for the particle data before the 7-8 μm and 8-9 μm classes were merged

Figure 4.8 An incorrect histogram for the particle size data with merged classes.

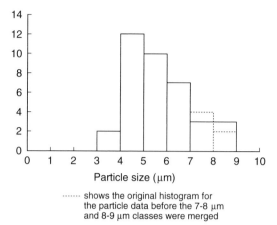

Particle size (μm)

------ shows the original histogram for
the particle data before the 7-8 μm
and 8-9 μm classes were merged

Figure 4.9 The correct histogram for the particle size data with merged classes.

would be very misleading as it gives the impression that particles in the range 7.0 to 9.0 μm are far more common than they actually are. Ideally the histogram for the frequency distribution with merged classes should be the same general shape as the original histogram, but with less detail. In this case the final block in the histogram is clearly too high.

In order to correct matters we must take into account that the last category, 7.0 to 9.0 μm, is twice as wide as all the others. If we did not know how many of the six observations within this class interval were in the ranges 7.0 to 8.0 μm and 8.0 to 9.0 μm, our best guess would have to be that three of the observations were in each grouping. Hence, the histogram that best approximates to the true situation would have a block drawn to a height of 3. This is shown clearly by Figure 4.9.

In general, if a class is twice as wide as the 'standard' class interval (see Example 4.4), then the block is drawn half as high as the frequency. Similarly, if a class is three times as wide as the standard class interval, the block is drawn one-third as high as the frequency, and so on.

You will have noticed that in all the histograms we have drawn so far the vertical axis has not been labelled. This is not a mistake! It is because the **shape** of the histogram is the important feature. The histograms drawn by two different people might have different vertical scales but will have the same general shape (see the discussion of **standard class intervals** in Example 4.3). It is customary **not** to label the vertical axis; in fact, the vertical axis itself is often omitted (see Example 4.4). (Of course if all the classes have the same width then the simple title **frequency** can be used on the vertical axis.)

Note: *It is possible to scale histograms such that the area of each block is equal to the proportion of observations within the class interval that the block represents.*

*The shape of histograms constructed this way is **identical** to those produced using the methods outlined in this chapter.*

Often the construction of a histogram requires a little thought, as the following example shows.

Example 4.4

The following data shows the number of notified cases of food poisoning in England and Wales during 1989. Represent this data in the form of a histogram.

Age	Number of cases
0 to 4	5,594
5 to 14	3,257
15 to 24	6,821
25 to 44	12,294
45 to 64	5,935
over 65	2,894

Method

1. **Tidy up the frequency distribution classes**
    We first need to clarify what the age ranges mean. For example, the 0 to 4 category includes all children aged under 5 years old, so a child aged 4 years 11 months and 28 days is classed as a 4-year-old. For the purposes of producing a histogram it is required to redefine the classes as 0 to under 5 years old, 5 years to under 15 years old, and so on.

    Secondly, the final category is shown as over 65 years of age. To draw a histogram we need an upper and lower limit for all classes. Open-ended classes such as this can be troublesome, the best solution is to use common sense, and a knowledge of the subject area to determine a reasonable upper limit for the class. In this case we could reasonably take an upper limit of around 110 years old as very few people live beyond this age.

    Finally, it is essential to note the width of each class, all of which gives rise to the following distribution:

Age	Class width	Frequency
0 to under 5	5	5,594
5 to under 15	10	3,257
15 to under 25	10	6,821
25 to under 45	20	12,294
45 to under 65	20	5,935
65 to under 110	45	2,894

2. **Choose a standard class interval**
    The widths of the above classes vary from 5 years to 45 years. We need to choose a standard width known as the **standard class interval**. Usually this interval is taken as being the class width which occurs most often, although absolutely any standard interval could be chosen. In this example we shall take 10 years as the standard class interval.

3. **Calculate the relative frequencies**
    The frequencies of food poisoning cases within each class cannot be compared as they stand because some of the class intervals are wider than others. To rectify this we find the frequencies relative to the standard class interval. For example, the 25 to under 45 class is of width 20 years

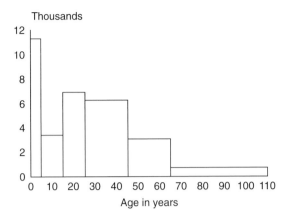

Figure 4.10 A histogram to show the age distribution of sufferers from food poisoning in the UK (1989).

while the standard class interval is 10 years, so the relative frequency is only half of the given frequency. In general:

$$\text{Relative frequency} = \text{Frequency} \times \frac{\text{Standard class interval}}{\text{Class interval}}$$

We can find the relative frequencies for all of the classes as shown below:

Age	Class width	Frequency	Relative frequency
0 to under 5	5	5,594	$5,594 \times (10/5) = 11,188.0$
5 to under 15	10	3,257	$3,257 \times (10/10) = 3,257.0$
15 to under 25	10	6,821	$6,821 \times (10/10) = 6,821.0$
25 to under 45	20	12,294	$12,294 \times (10/20) = 6,147.0$
45 to under 65	20	5,935	$5,935 \times (10/20) = 2,967.5$
65 to under 110	45	2,894	$2,894 \times (10/45) = 643.1$

4. **Draw the histogram**

Having calculated the relative frequencies, it is now a simple job to draw the histogram shown in Figure 4.10.

We said earlier that the vertical axis on a histogram was not particularly useful, apart from helping when drawing one. So we could draw the histogram in Figure 4.10 without a vertical axis, as shown in Figure 4.11.

4.3.4 Pie charts

The pie chart is used when we want to show how **constituent parts** make a **whole**. The general idea is that a circular pie is drawn to represent the whole, and appropriately sized slices of the pie show how large each constituent part of the whole is.

For example, we might want to show how the total energy production of the UK for 1991 was produced from solid fuels, electricity, petroleum and gas (Table 4.10).

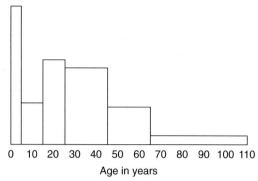

0 10 20 30 40 50 60 70 80 90 100 110

Age in years

Figure 4.11 An alternative histogram to show the age distribution of sufferers from food poisoning in the UK (1989).

Remembering from our schooldays that a circle has 360°, the slice representing solid fuel energy is drawn such that it accounts for a proportion of $5.44/60.45 = 0.09$ of the 360°. Similarly, the slice representing the contribution of electrical energy consumption accounts for 0.16 of the 360°, and so on. The calculations below show how the angle of each slice is arrived at.

Source	Production (10^9 therms)	Angle of slice
Solid fuel	5.44	$360° \times (5.44 \div 60.45) = 32.4°$
Electricity	9.67	$360° \times (9.67 \div 60.45) = 57.6°$
Petroleum	25.39	$360° \times (25.39 \div 60.45) = 151.2°$
Gas	19.95	$360° \times (19.95 \div 60.45) = 118.8°$

The resulting pie chart is shown in Figure 4.12.

Figure 4.13 uses two pie charts to show how the energy production characteristics of the UK changed between 1960 and 1991. In this time the use of solid fuel has fallen dramatically, leading to the closure of countless coalmining pits in recent years. You will notice that the slices on each pie chart are drawn in the same anticlockwise order from the 3 o'clock position and use identical shading patterns. This helps enormously when trying to compare two or more pie charts. You may also notice that Figure 4.13 shows the **percentage** of production by each energy source.

4.3.5 Other useful statistical diagrams

As you might expect, there are a number of useful statistical diagrams which have not been covered in this chapter. One particularly useful diagram which has not been discussed is the **scatter plot**. This will be discussed in Section 10.2.

Table 4.10 Energy production in the UK (10^9 therms) by source (1991)

Solid fuels	Electricity	Petroleum	Gas	Total
5.44	9.67	25.39	19.95	60.45

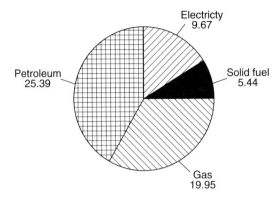

Figure 4.12 Energy production of the UK (10^9 therms), by source (1991).

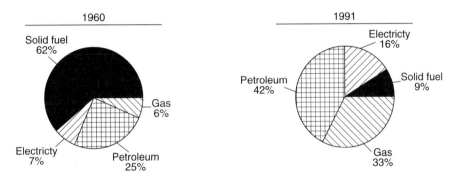

Figure 4.13 Percentage UK energy production by source, 1960 and 1991.

4.4 Data presentation with MINITAB and other software packages

Students often ask which software package is best for data presentation. There is no definitive answer to this question as different packages have different strengths and weaknesses. For example, MINITAB is one of the most widely used statistical packages, and EXCEL is one of the most popular spreadsheet packages, yet neither package alone is capable of presenting data in **all** the formats discussed in this chapter. In writing this chapter the authors used a mixture of EXCEL, MINITAB and a specialist package called HARVARD GRAPHICS.

As a rule, MINITAB is good for producing multi-way tables, stem-and-leaf displays, histograms and bar charts. In addition, MINITAB has the advantage of working well with raw data.

Spreadsheet packages such as EXCEL produce graphs of a superior visual quality to MINITAB, but will not readily produce a correct histogram, stem-and-leaf displays, or multi-way tables. In addition, before graphs are obtained the raw data often needs to be condensed to a tabular format.

The optimal solution is to be familiar with a statistical software package such as MINITAB **and** a spreadsheet package such as EXCEL!

Students should familiarize themselves with the data presentation facilities of the software they have available to them. A detailed discussion of the facilities offered by any particular software package is beyond the scope of this text. The following examples, however, illustrate some of the data presentation facilities offered by MINITAB for Windows and EXCEL.

4.4.1 Some MINITAB data presentations

Presentation 1: Tables with MINITAB

Refer back to the data introduced in Example 4.2, regarding the DDT levels of 27 falcons in an experiment. The data was typed into MINITAB as shown in Table 4.11.

Tables of this data can be obtained in MINITAB by using the selection sequence **Stat**, **Tables**, **Crosstabulation**.

This produces the menu shown in Exhibit 4.1, where the variables to be cross-tabulated can be specified.

For example, if the single variable **ddtcat** is selected, the following tabulation, which is equivalent to Table 4.6, is produced:

Table 4.11   DDT levels for 27 falcons

Column number	Column name	Contents	
c1	ddtcat	0 to under 30	– 1
		30 to under 60	– 2
		60 to under 90	– 3
		Over 90	– 4
c2	ddtlevel	ddt levels	
c3	site	Arctic	– 1
		Canada	– 2
		USA	– 3
c4	age	Young	– 1
		Middle aged	– 2
		Old	– 3

Note: Columns 1, 3 and 4 were **coded**. This means numbers were used to represent the possible values of categorical variables.

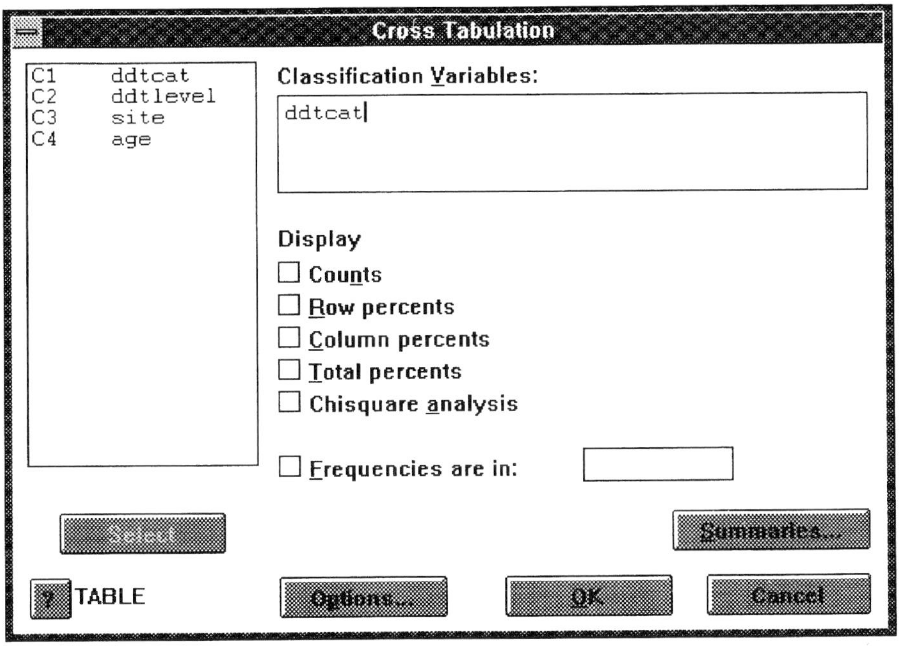

Exhibit 4.1 Cross-tabulation.

```
MTB > table c1
 ROWS: ddtcat

        COUNT

1        12
2         6
3         7
4         2
ALL      27
```

Similarly a two-way table equivalent to that shown in Table 4.7 can be produced by selecting the **ddtcat** and **site** variables.

```
MTB > table c1 c3
 ROWS: ddtcat        COLUMNS: site

             1        2        3      ALL

1            0        6        6       12
2            0        3        3        6
3            7        0        0        7
4            2        0        0        2
ALL          9        9        9       27

CELL CONTENTS -- COUNT
```

Presentation 2: Stem-and-leaf displays with MINITAB

Earlier, in Example 4.2, data relating to levels of SO_2 in urban and rural sites near Bristol was considered. The two sets of figures were typed into the first two columns of a MINITAB worksheet, and stem-and-leaf displays were produced by using the menu selection sequence:

Graph, Character Graphs, Stem-and-leaf

```
Stem-and-leaf of rural        N = 24
Leaf Unit = 1.0

        8    1 12566799
      (10)   2 0012333467
        6    3 2345
        2    4 12

Stem-and-leaf of city         N = 24
Leaf Unit = 1.0

        9    2 011345579
      (8)    3 01145888
        7    4 0135
        3    5 0
        2    6 23
```

The first column in the stem-and-leaf displays is not particularly useful to us at this stage, although it will be discussed and seen to be useful in Chapter 5. The first column apart, these stem-and-leafs are identical to those shown in Figure 4.3.

Presentation 3: Histograms with MINITAB

Referring to the same data as Example 4.2, we can obtain histograms to show the distribution of SO_2 levels for each site by using the menu selections:

Stat, Graphs, Histogram

The MINITAB histograms presented in Figures 4.14 and 4.15 show, respectively, SO_2 levels in one rural site, and one city centre site.

Note: *For MINITAB to produce correctly shaped histograms when unequal class widths are used, the histogram option* **frequency densities** *must be selected.*

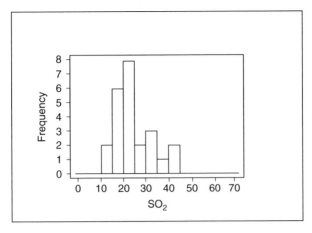

Figure 4.14 Rural site.

Presentation 4: Charts with EXCEL

EXCEL produces very smart graphs with relative ease. To do so the following procedure may be followed:

1. Highlight the region of the data of interest.
2. Select the **Chartwizard** icon.
3. Drag the Chartwizard icon into the highlighted region of data to be graphed.
4. Follow the step-by-step menus to produce the desired graph.

As an example, Figure 4.4 may be recreated by selecting the **Column** chart type, followed by option 5.

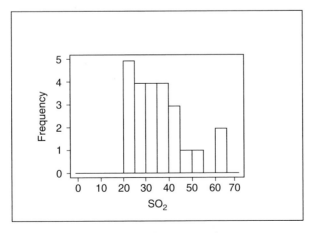

Figure 4.15 City centre site.

Exercises 4

Exercise 4.1

A road census was carried out to determine the level of traffic passing along a road which runs near a site of special scientific interest.

As part of the census, the number of vehicles passing by in one-minute intervals was counted, for each of the 30 one-minute intervals between 5.00 pm and 5.30 pm. The vehicle counts are shown below.

2	0	2	0	1	3
1	3	0	1	1	1
0	1	5	2	1	0
1	2	0	0	1	1
1	2	2	3	0	1

(a) Construct a frequency distribution to show the number of one-minute intervals with $0, 1, 2, \ldots, 5$ vehicles passing by.

(b) Present the information from your frequency distribution in the form of a bar chart.

Exercise 4.2

The following table shows the average concentrations of beta radiation (Bq/kg) in three species of fish in the Sellafield (off-shore) area from 1983 to 1991.

Species			
Year	Plaice	Cod	Whiting
1983	430	610	570
1984	320	420	480
1985	250	250	340
1986	170	240	270
1987	160	190	210
1988	130	190	170
1989	160	180	150
1990	130	190	170
1991	130	170	160

(a) The bar chart below was constructed by a student to show the above data pictorially. Why is this chart not appropriate?

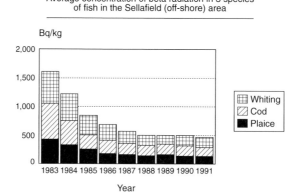

Average concentration of beta radiation in 3 species of fish in the Sellafield (off-shore) area

(b) Draw an appropriate chart to show the average beta radiation levels for all three species from 1983 until 1991.

Exercise 4.3

The national water council classify the quality of water into the following categories:

Class 1 Good quality
Class 2 Fair quality
Class 3 Poor quality
Class 4 Bad quality

The Westshire water region is subdivided into two subregions, North Westshire and South Westshire. Westshire water recently tested the quality of 26 rivers in the region, some of which were in North Westshire, the others being from South Westshire. The results of the testing were as follows:

River number	Sub-region	Water quality	River number	Sub-region	Water quality
1	North	2	14	South	2
2	North	1	15	South	1
3	North	1	16	South	1
4	North	3	17	South	2
5	North	1	18	South	1
6	North	2	19	South	3
7	North	4	20	South	1
8	North	1	21	South	2
9	North	1	22	South	1
10	North	2	23	South	1
11	North	1	24	South	1
12	North	2	25	South	1
13	South	1	26	South	2

(a) Produce a table to show clearly how many rivers from each of the two subregions are classified as good, fair, poor or bad.
(b) Draw pie charts to show the proportions of rivers classified in each of the four classifications, for both the Northern and Southern subregions.
(c) Construct a suitable bar chart to show the information from your table.

Exercise 4.4

The figures below show the percentage land use of the UK (1988). Show this data in the form of a pie chart.

Land use in the UK (1988)

Land use	Percentage of land
Arable and cropland	29%
Meadows and pasture	48%
Forests and woodland	10%
Other	13%

Source: The State of the World Environment, OECD (1991), Fig. 17, p. 96.

Exercise 4.5

Two recent field trips by environmental science students resulted in water samples being taken from different sections of the rivers Dee and Taff. Each water sample was analyzed, with the pH levels and nitrate concentrations being measured. The resulting data is shown below.

River Dee		River Taff	
pH	Nitrate (mg/lN)	pH	Nitrate (mg/lN)
7.4	1.86	7.9	1.40
7.3	1.98	8.0	1.20
7.1	1.96	8.0	1.42
7.6	2.04	7.8	1.48
7.5	1.88	7.8	1.48
7.1	1.66	7.9	1.45
7.7	1.32	8.0	1.44
7.4	2.11	8.0	1.41
7.3	1.68	8.2	1.90
7.6	1.69	7.9	1.65
7.6	1.58	7.8	1.63
7.7	1.37	7.9	1.67
7.6	1.91	8.0	1.33
7.5	1.65	8.0	1.93
7.6	1.35	8.0	1.71
7.5	1.53	7.9	1.50
7.6	1.74	7.8	1.52
7.6	1.79	8.0	1.34
7.4	1.94	7.9	1.57
		8.0	1.73

(a) Construct a back-to-back stem-and-leaf display to show the nitrate concentrations recorded for the water samples from the rivers Dee and Taff.

(b) Use your stem-and-leaf display to complete the tables below.

River Dee

Nitrate level	Frequency	Relative frequency
1.3 to under 1.5		
1.5 to under 1.7		
1.7 to under 1.9		
1.9 to under 2.2		

River Taff

Nitrate level	Frequency	Relative frequency
1.2 to under 1.4		
1.4 to under 1.6		
1.6 to under 1.8		
1.8 to under 2.0		

(c) Using the information from the tables above, draw histograms to show the distribution of nitrate concentrations for samples from the rivers Dee and Taff (two separate histograms, one for each river), and comment upon what they show.
Note: Use a standard class interval of 0.2 mg/lN for each histogram.

(d) **A tester:** Draw a histogram to show the distribution of pH levels recorded for samples from the river Dee.
Hint: All observations recorded as 7.1 actually refer to observations between 7.05 and 7.14999...

Exercise 4.6

In a woodland ecology study a transect of woodland was walked with measurements being made upon all trees and shrubs encountered on the transect line. As part of the study the girth of each tree (at 4 ft above ground level) was measured. The girth distribution for two of the most common trees encountered were as follows:

Girth size (mm)	Birch	Rowan
under 12.5	56	53
12.5 to under 25.0	31	4
25.0 to under 50.0	24	1
50.0 to under 75.0	0	0
75.0 to under 100.0	2	0
100.0 to under 125.0	1	0
over 125.0	0	0

Using a standard class interval of 25 mm, construct histograms to represent the girth size distributions for the two species. Comment upon what the histograms show.

Exercise 4.7

You should now be able to spot misleading diagrams, even when the data they portray is unavailable.
What could be misleading about the bar chart (a) and the histogram (b) shown below?

(a) Value of Ecologic Shares, 1990-1994

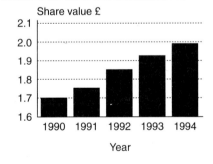

(b) Salaries of Ecologic Workforce (1994)

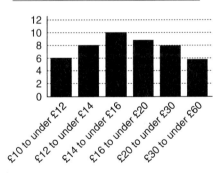

Exercise 4.8

Use MINITAB, or a similar statistical package to complete Exercise 4.1.

Exercise 4.9

Use MINITAB to carry out Exercise 4.3(a).

Exercise 4.10

Carry out Exercise 4.5(a), (c) and (d), using MINITAB or any other statistical software package.

Exercise 4.11

Experiment with a spreadsheet package such as EXCEL to see how easy it is to produce a graph. Once you have mastered the graphics, try drawing the graphs you drew earlier in the following exercises:

Exercise 4.1(b)
Exercise 4.2(b)
Exercise 4.3(b) and (c)
Exercise 4.4

5

Summarizing data numerically

5.1 Introduction
5.2 Measures of central tendency
5.3 Measures of dispersion
5.4 Examining the skewness of data
5.5 Aids to computing summary statistics
Exercises 5

5.1 Introduction

In Chapter 4 we saw how the key features of large datasets can be brought out by suitable methods of data presentation. It is usually a good idea to go a stage further and describe the key features of a set of data in **numerical** terms as well.

The data shown in Table 5.1 will be familiar to you if you tackled Exercise 4.5. This data is ideal for demonstrating many of the ideas in this chapter so it will be referred to regularly over the next few pages.

Exhibit 5.1 shows the data for Table 5.1 in the form of a dot plot (obtained from MINITAB). Dot plots are an alternative to histograms; they are particularly useful when comparing the distributions of two or more sets of data. Using the dot plot in Exhibit 5.1 it is clear that the pH levels recorded from specimens from the Taff tend to be higher than those recorded from the Dee, and also that the pH levels are more varied from the river Dee specimens than from the river Taff samples. The trouble is that Exhibit 5.1 does not enable us to be more precise and state *how much* higher the pH levels are from the Taff samples than the Dee samples, nor *how much* more variable the Dee samples were than the Taff samples. In order to do so we need:

1. A numerical measure of what constitutes a typical pH level for each river (i.e. an 'average'). Such measures are known as **measures of central tendency**.
2. A numerical measure of the variability in the pH levels recorded in samples from each river, known as **measures of dispersion** (or **measures of variability**).

Table 5.1   pH levels and nitrate concentrations (mg/l N) recorded in water specimens from the rivers Dee and Taff

River Dee		River Taff	
pH	Nitrate (mg/l N)	pH	Nitrates (mg/l N)
7.4	1.86	7.9	1.40
7.3	1.98	8.0	1.20
7.1	1.96	8.0	1.42
7.6	2.04	7.8	1.48
7.5	1.88	7.8	1.48
7.1	1.66	7.9	1.45
7.7	1.32	8.0	1.44
7.4	2.11	8.0	1.41
7.3	1.68	8.2	1.90
7.6	1.69	7.9	1.65
7.6	1.58	7.8	1.63
7.7	1.37	7.9	1.67
7.6	1.91	8.0	1.33
7.5	1.65	8.0	1.93
7.6	1.35	8.0	1.71
7.5	1.53	7.9	1.50
7.6	1.74	7.8	1.52
7.6	1.79	8.0	1.34
7.4	1.94	7.9	1.57
		8.0	1.73

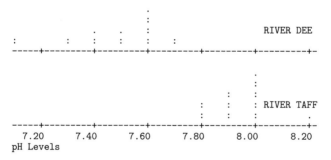

Exhibit 5.1 The distributions of pH levels from water specimens from the rivers Dee and Taff.

A wide variety of measures of central tendencies and measures of spread exist, and in this chapter a number of the most useful measures will be introduced, namely

- *measures of central tendency*
  - the mean
  - the median
  - the mode
- *measures of dispersion*
  - the range

- quartiles, and the interquartile range
- the variance
- the standard deviation
- the coefficient of variation

5.2 Measures of central tendency

A measure of central tendency is a guide to what constitutes a typical data value. In essence this section deals with what non-statisticians loosely refer to as 'averages'.

5.2.1 The arithmetic mean

This is probably the most familiar and important measure of central tendency. In its simplest form the arithmetic mean is

$$\frac{\text{The sum of all data values}}{\text{The number of data values}}$$

So the arithmetic mean of the values 4, 3, 6, 7 is

$$\frac{4+3+6+7}{4} = \frac{20}{4} = 5$$

The arithmetic mean is usually denoted by $\bar{x}$ and the formula for calculating the arithmetic mean can be written as:

$$\bar{x} = \frac{\sum x}{n}$$

(Equation 5.1)

where $\sum$ means the sum of, n stands for the number of data values and x represents an observation on the variable of interest.

Example 5.1

In an experiment the DDT levels of 9 falcons nesting in the United States were as follows.

19, 17, 16, 25, 24, 29, 34, 37, 36

Calculate the mean DDT level for these birds.

Solution

DDT level, x
19
17
16
25
24
29
34
37
36
$\overline{237}$

Therefore, the arithmetic mean is

$$\bar{x} = \frac{\sum x}{n} = \frac{237}{9} = 26.333$$

The mean of a frequency distribution

Often data is presented in the form of a frequency distribution, either grouped or ungrouped. For ungrouped data the exact mean can be found by using the formula

$$\bar{x} = \frac{\sum fx}{\sum f}$$ (**Equation 5.2**)

where f is the frequency of occurrences of the value x.

For grouped data the same formula is used, but as we don't know all the individual data values we obtain only an estimate of the true mean. Example 5.2 demonstrates how Equation 5.2 is used.

Example 5.2

Supposing the full data relating to the nitrate concentrations of the specimens from the river Dee were not available and, instead, only the frequency distribution below was supplied.

Nitrate concentration (mg/l N)	Number of specimens
1.3 to under 1.5	3
1.5 to under 1.7	6
1.7 to under 1.9	4
1.9 to under 2.1	5
2.1 to under 2.3	1

Estimate the mean nitrate concentration for the 19 specimens.

Solution

Nitrate concentration (mg/l N)	Midpoint, x	Number of specimens, f	fx
1.3 to under 1.5	1.4	3	$3 \times 1.4 = 4.2$
1.5 to under 1.7	1.6	6	$6 \times 1.6 = 9.6$
1.7 to under 1.9	1.8	4	$4 \times 1.8 = 7.2$
1.9 to under 2.1	2.0	5	$5 \times 2.0 = 10.0$
2.1 to under 2.3	2.2	1	$1 \times 2.2 = 2.2$
		$\sum f = 19$	$\sum fx = 33.2$

$$\bar{x} = \frac{33.2}{19} = 1.75$$

The mean nitrate concentration of the 19 specimens is estimated at 1.75 (mg/l N). (The reader might like to verify that this is very close to the true mean of 1.74 (mg/l N).

The mean is the most widely used measure of central tendency. The main reason for this is that it possesses nice mathematical features. The crucial point being that inferences about a population can be made from a sample arithmetic mean, and we shall discuss this in detail in Chapters 7 and 8.

The arithmetic mean, however, does have one major drawback: it can be heavily influenced by extreme data values. For example, the mean of the following wages

£15,000   £18,000   £17,000   £16,000   £65,000

is £26,250, but does this value really represent a 'typical' wage?

5.2.2 The median

Another measure of a 'typical' value is the 'middle value' known by statisticians as the **median**. For example, to find the median of the wages

£15,000   £18,000   £17,000   £16,000   £65,000

we put them in ascending order, and the middle wage in the list is the median:

£15,000   £16,000   **£17,000**   £18,000   £65,000

In this case the median is £17,000, which is more typical than the mean wage of £26,250.

Example 5.3 shows how the median can be calculated for a slightly more complex example.

Example 5.3

With reference to Table 5.1, find the median nitrate concentration for the 20 samples from the river Taff.

Solution

Neither the 10th nor the 11th value in ascending order will be exactly in the middle. The solution in such cases is to define the median as being the arithmetic mean of the middle two items.

To find the middle item(s) to calculate a median it is often useful to construct a stem-and-leaf display. We shall use this approach (read Section 4.4 if you have forgotten how to construct a stem-and-leaf display).

A stem-and-leaf display for the nitrate concentration (mg/l N) from the river Taff would be:

```
1.2  0
1.3  3  4
1.4  0  2  8  8  5  4  1
1.5  0  2  7
1.6  5  3  7
1.7  1  3
1.8
1.9  0  3
```

The 10th and 11th concentrations in ascending order are 1.48 and 1.50 respectively. Therefore the median nitrate concentration is

$$\frac{1.48 + 1.50}{2} = 1.49 \,(\text{mg/l N})$$

Estimating the median from a grouped frequency distribution

Consider Table 5.2. It shows the age distribution of meningitis sufferers for England and Wales in 1989. Meningitis is known to be, predominantly, a young person's disease, but what is the 'average' age of sufferers?

The median would be a reasonable measure to use, but there are two reasons why the approaches taken so far are inappropriate.

1. There are 2,673 cases. Finding the middle age, in order, of 2,673 cases would be very time consuming.

Table 5.2   The age distribution of meningitis sufferers for England and Wales (1989)

Age (years)		Number of cases
Under	1	673
1 to under	2	354
2 to under	3	193
3 to under	4	129
4 to under	5	79
5 to under	10	204
10 to under	15	144
15 to under	25	345
Over	25	552
		2,673

Table 5.3

Age (years)		Number of cases	Cumulative frequency	Percentage cumulative frequency
Under	1	673	673	25.18%
1 to under	2	354	1,027	38.47%
2 to under	3	193	1,220	45.64%
3 to under	4	129	1,349	50.47%
4 to under	5	79	1,428	53.47%
5 to under	10	204	1,632	61.05%
10 to under	15	144	1,776	66.44%
15 to under	25	345	2,121	79.35%
Over	25	552	2,673	100.00%
		2,678		

2. The ages of each case are not in fact given; instead only an age distribution is available, so ordering the ages is impossible.

When either or both of these problems occur the solution is to estimate the median through drawing an **ogive** or **cumulative frequency curve**.

For our example the cumulative frequencies and percentage cumulative frequencies are shown in Table 5.3 (re-read Section 4.2 if you cannot see where the figures come from).

We can see that 25.18% of cases were from children under 1 year of age, 38.47% of cases were from children under 2 years and so on. If we plot the percentage cumulative frequencies against the **upper class boundaries** of the age categories we obtain the **cumulative frequency curve** (sometimes known as an ogive) shown in Figure 5.1.

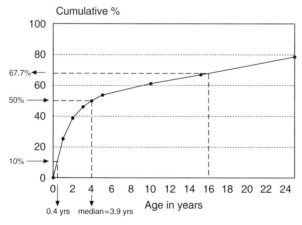

Figure 5.1 A cumulative frequency curve for the meningitis data shown in Table 5.3.

We can use the ogive in two ways. For example if we want to know what percentage of cases were children under 16 years of age, we can read off the value of around 67.7%. Alternatively we might want to estimate the age relating to the youngest 10% of cases, and in this event we would estimate that 10% of the cases were in children aged under 0.4 years of age.

The median age, of course, is the halfway age of all the cases, represented by the 50% cumulative frequency. From the graph the median age can be seen to be around 3.90 years.

5.2.3 The mode

The final measure of location to be considered is the **mode**. This is simply the most frequently occurring value, as demonstrated by Example 5.4.

Example 5.4

The data below show the number of sparrows' nests per hectare for 3.6 hectares of farmland. (This data was introduced in Section 4.2.) What is the modal number of nests per hectare?

Number of sparrows' nests	Number of hectares
0	10
1	18
2	5
3	2
4	1

Solution

The most frequently occurring number of nests per hectare is 1 nest, observed on 18 occasions. Thus the mode is 1 nest per hectare.

The mode for continuous data

When dealing with truly continuous data there may not be any values of a variable that occur more than once, so quoting a single mode is meaningless. Instead, the **modal class** is sometimes quoted. The modal class is the class in a frequency distribution that has the highest relative frequency; that is, the class that would result in the highest block in a histogram.

For example, consideration of Table 5.2 shows that the most common class, both in absolute and relative frequency terms, is the under 1 year class. Hence the **modal class** is the **under 1 year class**.

Bimodal distributions

There can of course be more than one mode. For example, if we consider the following data

   0   1   2   2   1   4

we have two modes, namely the values of 1 and 2. This attribute can be useful in that finding the mode(s) can often pinpoint when a data distribution has more than one peak.

Some concluding comments

The most used measure of central tendency is the arithmetic mean. This is largely because it is amenable to statistical inference and testing procedures. The reader will see this in Chapters 7, 8 and 10.

     If data is clearly skewed (see Section 5.3), then a median measure might be more 'typical' than a mean. The median, though not as useful as the arithmetic mean, is still useful as the reader will see in Chapter 9.

     The mode is rarely used, other than as a quick guide to what constitutes a typical data value. In Section 5.4 the reader will see that it is often beneficial to calculate all three measures of location for a set of data, in order to gain appreciation or the skewness of data.

5.3   Measures of dispersion

A measure of dispersion (or measure of variability) provides a guide as to the variability of a set of data.

Example usage

The MINITAB example file 'FALCON.MTW' contains data relating to a study of the levels of the pesticide DDT in falcons nesting in different nesting areas. The DDT levels found in falcons nesting in the United States and Canada were as follows:

United States	19	17	16	25	24	29	34	37	36
Canada	16	13	16	28	24	26	36	39	37

It would be interesting to determine whether the DDT levels are more varied in birds nesting in one area than the other. Looking at the numbers it is not immediately clear which set of DDT levels is the most variable. In this section we will discuss some of the methods of measuring variability that are commonly used.

5.3.1 The range

The simplest measure of variability is the difference between the smallest and the largest values in a set of data. This is known as the **range**. The calculation of the range is demonstrated by Example 5.5.

Example 5.5

For the DDT data on falcons the ranges of DDT levels for the birds from each nesting site can be found as follows.

Birds nesting in the USA
Highest DDT level = 37
Lowest DDT level = 16
Range   = 37 − 16 = 21

Birds nesting in Canada
Highest DDT level = 39
Lowest DDT level = 13
Range   = 39 − 13 = 26

So, according to the ranges, the DDT levels of birds nesting in Canada are more variable than for birds nesting in the United States. This might have important connotations: perhaps the use of DDT as a pesticide was more uneven in Canada than the USA, or perhaps falcons nesting in Canada have a wider range of diets.

The range is very useful as a quick guide to the variability in data, but has little use as a serious statistical tool. One reason for this is that, by definition, only the smallest and largest values are considered. These values may be atypical of the data as a whole, for example the range of

    1   2   1   2   20

is higher than the range of

    1   12   6   5   19

but the reader might well consider that the second set of data seems more varied.

One way of overcoming this problem is to find the range of the middle 50% of data points, which is known as the interquartile range.

5.3.2 The interquartile range

Earlier in Section 5.3 we defined the median as the data value which has 50% of observations below it, and 50% above it. In a similar way we can define the 25% point and the 75% point of a measured variable as the **first quartile** (or **Q1**) and the **third quartile** (or **Q3**) respectively. (The median is often referred to as the **second quartile**, or **Q2**.)

If we have n observations of a measured variable, then the rank positions of the quartiles are:

Rank position of the first quartile (Q1) $= 0.25(n + 1)$
Rank position of the second quartile (Q2) $= 0.50(n + 1)$
Rank position of the third quartile (Q3) $= 0.75(n + 1)$

The **interquartile range** (often denoted by **IQR**) is defined as the difference between the third and the first quartile, i.e.

$$IQR = Q3 - Q1$$

Example 5.6 shows how the interquartile range is calculated and used.

Example 5.6

Find the interquartile range of the levels of DDT recorded in the 9 falcons nesting in the United States.

Solution

Original data: 19   17   16   25   24   29   34   37   36
Ordered data: 16   17   19   24   25   29   34   36   37

The rank positions of the quartiles are:

Rank position of Q1 $= 0.25(9 + 1) = 2.5$
Rank position of Q3 $= 0.75(9 + 1) = 7.5$

The quartiles themselves are:

Q1:   Rank 2.5 means the average of the observations occupying ranks 2 and 3, i.e.
         Q1 $= (17 + 19)/2 = 18$
Q3:   Similarly a rank of 7.5 means the average of the observations occupying ranks 7 and 8, i.e.
         Q3 $= (34 + 36)/2 = 35$

The first quartile is 18, the third quartile is 35, so the interquartile range is:

1QR $= Q3 - Q1 = 35 - 18 = 17$

This means that the middle 50% of falcons have a range of DDT levels of 17.
    Readers might like to verify that the interquartile range for birds nesting in Canada is 20.5, so this measure of dispersion once again shows that the DDT levels are more variable in birds which nested in Canada.

Estimating the interquartile range from a frequency distribution

In Section 5.2 we discussed how the median could be estimated from a frequency distribution by the use of an ogive. The same is true for the interquartile range.

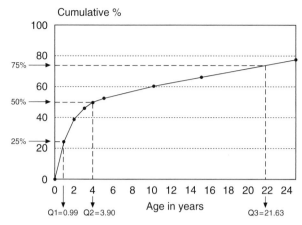

Figure 5.2 A cumulative frequency curve to find the IQR of the meningitis data.

Example 5.7

Referring back to Table 5.2, find the interquartile range of the ages of meningitis cases in England and Wales during 1989.

Solution

We draw an ogive, in the same way that we drew Figure 5.1. This time we read off the ages corresponding to the 25% and 75% cumulative percentages. As Figure 5.2 shows, the first quartile is 0.99 years, the third quartile is 21.63 years, so the interquartile range is:

$$IQR = 21.63 - 0.99 = \textbf{20.64 years}$$

Further comments regarding quartiles

In Section 5.4 we shall see how quartiles can be useful to examine possible skewness in data distributions. It should also be pointed out that often ogives are used to determine not the 25% or 75% values, but, perhaps, the top 10% or lowest 1%, depending upon the needs of the user.

5.3.3 Measuring variability from the mean

The remaining measures of variability that we shall consider, all aim to show how much the individual items in a set of data vary from the mean of the set of data. In order to sequentially develop the rationale behind these measures we shall initially consider a situation in which all the observations in a finite population of interest are sampled. Here the sample size n, and the population size N, are of course the same.

Intuitively, finding the average difference from the mean of all the observed values of a variable seems like a good idea, where this could be defined as:

$$\text{Average difference} = \sum \frac{(x - \bar{x})}{n}$$

Let us try this measure for the following observed values from a population of size 5:

1 2 3 4 5

The mean is clearly 3, so the calculation would proceed as follows:

x	$x - \bar{x}$
1	$1 - 3 = -2$
2	$2 - 3 = -1$
3	$3 - 3 = 0$
4	$4 - 3 = 1$
5	$5 - 3 = 2$
	$\sum (x - \bar{x}) = 0$

$$\text{Average difference} = \frac{0}{5} = 0!$$

Clearly this approach doesn't work; the differences from the mean always sum to zero.

5.3.4 The variance of a finite population

The **variance** gets around the problematical result that $\sum(x - \bar{x}) = 0$ by squaring all the differences $(x - \bar{x})$ and finding the average squared difference from the mean:

$$\text{Variance} = \frac{\sum(x - \bar{x})^2}{n} \qquad \text{(Equation 5.3)}$$

So, for the previously used data, 1 2 3 4 5, the calculation of the population variance would be as follows:

x	$(x - \bar{x})$	$(x - \bar{x})^2$
1	-2	4
2	-1	1
3	0	0
4	1	1
5	2	4
	$\sum (x - \bar{x})^2 = 10$	

$$\text{Population variance} = \frac{\sum(x - \bar{x})^2}{n} = \frac{10}{5} = 2$$

For reasons that will become apparent soon, the variance of a population is denoted by the symbol σ^2.

5.3.5 The standard deviation of a finite population

The **standard deviation** of a finite population, denoted by the greek letter σ (sigma), is the square root of the variance of a population, that is:

$$\sigma = \sqrt{\left(\frac{\sum(x - \bar{x})^2}{n}\right)}$$

(**Equation 5**.4)

This probably looks a little confusing to the reader at first sight, but in a few weeks' time you will have used the standard deviation in so many ways that it will have become a familiar friend!

Example 5.8 demonstrates how the standard deviation of a population can be calculated.

Example 5.8

The ten employees of a small waste management company earn the following salaries:

£10,000   £15,000   £17,000   £8,500   £23,000
£14,000   £10,000   £18,000   £16,000   £11,000

Find the standard deviation of these salaries.

Solution

A handy tip is to note that we can express the figures as 000s to facilitate an easier calculation without altering the standard deviation.

The first calculation step is to find the arithmetic mean, $\bar{x}$. We leave the reader to check that the arithmetic mean is 18.3 (£000s). The standard deviation calculation then proceeds as follows:

Calculation

x (£000's)	$x - \bar{x}$	$(x - \bar{x})^2$
10.0	$10.0 - 18.3 = -8.3$	68.89
15.0	$15.0 - 18.3 = -3.3$	10.89
12.0	$12.0 - 18.3 = -6.3$	39.69
8.5	$8.5 - 18.3 = -9.8$	96.04
23.0	$23.0 - 18.3 = 4.7$	22.09
14.0	$14.0 - 18.3 = -4.3$	18.49
10.0	$10.0 - 18.3 = -8.3$	68.89
18.0	$18.0 - 18.3 = -0.3$	0.09
16.0	$16.0 - 18.3 = -2.3$	5.29
11.0	$11.0 - 18.3 = -7.3$	53.29

$$\sum(x - \bar{x})^2 = 383.65$$

$$\sigma = \sqrt{\frac{\sum(x - \bar{x})^2}{n}} = \sqrt{\frac{383.65}{10}} = \sqrt{38.365} = 6.1939$$

Remembering that the figures were in £000s this means that the standard deviation of the salaries is £6,193.90.

Interpreting a standard deviation can seem difficult until these sections have been studied. The most important thing to realize is that highly variable data produces larger standard deviations than less variable data (although the situation is a little more complicated than this, see the section on the 'coefficient of variation').

Many data distributions are approximately symmetrical about a central peak. For such data a useful result applies which aids an understanding of the standard deviation. The result is that around 68% of observations fall within 1 standard deviation of the mean, around 95% of observations lie within 2 standard deviations of the mean, and nearly all observations lie within 3 standard deviations of the mean. Even more precise statements can be made when data follows a distribution known as the normal distribution. This will be considered in Section 6.4.

The sample standard deviation

In the environmental sciences most of the data that are dealt with comes from samples, the hope being that these samples accurately reflect the population as a whole. For example, the data shown in Table 5.1 is hoped to be representative of rivers Taff and Dee as a whole. When we calculate a standard deviation from our sample we want the results to be a good estimate of the standard deviation of **all** possible water specimens from the river. It can be shown that the definition given in Equation 5.4 is not suitable for estimating the standard deviation of a population from a sample, as it results in estimates which underestimate the degree of variability in the population.

The unknown population standard deviation, σ, can be best estimated from samples by using the sample standard deviation, denoted by s, where

$$s = \sqrt{\frac{\sum(x - \bar{x})^2}{n - 1}}$$
(**Equation 5.5**)

The reader will notice that the only visible difference between this equation, and Equation 5.4 is the replacement of the divisor n by $n - 1$. (The other difference being that in Equation 5.4 the x's consist of the entire population, whereas in Equation 5.5 the x's consist of a sample of values from the population.)

From this point on we shall deal exclusively with the sample standard deviation as environmentalists almost invariably deal with samples.

An alternative formula for s
Using the definition shown in Equation 5.5, the sample standard deviation can be a time-consuming statistic to calculate, as it requires the mean, $\bar{x}$, to be calculated beforehand. An alterative but equivalent way of expressing the sample standard

deviation is:

$$s = \sqrt{\left(\frac{\sum x^2 - [(\sum x)^2/n]}{n-1}\right)}$$

(Equation 5.6)

This looks more complicated, but in fact is quicker to calculate. An example calculation is shown in Example 5.9.

Note: *The reader should note that $\sum x^2 \neq (\sum x)^2$.*

Example 5.9

An example calculation of s

With reference to Table 5.1, calculate the sample standard deviation of the nitrate concentrations recorded in the river Dee.

Solution

Nitrate concentrations, x	x^2
1.86	3.4596
1.98	3.9204
1.96	3.8416
2.04	4.1616
1.88	3.5344
1.66	2.7556
1.32	1.7424
2.11	4.4521
1.68	2.8224
1.69	2.8561
1.58	2.4964
1.37	1.8769
1.91	3.6481
1.65	2.7225
1.35	1.8225
1.53	2.3409
1.74	3.0276
1.79	3.2041
1.94	3.7636
$\sum x = 33.04$	$\sum x^2 = 58.4488$

$$s = \sqrt{\frac{\sum x^2 - [(\sum x)^2/n]}{n-1}} = \sqrt{\frac{58.4488 - [(33.04)^2/19]}{19-1}}$$

$$s = \sqrt{\frac{58.4488 - 57.4548}{18}} = \sqrt{0.0552} = 0.2350\,(mg/lN)$$

Given that the mean nitrate concentration from the river Dee samples was 1.7389, and assuming the distribution of nitrate concentrations from specimens would be approximately symmetrical, then we

66

could estimate that:

1. Around 68% of water specimens from the river Dee will have nitrate concentrations within 0.235 mg/l N of the mean concentration of 1.7389, i.e. between 1.5039 and 1.9739 mg/l N. (In our sample, 13 of the water specimens or 68.4% of samples were in this range.)
2. Similarly, around 95% of water specimens will have concentrations within 2 × 0.235 = 0.47 mg/l N of the mean, i.e. within the range 1.2689 to 2.2089 mg/l N. (In our sample all 19, or 100%, of the water specimens had nitrate concentrations within this range.)
3. Virtually all water specimens will have concentrations within 3 × 0.235 = 0.705 mg/l N of the mean, i.e. within the range 1.0339 to 2.4439 mg/l N. All our water specimens were in this range.

Estimating the sample standard deviation from a frequency distribution

As we have seen before, data is often presented in the form of a frequency distribution. For ungrouped data the formula

$$s = \sqrt{\frac{\sum fx^2 - [(\sum fx)^2 / \sum f]}{\sum f - 1}}$$
(Equation 5.7)

(where f is the frequency of occurrences of the value x) yields the sample standard deviation. When the data is of the grouped variety the same formula can be used, but the result is only an approximation (though usually a close approximation) of the sample standard deviation. Example 5.10 demonstrates how this formula is used.

Example 5.10

In Example 5.9, the sample standard deviation was found for the nitrate concentrations found in 19 water specimens from the river Dee. If this data was only available in the form of a frequency distribution, how could the sample standard deviation be approximated?

Solution

Nitrate concentration (mg/l N)	Midpoint, x	Number of specimens, f	x^2	fx	fx^2
1.3 to under 1.5	1.4	3	1.96	4.2	5.88
1.5 to under 1.7	1.6	6	2.56	9.6	15.36
1.7 to under 1.9	1.8	4	3.24	7.2	12.96
1.9 to under 2.1	2.0	5	4.00	10.0	20.00
2.1 to under 2.3	2.2	1	4.84	2.2	4.84
		$\sum f = 19$		$\sum fx = 33.2$	$\sum fx^2 = 59.04$

Note: As was the case when estimating the mean from a grouped frequency distribution, the x *values* are taken as being the *midpoints* of each class interval.

67

Substituting the above summations into Equation 5.7, we obtain:

$$s = \sqrt{\frac{59.04 - [(33.2)^2/19]}{19 - 1}}$$

$$s = \sqrt{\frac{59.04 - 58.0126}{18}} = \sqrt{0.0571} = 0.239 \,(\text{mg/I N})$$

So we approximate that the standard deviation of the nitrate concentrations from water specimens collected from the river Dee is around 0.239 mg/I N. This is close to the true sample standard deviation of 0.235 that we found earlier.

5.3.6 The coefficient of variation

The data in Table 5.4 relates to the February climate for England and Wales from 1980 to 1990.

Looking at the summary statistics in the table it is easy to think that the rainfall is far more variable than the temperature because the respective standard deviations are 34.6644 mm as opposed to a much smaller looking 2.2622 °C. This however is misleading. The standard deviation of the rainfall is larger in part because of the larger values it is dealing with. In fact it is misleading to compare the standard deviations from two samples unless the two sample means are similar; particularly if the variables being considered are measured on incomparable scales as they are in this example.

The correct way to examine the degree of variability in two or more samples simultaneously is to use the coefficient of variation.

$$\text{Coefficient of variation} = \frac{\text{Sample standard deviation}}{\text{Sample mean}} \times 100\%$$

Table 5.4   February climate for England and Wales, 1980–90

Year	Temperature (°C)	Rainfall (mm)
1980	6.3	93
1981	3.7	52
1982	5.5	44
1983	2.6	42
1984	3.5	57
1985	2.8	29
1986	−0.4	17
1987	4.1	58
1988	5.2	63
1989	6.4	88
1990	7.8	142
Sample means	4.3182 °C	62.2727 mm
Sample sd's	2.2622 °C	34.6644 mm

In our climatic example the variability of the two climatic variables can be measured as follows:

$$\textit{Temperature: Coefficient of variation} = \frac{2.2622\,°\mathrm{C}}{4.3182\,°\mathrm{C}} \times 100\%$$

$$= 52.39\%$$

$$\textit{Rainfall: Coefficient of variation} = \frac{34.6644\,\mathrm{mm}}{62.2727\,\mathrm{mm}} \times 100\%$$

$$= 55.67\%$$

So in fact, the degree of variability is very similar for the two climatic variables.

Some concluding comments

The most widely used measure of dispersion is the standard deviation. This is because it is amenable to a wide variety of statistical inference. Scientists in general, and environmental scientists in particular, deal with the sample standard deviation, s. Usually when summarizing data, the sample standard deviation is used hand in hand with the arithmetic mean. When the interquartile range is used it is usually in conjunction with the median.

5.4 Examining the skewness of data

Through considering histograms and dot plots in Chapter 4, the reader will by now realize that data distributions may be symmetrical or they may be skewed. It can often be useful to 'get a feel' for the shape of the distribution of a set of data without necessarily having to present the data graphically (although a graphical presentation is usually a good idea). A detailed examination of measures of skewness is beyond the scope of this text; however, some of the summary statistics we have looked at in this chapter provide useful information regarding the skewness of data. The notes that follow show that various summary statistics can indicate the symmetry or otherwise of a set of unimodal data.

Case A: A symmetrical distribution

If a distribution is approximately symmetrical:

(i) The mean, median, and mode are all very similar

  mean ≈ median ≈ mode

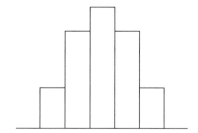

(ii) The difference between the third quartile and the median is very similar to the difference between the median and the first quartile

$$Q3 - Q2 \approx Q2 - Q1$$

Case B: A positively skewed distribution

If a distribution is positively skewed:

(i) mean > median > mode
(ii) Q3 − Q2 > Q2 − Q1

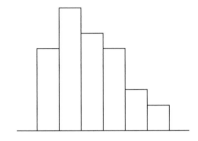

Case C: A negatively skewed distribution

If a distribution is negatively skewed:

(i) mode > median > mean
(ii) Q3 − Q2 < Q2 − Q1

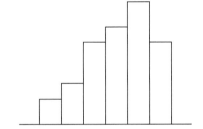

5.5   Aids to computing summary statistics

The reader will have noticed that calculating summary statistics using hand calculations can be a time-consuming and laborious task. Fortunately there are easier ways to obtain summary statistics allowing the scientist more time to concentrate on the interpretation of the results.

5.5.1 Scientific calculators

A scientific calculator with a standard deviation function is a wise investment for anyone who uses statistics. For less than £10 calculators can be purchased which allow the input of data. Such calculators can provide the arithmetic mean, the standard deviation and the sample standard deviations of data at the touch of a button.

5.5.2 *Spreadsheet packages*

Spreadsheet packages can usually calculate a variety of summary statistics. EXCEL 5.0 produces a particularly wide range of summary statistics very easily, as Example 5.11 shows.

Example 5.11

Summary statistics for the data introduced in Table 5.1 were calculated using EXCEL 5.0. Firstly, the data was entered into an EXCEL spreadsheet in the following format:

	A	B	C	D
	A	B	C	D
1	pHD	NitrateD	pHT	NitrateT
2				
3	7.4	1.86	7.9	1.40
4	7.3	1.98	8.0	1.20
5	7.1	1.96	8.0	1.42
..	..	..	..	..
..	..	..	..	..
21	7.4	1.94	7.9	1.57
22			8.0	1.73

The menu selections **Tools**, **Data Analysis**, were then made, followed by the selection of the **Descriptive Statistics** option. This produced the menu shown in Exhibit 5.2 where the data to be summarized was specified, along with the region of the spreadsheet where the summary statistics were to be provided.

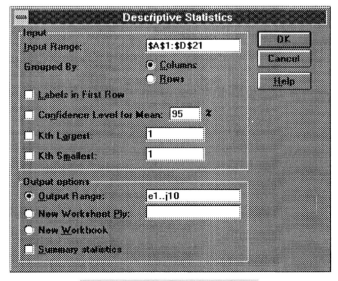

Exhibit 5.2 Descriptive statistics.

The resulting summary statistics provided by EXCEL are shown below.

Note: EXCEL provides more summary statistics than have been covered in this chapter. The measures of Kurtosis and Skewness shown are not covered by this text. The Standard Error is an important concept and will be introduced in Chapter 7. All the other statistics should by now make sense to the reader.

pHD		NitrateD		pHT		NitrateT	
Mean	7.478947	Mean	1.738947	Mean	7.94	Mean	1.538
Standard Error	0.040881	Standard Error	0.053911	Standard Error	0.022243	Standard Error	0.041755
Median	7.5	Median	1.74	Median	7.95	Median	1.49
Mode	7.6	Mode	#N/A	Mode	8	Mode	1.48
Standard Deviation	0.178198	Standard Deviation	0.234992	Standard Deviation	0.099472	Standard Deviation	0.186734
Variance	0.031754	Variance	0.055221	Variance	0.009895	Variance	0.034869
Kurtosis	0.251161	Kurtosis	-0.75016	Kurtosis	1.063763	Kurtosis	0.085908
Skewness	-0.96259	Skewness	-0.36473	Skewness	0.484828	Skewness	0.543717
Range	0.6	Range	0.79	Range	0.4	Range	0.73
Min	7.1	Min	1.32	Min	7.8	Min	1.2
Max	7.7	Max	2.11	Max	8.2	Max	1.93
Sum	142.1	Sum	33.04	Sum	158.8	Sum	30.76
Count	19	Count	19	Count	20	Count	20

5.5.3 Statistical software packages

Statistical software packages such as **MINITAB** can also provide a comprehensive range of summary statistics. With **MINITAB** for Windows summary statistics similar to those shown in Example 5.11 could be produced by entering the data into four columns of a MINITAB worksheet, and then using the menu selection sequence:

Stat, Basic Statistics, Descriptive Statistics

Exercises 5

Exercise 5.1

(a) What are the key advantages and disadvantages of using each of the following measures of central tendency:

the arithmetic mean
the median
the mode

(b) When is the sample standard deviation, s, used?

(c) What are the key advantages and disadvantages of using each of the following measures of dispersion:

the sample standard deviation
the range
the coefficient of variation

Exercise 5.2

A sample of seven employees of a waste disposal company was taken. The wages of the employees were as follows:

£200   £180   £240   £260   £220   £240   £2,000

(a) Find the mean and sample standard deviation of the wages.
(b) Find the median and interquartile range of the wages.
(c) It was later found that the final wage in the list was actually £200 and not £2,000. How different would your answers to (a) and (b) be using the correct wage of £200?

Exercise 5.3

A set of SO_2 readings was taken at monitoring stations around two large towns. Various statistics, shown below, were calculated to summarize the findings:

Mean	35	Mean	41
Median	25	Median	37
Sample standard deviation	12	Sample standard deviation	9
Range	46	Range	35

(a) Produce a paragraph or so of text which explains the similarities and differences in the distributions of SO_2 levels between the two towns.

Exercise 5.4

In Exercise 4.5 data relating to water specimens taken from the rivers Dee and Taff was introduced. The pH levels and nitrate levels for the 20 samples from the river Taff are once again shown below.

pH	Nitrate (mg/l N)	pH	Nitrate (mg/l N)
7.9	1.40	7.8	1.63
8.0	1.20	7.9	1.67
8.0	1.42	8.0	1.33
7.8	1.48	8.0	1.93
7.8	1.48	8.0	1.71
7.9	1.45	7.9	1.50
8.0	1.44	7.8	1.52
8.0	1.41	8.0	1.34
8.2	1.90	7.9	1.57
7.9	1.65	8.0	1.73

(a) Calculate the mean and sample standard deviation of the pH levels.
(b) Calculate the mean and sample standard deviation of the nitrate concentrations.
(c) Using the standard deviations calculated in parts (a) and (b) it would be difficult to determine whether the pH levels, or the nitrate concentrations are the most variable among water samples from the river Taff. Why is this?

(d) Calculate coefficients of variation for the pH levels and nitrate concentrations, and hence determine whether the pH levels or nitrate concentrations are the most variable in relative terms.

Exercise 5.5

In Example 4.1 data relating to the particle sizes of 37 grains from a sample of sediment from the Severn estuary was introduced. The data is summarized in the form of a frequency distribution below.

Particle Size (μm)	Frequency
3.0 to under 4.0	2
4.0 to under 5.0	12
5.0 to under 6.0	10
6.0 to under 7.0	7
7.0 to under 8.0	4
8.0 to under 9.0	2

(a) Using the frequency distribution given above, calculate estimates for the sample mean and the sample standard deviation of the particle sizes.
(b) Draw an ogive, and hence estimate the median particle size.
(c) In geological terminology particles between 2 and 6 μm are classified as fine silt, whereas particles between 6 and 20 μm are classified as medium silt.

(i) Would you classify this silt as being fine or medium?
(ii) Using your ogive from part (b), estimate the percentage of particles which fall into the medium silt category.

(d) All the above calculations only produce approximations of the summary statistics because a frequency distribution is used rather than the raw data. In this example the actual raw data is available and is shown below:

The particle sizes of 37 grains from sediment from the Severn estuary

8.2	6.3	6.8	6.4	8.1	6.3
5.3	7.0	6.8	7.2	7.2	7.1
5.2	5.3	5.4	6.3	5.5	6.0
5.5	5.1	4.5	4.2	4.3	5.1
4.3	5.8	4.3	5.7	4.4	4.1
4.2	4.8	3.8	3.8	4.1	4.0
4.0					

Use the **sd** or **stats** mode on your calculator to find the mean and sample standard deviation of the 37 grain sizes. These values should (hopefully) be close to those calculated in part (a).

Exercise 5.6

Type the data from Exercise 5.5 into MINITAB or EXCEL. Use the package to obtain summary statistics such as the mean, the median and the standard deviation.

6

Patterns in probability

6.1 Introduction

Whenever we take a sample or observe an event we can rarely, if ever, predict the outcome. For example, people have been trying to predict the weather for thousands of years, but in spite of billions of pounds spent world wide and today's sophisticated technology we still cannot predict tomorrow's weather with absolute certainty. We use words such as 'likely', 'probable', 'possible', 'improbable' and 'unlikely' to describe our feelings about the outcome of uncertain events. However, scientists, including environmental scientists, need to be more precise when expressing these feelings and make use of a quantitative measure of certainty known as *probability*.

Probability is measured on a scale of 0 to 1, where an impossible event has a probability of 0 and a certain event has a probability of 1. In an experiment that has only two possible outcomes which are equally likely (e.g. the tossing of a fair coin) each outcome has a probability of 0.5. You will sometimes see probability quoted as a percentage, for example there is a 50% probability of getting a head when tossing a fair coin. Recently meteorologists have begun to quantify their uncertainty with forecasts which include statements such as 'there is a 70% risk of showers tonight'.

The long-term frequency of an event in repeated trials is the easiest way of understanding the probability of most events. For example, the probability of one-sixth of getting a six on the throw of a fair die is interpreted as meaning that, if we were to throw this die a large number of times, we would expect to get a six on about one-sixth of the throws. Another (equivalent) way of interpreting this is by knowing that a die has six faces and, if it is a fair die, each face must be equally likely. However, we cannot interpret all probability statements in this way – in some cases it is simply an expression of one's belief that a particular outcome will occur.

6.2 The binomial distribution

The case when an observation or a trial results in one of only two possible outcomes is particularly common and important in environmental studies. For example, in surveys on environmental issues some of the questions may have Yes/No answers. As another example, soil samples may be taken to determine the absence or presence in the ground of a particular herbicide. In such experiments the result of an observation has one of two outcomes which, to generalize, we label a 'success' or 'failure'. If we know the probability of a single success it is possible to calculate the probabilities of each of the possible number of successes from a given number of observations. Suppose we take n observations (n questionnaires or n soil specimens) then the number of successes ('yes' answers or 'presence' of herbicide) can range from zero to n.

Consider a simple example in which we ask three people from a village whether they agree with a proposal for a new by-pass. We shall assume that only 1 in 5 (20%) of all villagers agree with the proposal and that the sample of three was chosen randomly (see Chapter 3) from the population of the village. The possible outcomes of this survey are that none, one, two or all three of the chosen villagers agree with the proposal. We shall calculate the probabilities of each of these outcomes. To do this we note that the probability of a randomly selected villager agreeing with the proposal is 0.20.

The list of all the possible responses to our survey is given in Table 6.1, which shows that there are eight potential outcomes. At the extremes we could get all

Table 6.1 Possible results from a survey of three villagers (Y = Yes, N = No and associated probabilities in brackets)

1st Villager	2nd Villager	3rd Villager	Outcome	Probability
Y (0.2)	Y (0.2)	Y (0.2)	YYY	$0.2 \times 0.2 \times 0.2 = 0.008$
Y (0.2)	Y (0.2)	N (0.8)	YYN	$0.2 \times 0.2 \times 0.8 = 0.032$
Y (0.2)	N (0.8)	Y (0.2)	YNY	$0.2 \times 0.8 \times 0.2 = 0.032$
Y (0.2)	N (0.8)	N (0.8)	YNN	$0.2 \times 0.8 \times 0.8 = 0.128$
N (0.8)	Y (0.2)	Y (0.2)	NYY	$0.8 \times 0.2 \times 0.2 = 0.032$
N (0.8)	Y (0.2)	N (0.8)	NYN	$0.8 \times 0.2 \times 0.8 = 0.128$
N (0.8)	N (0.8)	Y (0.2)	NNY	$0.8 \times 0.8 \times 0.2 = 0.128$
N (0.8)	N (0.8)	N (0.8)	NNN	$0.8 \times 0.8 \times 0.8 = 0.512$

Table 6.2   The probabilities of 0, 1, 2 and 3 'Yes' votes

No. of 'Yes' votes	Probability
0	$0.8 \times 0.8 \times 0.8 = 0.512$
1	$3 \times 0.2 \times 0.8 \times 0.8 = 0.384$
2	$3 \times 0.2 \times 0.2 \times 0.8 = 0.096$
3	$0.2 \times 0.2 \times 0.2 = 0.008$
Total	1.000

three villagers agreeing with the proposal (YYY), or all three disagreeing with the proposal (NNN). We can also see that there are three ways of getting one 'Yes' vote and three ways of getting two 'Yes' votes. The probabilities of a 'Yes' and a 'No' from each of the villagers are also displayed in brackets.

To calculate the probability that all three agree with the proposal we can use the long-term frequency interpretation of probability outlined in Section 6.1. Imagine that we take many samples of three villagers from the village. We would expect 1 sample in 5 to have the first selected villager answering 'Yes' and then for 1 in 5 of *these* samples the second villager would also answer 'Yes'. Thus, on average, 1 sample in 25 has the first two villagers agreeing with the proposals. Finally, for 1 in 5 of *these* samples the last selected villager also answers 'Yes'. Therefore, we expect only 1 sample out of every 125 (a probability of 0.008) to have all three villagers agreeing with the proposals. Thus the probability of three 'Yes' votes is obtained by multiplying the individual probabilities of a 'Yes' vote from each villager, i.e. $0.2 \times 0.2 \times 0.2 = 0.008$. (Further details of the rules for combining probabilities are given in an appendix to this chapter.) The same argument can be applied to the other outcomes and Table 6.1 also shows the results of these calculations. Four samples in every 125 (a probability of 0.032) have the first two villagers answering 'Yes' and the last 'No'. The same probability applies to the other outcomes in which exactly one villager answers 'No'. Thus there is a long-term frequency of 12 samples in 125 (a proportion of $3 \times 0.032 = 0.096$) in which just one of the sample villagers answers 'Yes'. Table 6.2 shows the full set of probabilities.

Notice that the probabilities add to one – since it is certain that one of these outcomes occurs. Thus the total probability of 1 has been divided or *distributed* over the set of possible outcomes. We have calculated the *probability distribution* for the case where each observation is either a 'success' or a 'failure' and when the probability of a success equals 0.2 and there are three observations. This is called a binomial distribution with $n = 3$ and $p = 0.2$. This probability distribution can be pictured graphically as in Figure 6.1.

The method of listing all possible outcomes as a way of calculating the binomial distribution, even for moderate values of n, is impractical but we have seen the way in which it was calculated for $p = 0.2$ and $n = 3$ and this can be generalized to any values of p and n. With a sample size of n and a probability of success

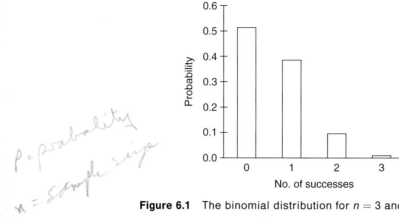

Figure 6.1 The binomial distribution for $n = 3$ and $p = 0.2$.

equal to p, we can see that

$$P(n \text{ successes}) = p \times p \times p \times \cdots \times p = p^n,$$

$$P(0 \text{ successes}) = (1 - p) \times (1 - p) \times (1 - p) \times \cdots \times (1 - p) = (1 - p)^n$$

and, in general,

$$P(r \text{ successes}) = (\text{Number of ways of selecting } r \text{ from } n) \times p^r \times p^{n-r}.$$

The number of ways of selecting r items from n items is given by the formula

$$\frac{n!}{r!(n-r)!}$$

where the symbol $n!$ (in words, n-factorial) represents the number n multiplied by all integers less than n. So, $3! = 3 \times 2 \times 1 = 6$ and $4! = 4 \times 3 \times 2 \times 1 = 24$. Note that, by convention, $0! = 1$.

Thus, the general formula for a binomial distribution is

$$P(r \text{ successes}) = \frac{n!}{r!(n-r)!} p^r (1-p)^{n-r}$$

The symbol ^nC_r is often used for the number of ways of choosing r items from n. That is,

$$^nC_r = \frac{n!}{r!(n-r)!}$$

and can be found on most scientific calculators.

Two assumptions have implicitly been made in the above. The first is that the probability, p, of a success on any one trial is the same for all trials. The second is that trials are assumed to be independent (see Section 6.7.1); that is, the chance of a success on each trial is not affected by what happens on any of the other trials.

Example 6.1

Childhood lead poisoning is a public health concern in the United States. In a certain population one child in eight a has high blood lead level. In a randomly chosen group of 10 children from the population, what is the probability that

(a)   none has a high blood lead level?
(b)   four have a high blood lead level?

This is an example of a binomial distribution with $n = 10$ and $p = 1/8 = 0.125$, where p is the probability that a child has a high blood lead level.

The probability that none of the 10 children has a high blood lead level is therefore

$$P(0) = (1 - 0.125)^{10} = 0.875^{10} = 0.263$$

The probability that exactly four of the 10 children have high blood lead is

$$P(4) = {}^{10}C_4 (0.125)^4 (0.875)^6 = 210 \times (0.125)^4 (0.875)^6 = 0.023$$

6.2.1 The mean and variance of the binomial distribution

Measures of location and spread, such as the mean, median, mode and variance, can be calculated for probability distributions such as the binomial distribution and are analogous to those you met for describing data in Chapter 5. The mean of a binomial distribution can be shown to be np and its variance is $np(1 - p)$. For example, the mean of a binomial distribution with $n = 12$ and $p = 1/6$ is $12 \times 1/6 = 2$. If the experiment of 'throw a fair die 12 times' was repeated on many occasions we would expect the average (mean) number of sixes (or indeed ones, twos, ..., fives) to be equal to 2. This is also called the expected number of successes.

Example 6.2

Calculate the mean and standard deviation of the number of children with high blood lead levels from a sample of 10 children (see Example 6.1).

The mean $= 10 \times 0.125 = 1.25$

The variance $= 10 \times 0.125 \times 0.875 = 1.09375$

Therefore the standard deviation $= \sqrt{1.09375} = 1.046$ (3 dp)

6.3   The Poisson distribution

In environmental studies the probability of a 'success' in a binomial distribution is often very small and the sample size relatively large; for example, $p = 0.01$ and $n = 200$, so that the mean of the distribution is 2.0 and the variance is 1.98.

**Table 6.3 A comparison of probabilities calcu-
lated for the binomial distribution with $n = 200$,
$p = 0.01$ and the Poisson distribution with $\mu = 2$**

r	Binomial	Poisson
0	0.1340	0.1353
1	0.2707	0.2707
2	0.2720	0.2707
3	0.1814	0.1804
4	0.0902	0.0902
5	0.0357	0.0361
6	0.0117	0.0120
7	0.0033	0.0034
8	0.0008	0.0009
9	0.0002	0.0002

In such cases the binomial distribution can be approximated by another probability distribution known as the Poisson distribution. This has a simpler formula
than the binomial distribution and is therefore useful in calculating probabilities
when n is large and p is small.

The Poisson probabilities are given by

$$P(r) = \frac{e^{-\mu}\mu^r}{r!} \quad (r = 0, 1, 2, 3, \ldots)$$

('e' is the mathematical constant 2.718... and the e^x function is available on all
scientific calculators).

The single parameter, μ, is the mean of the distribution. The variance is also equal
to μ. You will notice that the binomial distribution with $n = 200$ and $p = 0.01$ has a
mean of 2.0 and a variance of 1.98 (very close to 2). As an example, Table 6.3
compares the probabilities of the binomial distribution with $n = 200$, $p = 0.01$ with
the Poisson probabilities for $\mu = 2$, showing how good an approximation the Poisson
distribution is in this case.

The Poisson distribution occurs quite naturally in many circumstances since
data involving counts can be regarded as counting the number of occurrences of
an event which has a small probability of occurring, but such that the expected
number is relatively modest (e.g. between 1 and 10). Consider, for example, the
number of weeds per square metre in an area recently treated by a herbicide. A
square metre is made up of 10,000 centimetre squares and it is reasonable to suppose that a weed is either present or not in each of these squares (i.e. we assume
that only no weed or one weed is present in each square and it is impossible to
have two weeds in one centimetre square). The number of weeds per square
metre can thus be regarded as a binomial distribution with $n = 10,000$ and p
equal to the probability of finding a weed in one of the squares. Following application of the herbicide, the value of p should be quite small and thus we would
expect the number of weeds in a square metre to follow a Poisson distribution.

However, one of the assumptions of the binomial distribution is that the individual trials should be independent – i.e. the occurrence of a weed in one square does not affect the occurrence of a weed in an adjacent square. This is equivalent to assuming that the weeds occur **randomly** throughout the area being studied. Therefore, only if the weeds are randomly distributed over the area with a low density per square metre do we expect the number of weeds per square metre to have a Poisson distribution.

This allows us to test whether an event which has a low rate of occurrence (such as weeds after an application of herbicide) is randomly distributed in space. If it is random we would expect the number of occurrences per unit area to have a Poisson distribution. The first test is to calculate the mean and variance of the number of occurrences per unit area. For the Poisson distribution these should be approximately equal.

Example 6.3

In a large field of wheat the number of wild oats in each of 100 randomly placed quadrants was counted with the following results:

No. of wild oat plants per quadrat	0	1	2	3	4
Frequency	52	32	12	3	1

Calculate the mean and variance of the data. Does it appear that the wild oats occur at random within the field?

The mean $= [(1 \times 32 + 2 \times 12 + 3 \times 3 + 4 \times 1)]/100 = 0.69$

The variance $= 0.51$

These values are fairly close and indicate that the oats are likely to be randomly distributed throughout the field.

The appropriate statistical test to confirm that the data can be regarded as coming from a Poisson distribution is the chi-squared test, which will be discussed in Chapter 11.

If a spatial distribution is regular, or uniform, as in an area where plants have been sown on a rectangular grid, the variance of the number of plants per unit area will be less than the mean. At the other extreme, if the occurrence of an event at a particular point increases the probability that other events will occur nearby, then the events will be clumped together and the variance of the number of events per unit area will be greater than the mean. In Example 6.3, above, there is an indication that the wild oat plants may be more regular than random because the variance is less than the mean.

The same arguments apply to the number of rare events occurring over a period of time. This, too, has a Poisson distribution, provided the occurrence of an event at a particular point in time does not affect the chance of another event occurring soon afterwards. Thus, for example, the number of incidences of a rare type of accident over a year tend to follow a Poisson distribution.

Example 6.4

Over a period of 50 years the number of people each year suffering from a certain disease was as follows:

No. of deaths	0	1	2	3	4	5	6	7
Frequency	3	9	12	11	7	5	2	1

Assuming that the population size is constant, is there any evidence that the number of incidences of the disease cluster in time, or do they simply occur at random?

To test this we can assume that the probability of the disease is small, that the population is large and that the number of incidences per year will follow a Poisson distribution if the incidences occur at random and are not clustered in time. We therefore calculate the mean and variance of the above data. The mean equals 2.76 incidences per year and the variance equals 2.72. Since the mean and variance are almost equal it seems likely that the data do follow a Poisson distribution and, therefore, that the incidences of the disease do occur at random.

6.4 The normal distribution

The two probability distributions discussed so far arise from counting and are not appropriate for the many continuous variables observed by environmental scientists. By far the most important probability distribution for modelling the distribution of continuous data is the normal distribution. There are three reasons for this. First, it approximates the distribution of many measurements (or a transformation of these measurements – see next section) and, secondly, it plays a central role in statistical inference (see Chapters 7 and 8). It is also a useful approximation to the binomial and Poisson distributions when n is large. Figures 6.2 and 6.3 show the histograms of two sets of data (two of the sample datasets provided with MINITAB) and display common features. They are both unimodal with most of the data centred around the mode of the distribution; they are approximately symmetrical and they both have bell-shaped distributions.

This is a very common form of distribution and can often be closely approximated by the normal distribution curve. The equation of the normal distribution curve is

$$\frac{1}{\sigma\sqrt{(2\pi)}}\exp\left[-\frac{1}{2}\left(\frac{x-\mu}{\sigma}\right)^2\right]$$

where μ is the mean of the distribution and σ is its standard deviation.

The shape of the normal distribution is completely determined by its mean and its standard deviation. Since it is symmetrical the mean is the centre of the distribution. A range of normal curves, labelled $N(\mu, \sigma)$, is shown in Figure 6.4.

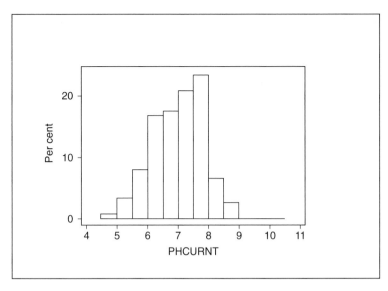

Figure 6.2 A histogram of pH levels of water samples taken from 149 lakes in Wisconsin between 1979 and 1983. (From MINITAB sample data set LAKES.MTW using the variable PHCURNT.)

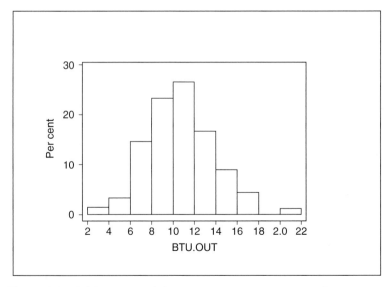

Figure 6.3 A histogram of the average energy consumption over a period of several weeks of 90 gas-heated homes in Wisconsin (See MINITAB sample data set FURNACE.MTW using the variable BTU.OUT.)

83

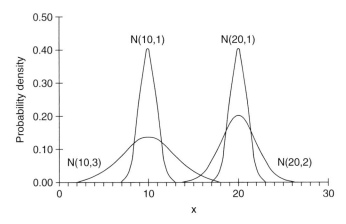

Figure 6.4 Normal distributions (a) $\mu = 10$, $\sigma = 1$; (b) $\mu = 10$, $\sigma = 3$; (c) $\mu = 20$, $\sigma = 1$; (d) $\mu = 20$, $\sigma = 2$.

From this figure you will see that virtually all the distribution is contained in a range covering three standard deviations either side of the mean. In fact about 99.7% of the distribution lies within three standard deviations of the mean. This is one of the important and useful properties of the normal distribution. Table 6.4 summarizes some of these.

We often need to calculate probabilities concerning measurements that we can assume are normally distributed. For example, what proportion of homes in Wisconsin have an average energy consumption greater than 14 BTU? In order to do this we make use of tables of the standard normal distribution which is the subject of the next section.

6.5 The standard normal distribution

If a variable X has a mean of μ and a standard deviation equal to σ, then the new variable, Z, defined by

$$Z = \frac{X - \mu}{\sigma}$$

Table 6.4   Important properties of a normal distribution

Approximately
68%	of a normal distribution lies within ± 1 SDs of its mean
95%	of a normal distribution lies within ± 2 SDs of its mean
99.7%	of a normal distribution lies within ± 3 SDs of its mean

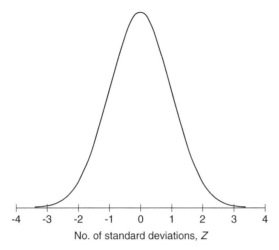

No. of standard deviations, Z

Figure 6.5   The standard normal distribution ($\mu = 0$, $\sigma = 1$).

is called the standard form of X, or the z-score, and has a mean of 0 and a standard deviation of 1. In addition, if X has a normal distribution then so does Z. The value of Z represents the number of standard deviations a value X is from the mean of the distribution. A positive value of Z indicates that X is larger than the mean while a negative value of Z shows that X is smaller than the mean.

Figure 6.5 shows how the value of Z represents the number of standard deviations an X value is from the mean. For example, $Z = 1$ corresponds to an X value that is 1σ greater than the mean and $Z = -2$ corresponds to an X value that is 2σ less than the mean.

Thus any normal distribution can be converted to one with a mean of zero and a standard deviation of 1. This very special normal distribution is called the standard normal distribution and tables of the probabilities associated with this distribution are widely available and are included in this book (Table B1 in Appendix B).

Table B1 gives the probability that a standard normal variable, Z, is greater than values of z, ranging from 0.00 to 2.99 in steps of 0.01 and 3.00 to 4.00 in steps of 0.1.

Note that areas under the normal curve represent probabilities. Thus the total area under the curve is equal to 1 and the mean divides this area into two equal halves. In Table B1 the probability of an observation from the standard normal distribution being greater than z is represented by the area under the curve to the right of z.

For example, the probability that $Z \geq 1.0$ is 0.15866 and the probability that $Z \geq 1.05$ is 0.14686. To use these tables to calculate probabilities for other normal distributions we adopt the following procedure, which we illustrate through an example.

Suppose X is a measurement from a normal distribution having a mean equal to 3 and a standard deviation of 2, then $Z = (X - 3)/2$ is a measurement from a standard normal distribution, so the probability that $X \geq 5$ is the same as the probability that

$Z \geq (5-3)/2$, or $Z \geq 1$, which, as we have seen, is 0.15866. Let us continue with this example and calculate the following probabilities:

(a) **$P(X \leq 5)$**

This is equal to $P(Z \leq (5-3)/2)$ or $P(Z \leq 1)$. $P(Z \leq 1)$ is represented by the area under the standard normal curve to the left of $z = 1$. However, Table B1 gives $P(Z \geq 1)$, the area to the right of $z = 1$. Since the total area under the curve is one we calculate $P(Z \leq 1)$ as

$$P(Z \leq 1) = 1 - P(Z \geq 1) = 1 - 0.15866 = 0.84134$$

Therefore

$$P(X \leq 5) = 0.84134$$

(b) **$P(X \leq -1)$**

This is equal to $P(Z \leq (-1-3)/2)$ or $P(Z \leq -2)$. You will notice that Table B1 only has values of z which are greater than 0. This is because we can deduce probabilities for negative values of z by the symmetry of the normal distribution. Clearly, by symmetry of the normal curve, $P(Z \leq -2)$ is the same as $P(Z \geq 2)$, which from Table B1 is equal to 0.02275. Therefore

$$P(X \leq -1) = 0.02275$$

(c) **$P(-1 \leq X \leq 5)$**

Probabilities of this form can be expressed as the difference between two probabilities. In this case

$$P(-1 \leq X \leq 5) = P(X \leq 5) - P(X \leq -1)$$

and we have seen how to calculate these probabilities in the examples above, so

$$P(-1 \leq X \leq 5) = 0.84134 - 0.02275 = 0.81859$$

6.6 The log-normal distribution

Data collected by environmental scientists often have a skewed distribution (see, for example, the particle size data of Example 4.1 whose distribution is shown in Figure 4.7). In such cases the symmetric normal distribution described in Section 6.5 is not an appropriate approximation for this data. However, in many cases, the logarithm of the data values displays an approximately normal distribution. If so, the original data is said to have a log-normal distribution. Figure 6.6 shows the distribution of the particle size data after taking logarithms to base e. The effect is to produce a more symmetrical distribution which may reasonably be approximated by a normal distribution. The mean and standard deviation of the $\log_e$ data are 1.6791 and 0.2269 in $\log_e(\mu m)$ units.

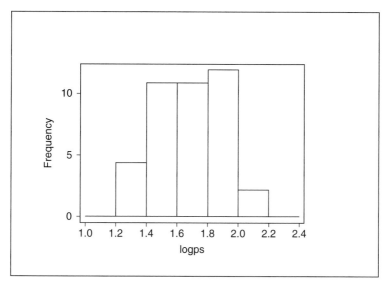

Figure 6.6 Distribution of $\log_e$ (particle size) from Example 4.1.

Thus, for example, to estimate the percentage of particles greater than 7.5 μm we can use the normal distribution with a mean of 1.6791 and a standard deviation of 0.2269 to estimate the percentage greater than $\log_e(7.5) = 2.0149$.

The corresponding z value is $(2.0149 - 1.6791)/0.2269 = 1.48$. Using Table B1, the probability that z is greater than 1.48 is equal to 0.06944. Thus, just under 7% of particles have a size greater than 7.5 μm.

Further details of how to deal with skewed data and the log-normal distribution in particular can be found in many textbooks; see, for example, Chapters 12 and 13 of Gilbert (1987).

6.7 Appendix

6.7.1 Rules for calculating probabilities

When combining the probabilities of simple events in order to calculate the probability of a compound event we have to consider whether the simple events are 'independent' and/or 'mutually exclusive'.

Independent events

Two events, A and B, are said to be independent if the probability of event A occurring does not affect the probability of B occurring. Formally, if we write $P(A)$

to symbolize the probability of A and $P(A|B)$ to symbolize the conditional probability of A given that B has occurred, then A and B are independent events if

$$P(A|B) = P(A) \quad \text{and} \quad P(B|A) = P(B)$$

For example, when throwing two dice, the probability of a six on the second die is independent of the outcome of the first die and

$$P(\text{six on second die}|\text{ six on first die}) = P(\text{six}) = 1/6$$

If two events are independent, then the probability of A and B occurring simultaneously is

$$P(A \,\&\, B) = P(A) \times P(B)$$

The probability of two sixes is equal to $(1/6) \times (1/6) = 1/36$, which can be confirmed by considering all the possible outcomes from throwing two dice.

If two events are not independent then the probability of their simultaneous occurrence is given by the probability of one event multiplied by the probability of the other, conditional on the first event occurring. That is,

$$P(A \,\&\, B) = P(A) \times P(B|A) \quad \text{or} \quad P(A \,\&\, B) = P(B) \times P(A|B)$$

Suppose we randomly select two people from four women and six men. What is the probability of selecting two women? The chances of our first selection being a women is 4/10, or 0.4. But the probability of our second selection also being female depends on our first selection. The two events are not independent. So the probability of selecting two women is

$$P = (\text{Women from first selection})$$

$$\times (\text{Women from second selection} \div \text{Women from first selection})$$

$$= (4/10) \times (3/9) = (2/5) \times (1/3) = 2/15$$

Again this can be confirmed by considering all possible ways of selecting pairs from the 10 people.

Mutually exclusive events

When two events, A and B, cannot occur simultaneously they are said to be mutually exclusive events and the probability that one or other occurs is equal to the sum of their probabilities, i.e.

$$P(A \text{ or } B) = P(A) + P(B)$$

So the chances of a six or an odd number on the throw of a die is $(1/6) + (1/2) = 4/6$, or 2/3, and can readily be confirmed by counting.

If the events can occur simultaneously, then

$$P(A \text{ or } B) = P(A) + P(B) - P(A \,\&\, B)$$

The probability of an even number or a number greater than 4 on the throw of a die is therefore

$$(1/2) + (1/3) - (1/2)(1/3) = 4/6.$$

6.7.2 Summary

$P(A \& B) = P(A) \times P(B)$	if A and B are independent
$P(A \& B) = P(A) \times P(B|A)$	if A and B are not independent
$\quad\quad\quad = P(B) \times P(A|B)$	
$P(A \text{ or } B) = P(A) + P(B)$	if A and B are mutually exclusive
$P(A \text{ or } B) = P(A) + P(B) - P(A \& B)$	if A and B are not mutually exclusive

Exercises 6

Exercise 6.1

A fair coin is tossed 10 times. Calculate the probabilities of the following outcomes:

(a) 5 heads and 5 tails.
(b) 8 heads and 2 tails.
(c) 2 tails and 8 heads.
(d) 10 heads.
(e) At least 8 heads.
(f) 4, 5 or 6 heads.

Exercise 6.2

Thirty per cent of students are known to support the activities of an environmental action group (EAG). For a tutorial group of 10 students calculate the following probabilities:

(a) All the tutorial group support EAG.
(b) None of the tutorial group supports EAG.
(c) Exactly half the tutorial group supports EAG.
(d) What assumptions have you made in calculating these probabilities?
(e) More than half the group supports EAG.

Exercise 6.3

The probability of getting an ear infection in normal circumstances is 1 in 1,000. One summer's day 2,000 people visit a beach in the south of England.

(a) Why can the Poisson probability distribution be used to model the number of ear infections among these people after their visit to the beach? What assumptions have been made?
(b) Calculate the probability that nobody has an ear infection that day.
(c) Calculate the probability that two or more of the beach visitors catch an ear infection on that day.

Exercise 6.4

The concentration of ozone (ppb) at midday at a sampling site near Bristol can be assumed to have a normal distribution with a mean of 12 ppm and a standard deviation of 3 ppm. Calculate the probability that the ozone level is

(a) greater than 12 ppm
(b) less than 14 ppm
(c) less than 16 ppm
(d) greater than 10 ppm
(e) less than 10 ppm
(f) less than 9 ppm
(g) between 11 and 14 ppm

Exercise 6.5

Gilbert (1987) shows that the concentration of mercury in swordfish can be assumed to follow a log-normal distribution. We can use the properties of the normal distribution on such data after transforming the data to logarithms. A sample of 10 swordfish had the following mercury levels:

   0.13   1.12   0.45   1.20   0.60   1.37   0.76   1.69   1.05   2.06

(a) Calculate the logarithms of this data.
(b) Calculate the mean and standard deviation of the values calculated in (a).
(c) Using these estimates, calculate the range over which 95% of the log (mercury) values are expected to lie.
(d) Hence calculate the range over which 95% of mercury levels are expected to lie.

7 Estimation from samples

7.1 Introduction

A set of measurements can almost always be regarded as measurements on a sample of items from a population of these items. It is usually too costly, too time consuming or simply impractical to measure every item in the population. Table 5.1 shows pH and nitrate measurements recorded from 19 specimens of water taken from the river Dee and 20 from the river Taff. Clearly it would have been impossible to measure all the water in these two rivers! Therefore, decisions based on pH and nitrate levels in these two rivers can only be based on samples of water. In this example we have two populations (of water) – the river Dee and the river Taff – and samples of water specimens from each river. The pH and nitrate levels of each specimen were then determined. From a sample we have to make inferences about the population as a whole.

The mean of the pH values from the river Dee is 7.48 and this is our best estimate of the mean level of pH in the river Dee. However, this value is unlikely to be equal to the true mean pH level in the river, simply because we have not measured all the water in the river. Providing we have taken care over the way we selected our water specimens, by ensuring that they are representative of water from the river (see Chapter 3), we can be confident that 7.48 is a 'good' estimate of the average pH in the river. What we mean by 'good' and ways of quantifying confidence are the subjects of this chapter. We shall assume that samples have been selected at random from the defined population and that we are interested in estimating the population mean value of a quantity.

7.2 The sampling distribution of the mean

When we estimate the mean of a population from the mean of a sample taken from that population it is very unlikely that the sample mean is exactly equal to the population mean. This discrepancy is called sampling error – it is not a mistake, but simply a consequence of incomplete information as we have only measured a fraction of the whole population. Clearly we would wish to minimize this sampling error and we shall see how we can do this later in this chapter. In addition, if we take another sample from the population we are most likely to find that the second sample has a different mean value from the first sample. In the face of all this variation how can we estimate the population mean with any confidence? In order to answer this question we shall consider an environmental monitoring system. Let us suppose that the benzene level (ppm) in the atmosphere is being regularly measured in Town A and that two specimens of air are taken every day from randomly chosen places in the town, to check that levels are not increasing. Let us also suppose that in fact the actual mean level of benzene does not change over a period of 30 days. Figure 7.1(a) shows a typical graph of the sample means for this 30 day period.

Although the mean concentration of benzene has not changed (about 1.6 ppm), the sample means vary around this value due to sampling error. Figure 7.2(a) shows the histogram of the 30 sample means.

Another town (Town B) takes eight specimens of air each day, again from randomly selected places, and we shall assume the that mean concentration and the natural variation in the benzene concentrations are the same as Town A. A typical set of results from Town B is shown in Figures 7.1(b) and 7.2(b).

Town A

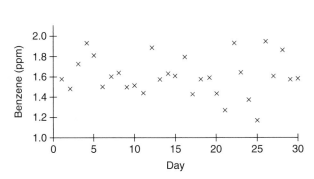

Figure 7.1(a) Mean benzene levels over 30 days (sample size = 2).

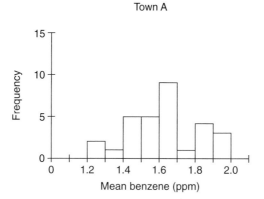

Figure 7.2(a) Histogram of 30 sample means (sample size = 2).

Notice how the variation in sample means is much less for Town B compared with that for Town A. This is because they are collecting more data (eight specimens per day rather than two, and so their sampling error is less). If they took even more, say 20 samples per day, we would expect to see even less variation about the true mean. The larger the sample the less the sample means vary about the population mean. This variation also depends on the variation of the measurement in the population. The greater this variation, the more variation will be seen between sample means for the same sample size. To demonstrate this, Figures 7.1(c) and 7.2(c) show results from samples of size 8 from Town C which has the same mean benzene concentration as the other towns, but has less consistent (i.e. more variable) benzene levels.

Standard deviation is a measure of the variation of a set of values (Chapter 5) and the standard deviation of a set of sample means is called the standard error of the mean. As we have seen, this will depend on the size of the sample and the variation

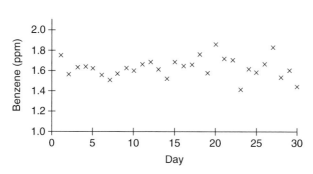

Figure 7.1(b) Mean benzene levels over 30 days (sample size = 8).

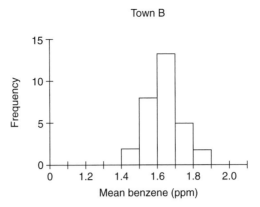

Figure 7.2(b) Histogram of 30 sample means (sample size = 8).

of the population. Table 7.1 gives the means and standard deviations of the data displayed in Figures 7.2(a) to 7.2(c).

The standard error of the mean is related to the standard deviation of the population, σ, and the sample size, n, by the following equation:

$$\text{s.e.}(\bar{x}) = \frac{\sigma}{\sqrt{n}}$$

This equation confirms our intuitive arguments. As the sample size n increases, the standard error will decrease (by a factor $1/\sqrt{n}$) and sample means from populations with large σ will, for the same sample size, have larger standard errors than sample means from populations with small σ. Note that the *standard deviation*, σ, is a population parameter whose value is dependent only on the variability of the population values. However, the *standard error of the mean*, which depends on the sample size and the population standard deviation, is a measure of the precision of the sample mean as an estimate of the population mean.

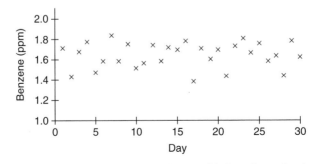

Figure 7.1(c) Mean benzene levels over 30 days (sample size = 8).

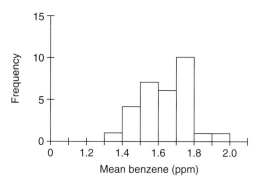

Figure 7.2(c) Histogram of 30 sample means (sample size = 8).

It can be shown that, if the population values have a normal distribution, the sample means will also have a normal distribution. More remarkably it can be shown that, when the sample size is large ($n > 30$ is often regarded as large enough), the sample means will have a normal distribution *whatever the distribution of the population values*. This result is usually referred to as the central limit theorem.

These results allow us to make use of the properties of the normal distribution, discussed in Sections 6.4 and 6.5, to make probability statements about our estimate of the population mean.

So, if we are sampling from a population with mean μ and standard deviation σ, the mean of a sample of size n can be regarded as coming from a normal distribution having a mean of μ and a standard deviation of $\sigma/\sqrt{n}$, providing the population distribution is normal or the sample size is large (typically $n > 30$).

Therefore, for example,

$$P\left(\mu - 1.96\frac{\sigma}{\sqrt{n}} \le \bar{x} \le \mu + 1.96\frac{\sigma}{\sqrt{n}}\right) = 0.95$$

The inequalities can be rearranged to give

$$P\left(\bar{x} - 1.96\frac{\sigma}{\sqrt{n}} \le \mu \le \bar{x} + 1.96\frac{\sigma}{\sqrt{n}}\right) = 0.95$$

Table 7.1   Mean and standard deviations of data in Figures 7.1(a) to 7.2(c)

Town	Mean	SD	Figures
A	1.62	0.19	7.1(a) and 7.2(a)
B	1.64	0.10	7.1(b) and 7.2(b)
C	1.64	0.12	7.1(c) and 7.2(c)

which states that there is a probability of 0.95 that the interval

$$\bar{x} - 1.96\frac{\sigma}{\sqrt{n}} \quad \text{to} \quad \bar{x} + 1.96\frac{\sigma}{\sqrt{n}}$$

contains the population mean μ. This is known as a 95% confidence interval for μ and we shall discuss this more fully in Section 7.4. At present we note that while this gives a range of values in which the true mean is very likely to lie, it assumes that we know the value of the population standard deviation, σ. This is rarely the case – but we can estimate it from our sample. It is tempting to simply replace σ in the formula above by its estimate s and while this is valid for very large samples it not correct for small samples. To overcome this problem we have to introduce another sampling distribution.

7.3   The *t*-distribution

In Section 6.5 we saw that the difference between a normally distributed variable and its mean divided by its standard deviation has a standard normal distribution, i.e. a mean of 0 and standard deviation of 1. In the previous section we established that, under certain conditions, the sampling distribution of the sample mean has a normal distribution with mean μ and standard deviation of $\sigma/\sqrt{n}$ which we call the standard error (s.e.) of the mean. Thus the quantity

$$\frac{(\bar{x} - \mu)}{\sigma/\sqrt{n}} \quad \text{or} \quad \frac{(\bar{x} - \mu)}{\text{s.e.}(\bar{x})}$$

has a standard normal distribution and, as we have seen, can be used to make probability statements about the sample mean.

However, as we rarely know the value of σ we have to replace it with its estimate, s. The new quantity

$$\frac{(\bar{x} - \mu)}{s/\sqrt{n}} \quad \text{or} \quad \frac{(\bar{x} - \mu)}{\text{s.e.}(\bar{x})}$$

no longer has a standard normal distribution. Note that henceforth we shall use s.e. to stand for the estimated standard error $s/\sqrt{n}$.

The distribution of this quantity was determined by Gossett in 1908, writing under the pseudonym of 'Student', who used the symbol t for this expression and its distribution is therefore known as Student's t-distribution. The distribution is very similar to the standard normal distribution, being bell-shaped with a mean of zero, but its width depends on the value of n. Table B2 in Appendix B gives values of t such that the probability of a value *greater* than t is equal to 10%, 5%, 2.5%, 1%, 0.5%, 0.1% and 0.05%, for a range of sample sizes – although these are expressed in terms of 'degrees of freedom' which, for a single sample of size n, is equal to $n - 1$ (the divisor in the sample standard deviation formula). These percentages are labelled as one-tailed percentages. The same table gives values of t such that the probability of t lying *outside* the range $-t$ to $+t$ equals 20%, 10%, 5%, 2%, 1%, 0.2% and 0.1%. These are labelled as two-tailed percentages. When the sample size is very large (infinite) the t-distribution is the same as the standard normal distribution. Thus on the bottom line of Table B2 you will see the familiar value of 1.9600 as being the z-value above which lies 2.5% of the standard normal distribution.

7.4 Confidence intervals for the mean

We can now set up a 95% confidence interval for the mean using an estimated value of σ, since we can use Table B2 in Appendix B to find the value of t such that

$$P\left(-t \leq \frac{(\bar{x} - \mu)}{\text{s.e.}(\bar{x})} \leq +t\right) = 0.95$$

As in Section 7.2, the inequalities can be rearranged to give

$$P[\bar{x} - t_{0.025}\,\text{s.e.}(\bar{x}) \leq \mu \leq \bar{x} + t_{0.025}\,\text{s.e.}(\bar{x})] = 0.95$$

In words, this says that there is a probability of 0.95 that the range

$$\bar{x} - t_{0.025}\,\text{s.e.}(\bar{x}) \quad \text{to} \quad \bar{x} + t_{0.025}\,\text{s.e.}(\bar{x})$$

contains μ. This is known as a 95% confidence interval for the population mean μ and is identical to the expression for the confidence interval given in Section 7.2 except that $t_{0.025}$ has replaced 1.96. If you refer to the bottom line of Table B2 in Appendix B which corresponds to very large (infinite) sample sizes, equivalent to known σ, you will see that the appropriate value of t is indeed 1.96. Even for moderate sample sizes of around 30 the appropriate value of t is close to 2.

Example 7.1

Calculate the 95% confidence interval for the mean pH of water in the river Dee. The sample mean and standard deviation of the 19 specimens of water from the river Dee are 7.479 and 0.1782. Therefore the 95% confidence interval for the mean pH level in the river Dee is

$$7.479 - 2.101 \times \frac{0.1782}{\sqrt{19}} \quad \text{to} \quad 7.479 + 2.101 \times \frac{0.1782}{\sqrt{19}}$$

i.e. 7.39 to 7.57, where the value of $t = 2.101$ was obtained from Table B2, Appendix B, using $19 - 1 = 18$ degrees of freedom.

Confidence intervals based on other probability levels can, of course, be calculated. The usual ones being, 90%, 99% and 99.9%, although the 95% confidence interval is the most common.

Example 7.2

Calculate the 99.9% confidence interval for the mean pH level of the water in the river Dee.

This is calculated as

$$7.479 - 3.922 \times \frac{0.1782}{\sqrt{19}} \quad \text{to} \quad 7.479 + 3.922 \times \frac{0.1782}{\sqrt{19}}$$

i.e. 7.32 to 7.64, where 3.922 was obtained from Table B2, Appendix B, using $19 - 1 = 18$ degrees of freedom.

7.5 Confidence intervals for the difference between two means

Much of the time we need to compare the results from two samples to see whether the means of the two populations differ. In such cases we would like to establish confidence in the difference between the two means. The method for doing this depends on the way the experiment was designed.

Two sets of samples can be regarded as being either paired or unpaired (independent). Paired samples can be regarded as being made up of pairs of observations from a number of different experimental units. For example, the randomized block design to compare two types of catalytic converter introduced in Section 4.2 is an example of paired observations in which the types of vehicle are the different experimental units. Unpaired samples are simply samples from two sources with no relation between the two sets of experimental units – as with the 19 specimens of water from the river Dee and 20 specimens from the river Taff.

The approach for paired samples is straightforward. We reduce the two sets of values from the two samples to one sample of differences by calculating the difference between the two values of each experimental unit. We can then apply the principles of Section 7.4 to these values to construct a confidence interval for the mean difference.

Thus we first calculate the difference between the treatments for each experimental unit and use these to calculate the mean of the differences and the standard deviation of the differences, s_d, and then the standard error of the differences $(s_d/\sqrt{n})$, where n is the number of units.

Example 7.3

Use the data from the randomized block design in Section 3.5 to estimate the difference between the mean CO_2 emissions of the two types of catalytic converter. Calculate the 95% confidence interval for this difference. The data is shown below again for convenience.

The estimated difference between the two types of converter is 0.16 with the 'Nonox Emissions' converter giving higher reading on average than the 'Cleanair Pipes' converter.

Table 7.2 CO$_2$ emissions per hour

	Cleanair Pipes	Nonox Emissions	Difference
Dustcart	1.3	1.5	+0.2
Transit van	1.1	1.1	0.0
Estate car	0.8	0.7	−0.1
Saloon car	0.7	0.8	+0.1
Mercedes van	1.2	1.8	+0.6
Mean			+0.16
Standard deviation			0.2702

The standard error of the mean equals $0.2702/\sqrt{5} = 0.1208$ and the t-value (4 degrees of freedom) is 2.776, so that the 95% confidence interval is

$$0.16 - 2.776 \times 0.1208 \quad \text{to} \quad 0.16 + 2.776 \times 0.1208$$

i.e.

$$0.16 - 0.34 \quad \text{to} \quad 0.16 + 0.34$$

or

$$-0.18 \quad \text{to} \quad 0.50$$

The form of a confidence interval for the difference between the means, μ_1 and μ_2, of two independent samples is similar to that for the paired-sample case. It is

Estimated difference $\pm t_{0.025}$ s.e.(difference)

or

$$(\bar{x}_1 - \bar{x}_2) \pm t_{0.025} \text{ s.e.}(\bar{x}_1 - \bar{x}_2)$$

The method of calculation of the standard error of the difference between the two means depends on whether we are willing to assume, or have evidence to support, that the standard deviations of the populations are equal. Further discussion of this point appears in Section 8.4, but for the purposes of this chapter we shall assume that they are equal. If so, we have two estimates of σ – one from each sample – and it is natural to combine these to get a single estimate. Also, since the estimates may come from different sized samples, we have to weight the estimates. The appropriate weights are the degrees of freedom in each sample. Thus the estimate of σ is

$$s = \sqrt{\frac{(n_1 - 1)s_1^2 + (n_2 - 1)s_2^2}{(n_1 + n_2 - 2)}}$$

This is often called the pooled standard deviation (s.d.) and has $(n_1 + n_2 - 2)$ degrees of freedom; $(n_1 - 1)$ from the first sample and $(n_2 - 1)$ from the second sample.

When the two samples are of the same size $(n_1 = n_2 = n)$ the formula for the pooled s.d. simplifies to

$$s = \sqrt{\frac{s_1^2 + s_2^2}{2}}$$

The standard error of the difference between means from two unpaired samples is

$$\text{s.e.}(\bar{x}_1 - \bar{x}_2) = s\sqrt{\left(\frac{1}{n_1} + \frac{1}{n_2}\right)}$$

which, again, simplifies when the sample sizes are equal to

$$\text{s.e.}(\bar{x}_1 - \bar{x}_2) = s\sqrt{\frac{2}{n}} = \sqrt{2}\,\frac{s}{\sqrt{n}}$$

Example 7.4

Calculate the 99% confidence interval for the difference in the mean SO_2 levels in the atmosphere of two sites in the Bristol area (see Example 4.2 for the data. Twenty-four samples were taken from each site).

The mean and standard deviation of the data from the two sites are

Site 1: $\bar{x}_1 = 34.75\,\text{ppm}$, $s_1 = 11.8478\,\text{ppm}$.

Site 2: $\bar{x}_2 = 23.79\,\text{ppm}$, $s_2 = 8.4954\,\text{ppm}$.

and the pooled standard deviation is therefore

$$s = \sqrt{\frac{11.8478^2 + 8.4954^2}{2}} = 10.3088$$

and

$$\text{s.e.}(\bar{x}_1 - \bar{x}_2) = \sqrt{2} \times \frac{10.3088}{\sqrt{24}} = 2.9759$$

Using Table B2 the value of t (45 degrees of freedom, being the closest to $24 + 24 - 2 = 46$ degrees of freedom) is 2.6896 so that the 99% confidence interval equals

$$(34.75 - 23.79) \pm 2.6896 \times 2.9759$$

or

$$10.96 - 8.01 \quad \text{to} \quad 10.96 + 8.01$$

i.e.

$$2.95\,\text{ppm} \quad \text{to} \quad 18.97\,\text{ppm}$$

7.6   Confidence intervals for percentages

In many environmental experiments or surveys one of the variables of interest is often expressed as a percentage. For example, in attitude surveys the number of respondents holding a certain opinion are counted and this number is converted to the percentage, p, of respondents with that opinion. If the respondents can be regarded as representative of the population sampled, this percentage is an estimate of the percentage of the population holding this opinion. This is how an opinion pollster operates. We shall follow our previous convention of using Greek letters for population parameters and call the population percentage π. Note that this is merely a symbol for the unknown population percentage and is not the mathematical constant 3.142...

The sample percentage, p, is our best estimate of the population percentage, π, but is subject to sampling errors in the same way as the sample mean when estimating a population mean. We therefore construct confidence intervals for a percentage to indicate the degree of precision with which the percentage has been estimated. Assume that we have taken a sample of n individuals, or items, and that r of these possess the attribute of interest. We shall also assume that the sample size is large enough to apply the central limit theorem of Section 7.2, and since the sample proportion r/n is the mean number of successes per trial its sampling distribution is normal.

The sample percentage, $p = 100r/n$, has a mean of π and its standard error is estimated as

$$\text{s.e.}(p) = \sqrt{\frac{p(100-p)}{n}}$$

Since p has a normal distribution, for large values of n, the 95% confidence interval for π is given by

$$p - 1.96\,\text{s.e.}(p) \quad \text{to} \quad p + 1.96\,\text{s.e.}(p)$$

To obtain the 99% and 99.9% confidence intervals the factor 1.96 is replaced by 2.5758 and 3.2905, respectively.

Example 7.5

In a sample of 300 students who were asked whether they were aware of their university's environmental policy, 57 answered 'Yes'. Calculate the 99% confidence interval for the percentage, π, of students at the university who are aware of the policy.

The estimate of π is $100 \times 57/300 = 19\%$ and its standard error is $\sqrt{(19(100-19)/300)} = 2.265$. The 99% confidence interval is, therefore, $19 \pm 2.5758 \times 2.265$ or 19 ± 5.8, i.e. 13.2% to 24.8%.

The standard error of the difference between two percentages, estimated from two independent samples, is

$$\text{s.e.}(p_1 - p_2) = \sqrt{\left(\frac{p_1(100-p_1)}{n_1} + \frac{p_2(100-p_2)}{n_2}\right)}$$

so that the 95% confidence interval is

$$(p_1 - p_2) - 1.96\,\text{s.e.}(p_1 - p_2) \quad \text{to} \quad (p_1 - p_2) + 1.96\,\text{s.e.}(p_1 - p_2)$$

Example 7.6

A sample of 200 students from another university were also asked whether they were aware of their university's environmental policy. Fifty of these students said 'Yes'. Calculate the 95% confidence interval for the difference between the percentages of students at the two universities.

$$\text{s.e.}(p_1 - p_2) = \sqrt{\left(\frac{19 \times 81}{300} + \frac{25 \times 75}{200}\right)} = 3.8085$$

The 95% confidence interval is $(25 - 19) \pm 1.96 \times 3.8085 = 6.0 \pm 7.5$, or -1.5% to 13.5%.

7.7 Calculations using MINITAB and EXCEL

Section 5.5 showed how both MINITAB and EXCEL can be used to obtain a wide range of summary statistics for a set of data. Among these were the sample mean, which estimates the population mean, μ, and the sample standard deviation, s, which estimates the population standard deviation, σ.

Sample values should be entered into a column of a MINITAB worksheet or an EXCEL spreadsheet. Although EXCEL will calculate the summary statistics of any range of cells, it is generally good practice to enter data in columns, especially if you wish to copy data between the two applications.

In MINITAB the standard error of a mean is calculated as part of the output obtained by selecting the menu sequence

Stat, Basic Statistics, Descriptive Statistics . . .

and entering the name(s) of the data column(s) in the **Variables** box.

Example 7.7

The pH and nitrate data from the rivers Dee and Taff were entered into a MINITAB worksheet as shown in Example 5.11 and the descriptive statistics obtained as described above. The resulting output in the Session Window is shown below and includes the estimates of the population mean (MEAN), standard deviation (STDEV) and the standard error of the mean (SEMEAN).

	N	MEAN	MEDIAN	TRMEAN	STDEV	SEMEAN
pHD	19	7.4789	7.5000	7.4882	0.1782	0.0409
Nitrate	19	1.7389	1.7400	1.7418	0.2350	0.0539
pHT	20	7.9400	7.9500	7.9333	0.0995	0.0222
Nitrate	20	1.5380	1.4900	1.5350	0.1867	0.0418

	MIN	MAX	Q1	Q3
pHD	7.1000	7.7000	7.4000	7.6000
NitrateD	1.3200	2.1100	1.5800	1.9400
pHT	7.8000	8.2000	7.9000	8.0000
NitrateT	1.2000	1.9300	1.4125	1.6650

Confidence intervals for a mean are obtained by selecting the menu sequence:

Stat, Basic Statistics, 1-Sample t . . .

entering the name(s) of the data column(s) in the **Variables**: box and selecting **Confidence interval**. Enter the required level, 95 (the default), 99 or 99.9, in the **Level** box and click on **OK**.

For the pH and nitrate data the output is:

	N	MEAN	STDEV	SE MEAN	95.0 PERCENT C.I.
pHD	19	7.4789	0.1782	0.0409	(7.3930, 7.5649)
NitrateD	19	1.7389	0.2350	0.0539	(1.6257, 1.8522)
pHT	20	7.9400	0.0995	0.0222	(7.8934, 7.9866)
NitrateT	20	1.5380	0.1867	0.0418	(1.4506, 1.6254)

Confidence intervals for the difference between two means may also be calculated using MINITAB. When the data is paired, a column of differences between the pairs of values must be first calculated using

Calc, Mathematical Expressions . . .

Basic statistics may then be calculated on this new column of difference as described above.

When the data form two unpaired or independent samples the confidence interval for the difference between the two mean values is obtained using

Stat, Basic Statistics, 2-Sample t . . .

Example 7.8

To obtain the 95% confidence interval for the difference in pH values of water from the rivers Dee and Taff, select **Samples in different columns** from the **2-Sample t** dialogue box and enter pHD as the **First:** sample and pHT as the **Second:** sample. Ignore **Alternative** (see next chapter), enter the required **Confidence level:** and click on **Assume equal variances** and **OK**. The following output is obtained showing the samples sizes, means, standard deviations and standard error of the means. The 95% confidence interval for the difference in mean pH, $\mu_{Dee} - \mu_{Taff}$ is -0.554 to -0.368. Ignore the next line of output as this refers to the t-test which is will be covered in Chapter 8. Note that the pooled standard deviation is equal to 0.143.

```
TWOSAMPLE T FOR pHD VS pHT
         N    MEAN    STDEV   SE MEAN
pHD 19   7.479    0.178     0.041
pHT 20   7.9400   0.0995    0.022

95 PCT CI FOR MU pHD - MU pHT: ( -0.554, -0.368)

TTEST MU pHD = MU pHT (VS NE): T= -10.04 P= 0.0000 DF= 37

POOLED STDEV = 0.143
```

EXCEL provides functions and a data analysis tool to calculate the estimates of the population mean and standard deviation from a sample. However, EXCEL 5.0 will only automatically calculate confidence intervals assuming that the population standard deviation is known.

The appropriate functions are =**AVERAGE(range)** and =**STDEV(range)**. Do not use =STDEVP as this assumes the data is the whole population and thus uses the n-divisor rather than the $(n-1)$-divisor to calculate the standard deviation. A standard error function is not available and must therefore be calculated as =**STDEV(range)/SQRT(COUNT(range))**.

Output from the data analysis tool obtained by using the menu selection

T̲ools, D̲ata Analysis, D̲escriptive Statistics

is shown in Section 5.5. Note however that selecting **Confidence Level for Mean:** in the **D̲escriptive Statistics** dialogue box will calculate the confidence interval assuming the estimated standard deviation is the true population value. This is therefore best avoided as, for the same reason, is the =**CONFIDENCE** function.

Exercises 7

Exercise 7.1

The mercury concentrations (ppm) measured in 10 swordfish were as follows (Source: Gilbert 1987)

    1.20   0.45   0.60   0.76   1.69   1.05   2.06   0.13   1.12   1.37.

(a) Calculate the mean and standard error of the mean for this data.
(b) Hence calculate a 95% confidence interval for the mean level of mercury.
(c) Calculate, also, a 99% confidence interval for the mean level of mercury.

Exercise 7.2

Over many years, weekly readings of pH levels in the river X have averaged 6.5 with a standard deviation of 0.5.

(a) In what range of pH (centred on 6.5) you would expect 95% of these readings to fall?
(b) Assuming no changes in the condition of the river X, what is the probability that a weekly reading exceeds (i) 6.75; (ii) 7.0?

Exercise 7.3

In order to estimate the total emissions of carbon monoxide from a fleet of 500 vehicles a sample of 5 of the vehicles was selected at random and each vehicle driven 100 miles. The total CO emissions were

501, 446, 860, 442 and 495 g/100 miles
(Based on Gilbert 1987.)

(a) Calculate a 95% confidence interval for the mean CO emission per vehicle in the fleet.
(b) Write a sentence describing the meaning of this 95% confidence interval.
(c) How many vehicles would have to be measured if it was required to reduce the width of this interval by half?

Exercise 7.4

A year after the swordfish in Exercise 7.1 was sampled a second sample of 20 fish were analyzed for mercury. The mean and standard deviation of the second sample were 0.703 and 0.666 ppm.

(a) Calculate a 95% confidence interval for the *change* in mercury level during the year.
(b) The Ministry of Fisheries claims that 'there has been a massive 30% reduction in mercury during the year'. Do you think that the data support this claim? Give reasons for your answer.

Exercise 7.5

Twenty-five specimens of air from inside a factory were analyzed for nitrogen dioxide and gave a mean of 79.50 ppb and a standard deviation of 5.00 ppb. Outside the factory a further 25 specimens had a mean of 74.20 ppb with a standard deviation of 7.74 ppb.

(a) Calculate a 99% confidence interval for the mean NO_2 levels (i) inside the building and (ii) outside the building.
(b) Calculate the 99% confidence interval for the difference in the level of NO_2 between the inside and outside of the building.

Exercise 7.6

Two hundred trees from a large forest were randomly selected and inspected for signs of damage from air pollutants. One hundred and ten showed signs of damage. Estimate the percentage of trees damaged and the standard error of this estimate. Hence calculate the 95% confidence interval for the percentage of trees in this forest that are suffering from pollutant damage.

Exercise 7.7

Two surveys were conducted to determine people's attitude to a proposed new road in their area. The first survey was carried out in January and the second during July. Random samples of 250 people were used on each occasion. In January 140 people opposed the new road and in July this had increased to 160.

Calculate the 95% confidence interval for the change between January and July in the percentage of people opposed to the new road. Does your result suggest that there has been a real change in this percentage?

8

Comparison of sample means

8.1 Introduction

We saw in the last chapter how to estimate the mean, μ, of a quantity in a population and also how to estimate a range, or confidence interval, which was very likely (with a specified probability such as 95%, 99% or 99.9%) to contain μ. In addition, we saw how to estimate the proportion, π, of a population having a specific property and estimate confidence intervals for its value. In this chapter we shall make use of and extend these ideas to test whether the estimated values support certain claims, or hypotheses, about a population mean or proportion.

Consider the example used in Chapters 5 and 7 about the pH levels in the river Dee. Suppose that an environmental pressure group had claimed the level to be 8.0. Does the evidence from the sample support or refute that claim? In Chapter 7 we calculated the 95% confidence interval for the mean level of pH to be 7.39 to 7.57 and the 99.9% confidence interval to be 7.32 to 7.64. This means that there is a probability of 0.95 that the range 7.39 to 7.57 contains the true level of pH (and a probability of 0.999 that 7.32 to 7.64 contains the true level of pH). It therefore appears very unlikely that the mean level of pH in the river Dee is equal to 8.0. Of course, we cannot be *absolutely* certain that it is not equal to 8.0 because we have only taken a small sample of the water, but the data provides us with some very strong evidence that the mean pH level is not as high as 8. The procedure we have followed here is called a **hypothesis test.** The hypothesis, in this case, is that the mean level of pH is 8.0 (called the **null hypothesis**, or H_0) and the implicit alternative hypothesis, H_1, is that the mean level is not equal to 8.0. The data was used to construct confidence intervals to determine which of these two hypotheses was the most likely. Hypothesis testing can always be performed by constructing an appropriate confidence interval and determining whether the value hypothesized under the null hypothesis lies inside (accept null hypothesis) or outside (reject null hypothesis in favour of the alternative). In practice, however, hypothesis testing is usually performed in a different but entirely equivalent way to that described above.

In the argument above we accepted the hypothesis if the hypothesized value, μ_0, was inside the 95% confidence interval

$$\bar{x} - t_{0.025} \text{ s.e.}(\bar{x}) \quad \text{to} \quad \bar{x} + t_{0.025} \text{ s.e.}(\bar{x})$$

where $t_{0.025}$ is obtained from tables of Student's t-distribution with $(n-1)$ degrees of freedom. This is equivalent to accepting the hypothesis if the difference between the sample and hypothesized means is not greater than $t_{0.025}$ s.e., i.e. if

$$-t_{0.025} \text{ s.e.}(\bar{x}) < \bar{x} - \mu_0 < t_{0.025} \text{ s.e.}(\bar{x})$$

or, if

$$-t_{0.025} \text{ s.e.} < \frac{\bar{x} - \mu_0}{\text{s.e.}(\bar{x})} < t_{0.025}$$

The conventional way of performing this hypothesis test is to calculate the quantity in the centre of these inequalities (called the test-statistic) and accept H_0 if its value lies between $-t_{0.025}$ and $t_{0.025}$. The value $t_{0.025}$ is called the **critical value** of t. In the next section this approach is formalized and extended.

In this chapter we shall assume that we are dealing with a large sample or, if not, that the population values are approximately normally distributed so that the sample mean can be assumed to have a normal distribution (see Section 7.2). We shall consider the case of small samples from non-normal distributions in the next chapter. Tests for normality are available and MINITAB offers two of these (the Anderson–Darling and Ryan–Joiner tests) under **Graph > Normal Plot...**

Example 8.1

Using the data from Example 5.9, test the claim that the level of nitrate in the river Dee is 2. The null hypothesis is H_0: $\mu_0 = 2$ and the alternative hypothesis is H_1: $\mu_0 = 2$.

The sample of 19 specimens of water from the river has a mean of 1.7389 and a standard deviation of 0.2350. The standard error of the mean $= 0.2350/\sqrt{19} = 0.0539$ and the test-statistic is therefore equal to $(1.7389 - 2)/0.053 = -4.844$.

The critical value (Table B2) is 2.1009 and the test-statistic lies outside the range -2.1009 to 2.1009. Thus we reject the hypothesis that the mean level of nitrate in the river Dee is equal to 2. We say it is *significantly* less than 2, with an estimated value of 1.74.

8.2   Single sample *t*-test

Suppose we wish to test the hypothesis, H_0, that a population mean, μ, is equal to a specific value, say μ_0. We have seen in the previous chapter that the quantity

$$t = \frac{(\bar{x} - \mu_0)}{\text{s.e.}(\bar{x})}$$

has Student's *t*-distribution when the population mean is equal to μ_0. Therefore if the hypothesis, H_0, is correct we expect the value of the sample mean to be close to μ_0 and the value of *t* to be small. Any large deviation from zero would be seen as evidence for rejecting the hypothesis H_0. The above quantity, *t*, is called a **test-statistic**.

We may express this formally by saying that if

$$-t_{\text{cv}} < \frac{(\bar{x} - \mu_0)}{\text{s.e.}(\bar{x})} < t_{\text{cv}}$$

we accept H_0 and reject the alternative hypothesis, H_1 (μ is not equal to μ_0), where t_{cv} is called the **critical value of** *t* and is chosen to reflect the risk we are willing to take of rejecting H_0 when, in fact, it is true. If the value of the test-statistic is outside the range from $-t_{\text{cv}}$ to t_{cv} we reject H_0 in favour of the alternative hypothesis, H_1, that the population mean is not equal to μ_0. Figure 8.1 represents this pictorially, showing the sampling distribution of the test-statistic and the critical values which determine whether H_0 is to be accepted or rejected. The question remains of how to determine the value of t_{cv}. This is chosen from tables of Student's *t*-distribution such that the probability of rejecting H_0 (when it is true) is tolerably small. By convention this probability is set at 0.05 (or occasionally at 0.01 or 0.001) and is called the **Type I error** or **significance level** of the test. It cannot be set arbitrarily small as deceasing the Type I error increases the probability of accepting H_0 when it is false (called the **Type II error**).

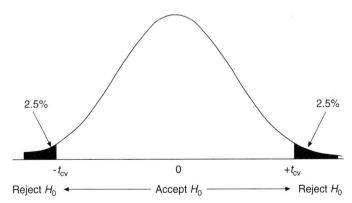

Figure 8.1 Student's *t*-distribution showing the ranges of *t* for which the null hypothesis would be accepted (Accept H_0) and rejected (Reject H_0). The value of t_{cv} is found from Table B2 using the required significance level (two-tailed test) and appropriate degrees of freedom.

Example 8.2

Test the hypothesis, at the 5% level of significance, that the mean DDT level of falcons nesting in the United States is 30 (see Example 5.1).

The null hypothesis is H_0: $\mu_0 = 30$
The alternative hypothesis is H_1: $\mu_0 = 30$

The mean level of DDT is estimated to be 26.333 and the sample standard deviation is 8.1240. Thus the standard error of the mean equals $8.1240/\sqrt{9} = 2.7080$ and the test-statistic is

$$\frac{26.333 - 30}{2.7080} = -1.354$$

$P_9 235$

The critical value of t at the 5% level of significance, with 8 degrees of freedom, is 2.306. Thus, since the value of the test statistic lies inside the range, -2.306 to 2.306, we accept the null hypothesis.

In the above we have assumed that the alternative hypothesis, H_1, is that the population mean is not equal to the hypothesized value, μ_0. In some experiments the alternative hypothesis is directional, that is, we only wish to determine whether the population mean is greater (or less) than μ_0. For example, the environmental pressure group would be interested in knowing whether the pH level in the river Dee was greater than 8.0. In this case the alternative hypothesis is H_1: $\mu > 8.0$ and we only accept this hypothesis for large positive values of t and reject H_1 for all other values of t. However, we still retain our chosen level of significance and the critical value changes to reflect the directional nature of the alternative hypothesis. This is called a **one-tailed test**. Figure 8.2 shows this situation. Tests in which the alternative hypothesis is not directional are called **two-tailed tests**.

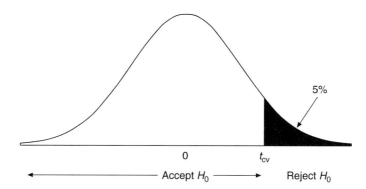

Figure 8.2 Student's t-distribution showing the ranges of t for which the null hypothesis would be accepted (Accept H_0) and rejected (Reject H_0) when the alternative hypothesis is directional. The value of t_{cv} is found from Table B2 (Appendix B) using the required significance level (one-tailed test) and appropriate degrees of freedom.

Example 8.3

The starting salaries of 10 recent graduates of an environmental science degree are shown below. Assuming these to be a random sample of these graduates, test the hypothesis that on average these graduates have a starting salary which is higher than the national average of £12,000 for all graduates.

Starting salaries (£000): 13.0, 12.2, 13.0, 13.5, 12.5, 11.5, 12.9, 12.9, 11.4, 12.0

The null hypothesis is $H_0: \mu_0 = 12,000$
The alternative hypothesis is $H_1: \mu_0 > 12,000$

The sample mean and standard deviation are £12,490 and £696.74. Thus the standard error of the mean is £696.74/$\sqrt{10}$ = £220.33 and the test-statistic is $(12,490 - 12,000)/220.33 = 2.225$.

As the alternative hypothesis is directional, this is a one-sided test, using the left-hand tail of the t-distribution, and the critical values of t (from Table B2 with 9 degrees of freedom) at the 5%, 1% and 0.1% levels of significance are 1.833, 2.821 and 4.297. The test-statistic lies between the 5% and 1% values and we therefore reject the null hypothesis at the 5% level of significance.

The significance level of a hypothesis should be chosen before the data is collected and is conventionally chosen to be 5%, although, depending on the risk the investigator is willing to accept, 10%, 1% and 0.1% are sometimes used. In this book we shall always use 5% and, thus, compare the test-statistic with the tabulated critical value in order to decide whether to accept or reject the null hypothesis at the 5% level of significance. When the null hypothesis is rejected it is conventional to quote the significance level at which H_0 would just be rejected. This is called the *p-value* and is usually expressed as a probability rather than a percentage. In Example 8.3 we rejected H_0 because the test-statistic, 2.225, was greater than the critical value of 1.833. The critical value at the 1% level of significance is 2.821, which implies that the significance level at which H_0 would just be rejected lies somewhere between 1% and 5%, i.e. the p-value lies between 0.01 and 0.05. In a report on the outcome of this study we would state that graduates have a significantly higher salary than £12,000 ($p < 0.05$). In Section 8.5 we shall see that when using computer software to perform a hypothesis test the exact p-value is given. In our example it is 0.02657. We would have just rejected H_0 if the significance level had been set at 2.7%. Figure 8.3 shows the sampling distribution of the t-statistic and the calculated value of $t = 2.225$ for our example. The area to the right of 2.225 represents the p-value (since this is a one-tailed test). For two-tailed tests the areas in both tails make up the p-value. The p-value can also be interpreted as the probability of obtaining the observed test-statistic, or one more extreme, when the null hypothesis is true. Thus we reject H_0 at the 5% level of significance when the p-value is smaller than 0.05.

8.3 Paired samples t-test

In the previous section we compared the mean of a single sample with a hypothesized mean and, on the basis of the value of the t test-statistic, declared the difference

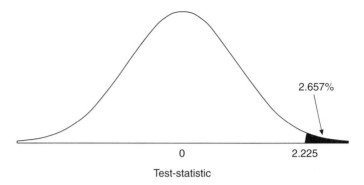

2.657%

0   2.225

Test-statistic

Figure 8.3 Student's *t*-distribution showing the value of the test-statistic for the starting salaries example and its corresponding *p*-value.

between the two to be significant or not. This provided an introduction to the concept of a hypothesis test. However, usually an experimenter has two samples to compare and wishes to know whether they can be regarded as coming from the same population. For example, are the average pH levels in the rivers Dee and Taff the same? Such questions can also be answered using a *t*-test. There are two cases we need to consider, depending on how the experiment was performed.

Two samples can be regarded as being either paired (dependent) or unpaired (independent). Paired samples are usually the result of applying two treatments to a single set of experimental units or to matched pairs of experimental units. A randomized block design with two treatments (Chapter 3) provides an example of matched pairs of experimental units. Unpaired samples are simply random samples from two sources with no relation between the two sets of experimental units and correspond to a completely randomized design with two treatments.

If the object of taking two samples is to compare the means of the populations from which the samples have been taken, the null hypothesis is that there is no difference between the population means. The alternative hypothesis is either that there is some difference between the population means or that one population has a mean that is bigger than the other (a directional hypothesis).

The approach for a paired sample is straightforward. We reduce the n pairs of values from the two samples to one sample of n differences by calculating the difference between the two values for each experimental unit. We can then apply the principles of the single sample t-test to these differences in order to test whether the mean difference, μ_d, is significantly different from zero. To do this we must first calculate the mean of the differences $\bar{d}$ and their standard deviation, s_d.

The null hypothesis is H_0: $\mu_d = 0$.
The alternative hypothesis is H_1: $\mu_d \neq 0$,

or

H_1: $\mu_d < 0$ or H_1: $\mu_d > 0$,

whichever is appropriate. The test-statistic is

$$\frac{\bar{d}}{\text{s.e.}(\bar{d})}$$

and this is compared with the 5%, 1% and 0.1% critical values of t from tables of Student's t-distribution with $(n-1)$ degrees of freedom as described in the previous section.

Example 8.4

Use the data from the randomized block design in Sections 3.5 and 7.5 to test whether there is a difference between the mean CO_2 emissions of the two types of catalytic converter.

The null hypothesis is H_0: $\mu_d = 0$
The alternative hypothesis is H_1: $\mu_d \neq 0$

The mean and standard deviation of the differences (see Section 7.5) are 0.16 and 0.2702.
Thus the standard error of the mean is $0.2702/\sqrt{5} = 0.1208$ and the test-statistic is $0.16/0.1208 = 1.325$.
The critical values of t, with 4 degrees of freedom, at 5%, 1% and 0.1% are 2.776, 4.604 and 8.610 and we therefore accept the null hypothesis. That is, the data does not provide any evidence to suggest that there is any difference between the average CO_2 emissions of the two types of catalytic converter.
Note that the 95% confidence interval for the difference in CO_2 emissions between the two converters was calculated in Section 7.5 to be −0.18 to 0.50. This also tells us that there is no significant difference between the two types of converter since the interval contains zero.

8.4 Unpaired samples *t*-test

The test statistic for an unpaired samples t-test to compare the means from two unpaired samples has the same form as those we have considered before – it is the ratio of the difference between the means divided by the standard error of this difference. The ratio

$$\frac{\bar{x}_1 - \bar{x}_2}{\text{s.e.}(\bar{x}_1 - \bar{x}_2)}$$

has a t-distribution under the hypothesis that the two samples came from populations with the same mean. We have already seen in Chapter 7 how to calculate the standard error of the difference between two means from two independent samples when the population standard deviations can be assumed to be equal. In the next section we shall show how to test whether this assumption is reasonable. For the purposes of calculation we shall continue to make the same assumption here and therefore use the pooled standard deviation in the calculation of the standard error of the difference between the two means. The calculations are best described by an example.

113

Example 8.5

Environmental scientists working for a water authority were asked to establish whether a change in the method of treating effluent would increase the level of dissolved oxygen in a lake into which the effluent was discharged. Prior to the change nine specimens of water were taken from the lake and analyzed for dissolved oxygen. Sometime after the introduction of the new method a further eight specimens were taken (one specimen was lost) and the levels of dissolved oxygen determined. The results were as follows:

Before change: 10.2   10.4   10.6   10.8   10.9   11.1   10.7   10.6   11.3
After change: 11.6   10.8   11.9   11.4   10.7   11.0   11.5   11.4

Is there any evidence that the new method has increased the level of dissolved oxygen in the lake?

The null hypothesis is H_0: $\mu_{after} = \mu_{before}$
The alternative hypothesis is H_1: $\mu_{after} > \mu_{before}$

This is a one-sided unpaired t-test and we shall reject the null hypothesis (and accept the alternative hypothesis) if the test-statistic is greater than the one-tailed critical values in Table B2.
    In order to calculate the test-statistic we use the following steps:

1.   Calculate the sample means and standard deviation for the two sets of data.

$\bar{x}_{before} = 10.7333$, $s_{before} = 0.3391$

$\bar{x}_{after} = 11.2875$, $s_{after} = 0.4155$

2.   Calculate the pooled standard deviation (Section 7.5)

$$s = \sqrt{\frac{8 \times 0.3391 + 7 \times 0.4155}{(9 + 8 - 2)}} = 0.6122$$

3.   Calculate the standard error of the difference between the means (Section 7.5)

$$\text{s.e.}(\bar{x}_{after} - \bar{x}_{before}) = 0.6122 \times \sqrt{\left(\frac{1}{9} + \frac{1}{8}\right)} = 0.2975$$

4.   Calculate the test-statistic

$$t = \frac{11.2875 - 10.7333}{0.2975} = 1.863$$

5.   Compare the value of the test-statistic with the critical values of t in Table B2. The appropriate degrees of freedom are $n_{after} + n_{before} - 2 = 8 + 9 - 2 = 15$. Thus the critical values at the 5%, 1% and 0.1% levels of significance are 1.7531, 2.6025 and 3.7329.

As the value of the test-statistic (1.863) is greater than the critical value at the 5% level of significance, but not greater than the critical value at the 1% level, we reject H_0 in favour of H_1 at the 5% level of significance.
    Our conclusion would be reported as follows: 'The new method of treating the effluent has significantly increased ($p < 0.05$) dissolved oxygen in the lake from an estimated value of 10.73 ppm (s.e. = 0.204 ppm) to an estimated value of 11.29 ppm (s.e. = 0.216 ppm).'
    The standard errors of the means were calculated using $s/\sqrt{n}$, where s is the pooled standard error. They have different values in this example since $n_{before} = 9$ and $n_{after} = 8$.

When the populations standard deviations cannot be assumed to be equal, the standard error of the difference between the two means is estimated as

$$\text{s.e.}(\bar{x}_1 - \bar{x}_2) = \sqrt{\left(\frac{s_1^2}{n_1} + \frac{s_2^2}{n_2}\right)}$$

and the ratio

$$\frac{\bar{x}_1 - \bar{x}_2}{\text{s.e.}(\bar{x}_1 - \bar{x}_2)}$$

no longer has a t-distribution with $(n_1 + n_2 - 2)$ degrees of freedom. However, by simply adjusting the number of degrees of freedom a valid t-test can be performed, although this adjustment often leads to non-integer degrees of freedom. However, some computer software including both MINITAB and EXCEL offer an option to perform the two-sample t-test when the standard deviations cannot be assumed to be equal (the Welch test) automatically calculating the adjusted degrees of freedom and p-value. In fact, this is the default option in MINITAB's two-sample test – Example 8.8 shows this.

8.5   The *F*-test

When calculating confidence intervals for the difference between two means (Section 7.5) and performing the t-test for the difference between two means (Section 8.4) we have made the assumption that the variances, σ_1^2 and σ_2^2, of the two populations are equal. We can test this assumption using a statistical hypothesis test known as the F-test.

The null hypothesis is H_0: $\sigma_1^2 = \sigma_2^2$ and the alternative hypothesis is H_1: $\sigma_1^2 \neq \sigma_2^2$.

The test-statistic, F, is the ratio of the two sample variances:

$$F = \frac{s_1^2}{s_2^2}$$

and is a two-tailed test.

Under the null hypothesis this ratio is distributed as the F-distribution with $(n_1 - 1)$ and $(n_2 - 1)$ degrees of freedom. If the null hypothesis is correct, we would expect the value of F to be equal to 1. Usually only critical values in the upper tail of the F-distribution are tabulated (e.g. Table B3 of Appendix B) so it is common to calculate the test-statistic with $s_1^2 > s_2^2$ (i.e. with the larger variance used as the numerator). We therefore use the critical value corresponding to 2.5% in the upper tail of the F-distribution, if available. However, an often used and useful rule-of-thumb is to take the population variances to be equal if one sample variance is less than three times the other.

Example 8.6

The estimated standard deviations in Example 8.5 were $s_{before} = 0.3391$ and $s_{after} = 0.4155$. Confirm that the hypothesis that $\sigma_{before}^2 = \sigma_{after}^2$.

The F test-statistic is $0.4155^2/0.3391^2 = 1.501$ with 7 and 8 degrees of freedom. The critical value at the 5% level of significance (two-tailed test) is 2.624. Since 1.501 is less than 2.624, we accept the null hypothesis that the two population variances are equal. It was therefore valid to pool the variances in Example 8.5.

8.6 Tests for percentages

Hypotheses concerning a population percentage may be tested using the normal distribution (Section 6.4). This approximation is only valid when the size of the sample is large. However this is rarely a problem as large samples are always required in order to get a reliable estimate of a percentage.

We follow the same procedure as with other hypothesis tests by establishing a null hypothesis and constructing a test-statistic with a known distribution when the null hypothesis is true. From a single sample we may wish to test the hypothesis, H_0, that the percentage of a population having a certain attribute is equal to a specific value, $\pi\%$ (note that π is used here as a symbol for the population percentage and not as the mathematical quantity 3.142...). The sample percentage $p\%$ has a normal distribution and when H_0 is true its mean is π and its standard error is estimated by

$$\text{s.e.}(p) = \sqrt{\frac{p(100-p)}{n}}$$

where n is the sample size. To test the hypothesis H_0: $\pi = \pi_0$ we use the test-statistic

$$z = \frac{p - \pi_0}{\text{s.e.}(p)}$$

which, under the null hypothesis, follows the standard normal distribution.

As usual the critical values depend on whether the alternative hypothesis is directional or not. For the non-directional alternative hypothesis, H_1: $\pi \neq \pi_0$ the critical values at 5%, 1% and 0.1% are 1.960, 2.576 and 3.291. For the directional hypothesis, H_1: $\pi > \pi_0$ the critical values are 1.645, 2.326 and 3.090.

Example 8.7

A random sample of 400 residents of a large town were asked whether they agreed with the town council's proposal to build a new out-of-town supermarket. 230 opposed the proposal. Is this sufficient evidence to suggest that more than half the residents are opposed to the proposal?

The null hypothesis is H_0: $\pi = 50\%$ and the alternative is H_1: $\pi > 50\%$. The estimated value of π is $(230/400) \times 100 = 57.5\%$ and the standard error of this estimate is

$$\text{s.e.}(p) = \sqrt{\frac{57.5(100 - 57.5)}{400}} = 2.47$$

Therefore the test-statistic is

$$z = \frac{57.5 - 50}{2.47} = 3.036$$

The alternative hypothesis is directional, so we use the one-tailed test and reject the null hypothesis at the 1% level of significance. There is strong evidence that more than 50% of the residents oppose the town council's proposal. Our estimate is that 57.5% are opposed to the proposal.

To compare the percentages, π_1 and π_2, of two populations we calculate the ratio of the difference between the sample percentages to their standard error:

$$\frac{p_1 - p_2}{\text{s.e.}(p_1 - p_2)}$$

to test the null hypothesis H_0: $\pi_1 = \pi_2$.

Under the null hypothesis that $\pi_1 = \pi_2 = \pi$, say, we can combine the two sample estimates p_1 and p_2 to obtain the pooled estimate, p, of π:

$$p = \frac{n_1 p_1 + n_2 p_2}{n_1 + n_2}$$

and the standard error of the difference between the two estimated percentages is

$$\text{s.e.}(p_1 - p_2) = \sqrt{\left[p(100 - p)\left(\frac{1}{n_1} + \frac{1}{n_2} \right) \right]}$$

The ratio

$$z = \frac{p_1 - p_2}{\text{s.e.}(p_1 - p_2)}$$

has a standard normal distribution under the null hypothesis that $\pi_1 = \pi_2$.

The critical values are the same as the single sample case. That is, for the non-directional alternative hypothesis, H_1: $\pi \neq \pi_0$, the critical values at 5%, 1% and 0.1% are 1.960, 2.576 and 3.291. For the directional hypothesis, H_1: $\pi > \pi_0$, the critical values are 1.645, 2.326 and 3.090.

Example 8.8

One hundred and twenty salmon were captured from the river X and the same number from the river Y. Each salmon was examined for evidence of poisoning to see whether there was any difference in the percentage of poisoned salmon in the two rivers. Thirty-two from the X showed evidence of poisoning, as did 25 from the Y.

The null hypothesis is H_0: $\pi_X = \pi_Y$ and the alternative is H_1: $\pi_X \neq \pi_Y$.

Our estimated values of π_X and π_Y are 26.67% and 20.83% with a pooled estimate of 23.75%. Therefore, under the null hypothesis, the standard error of the difference between the two estimated percentages is

$$\text{s.e.}(p_1 - p_2) = \sqrt{[23.75(100 - 23.75)(\tfrac{1}{25} + \tfrac{1}{25})]} = 12.036$$

and the test-statistic is

$$z = \frac{26.67 - 20.83}{12.306} = 0.475$$

which is less than the critical value at the 5% level (two-tailed test). We therefore conclude that there is no significant difference in the percentage of salmon showing effects of poisoning in the two rivers. This percentage is estimated to be about 24%.

8.7   Using MINITAB and EXCEL

Both MINITAB and EXCEL provide facilities for performing *t*-tests.
In MINITAB the *t*-tests are accessed using the menu sequence:

Stat, Basic Statistics

and selecting either **1-Sample t**, for a single sample *t*-test or a paired samples *t*-test (after calculating the differences between the pairs), or **2-Sample t**, for an unpaired samples *t*-test.

Example 8.9

Use MINITAB to test whether the level of nitrate is equal to 2 (see Example 8.1). Enter the name of the column (NitrateD) containing the data into the **Variables:** box of the **1-Sample t** dialogue box. Click on **Test mean:** and enter 2 (the mean level of nitrate we wish to test) into this box. The form of the alternative hypothesis is selected using the **Alternative:** options. In this case the alternative hypothesis is that the mean level of nitrate is *not equal* to 2. Finally click on **OK**. The output is shown below:

```
TEST OF MU = 2.0000 VS MU N.E.  2.0000

              N     MEAN    STDEV   SE MEAN       T  P VALUE
NitrateD  19   1.7389   0.2350    0.0539   -4.84   0.0001
```

The *p*-value indicates that the mean level of nitrate in the river Dee is significantly different from 2.

Example 8.10

Use MINITAB to test whether there is a mean difference between the mean CO_2 emissions of two types of catalytic converter (see Example 8.4).
The data is paired so that a paired *t*-test is appropriate. To perform a paired *t*-test in MINITAB a column containing the differences between the pairs must be calculated using **Calc, Mathematical Expressions...** and using a single sample *t*-test on these. In the **1-Sample**

t dialogue box, the name of the column of differences is entered in the **Variables:** box and 0.0 (zero) in the **Test mean:** box. Click on **OK** after selecting the appropriate alternative hypothesis.

The output for the catalytic converter data is:

```
TEST OF MU=0.0000 VS MU N.E. 0.0000

          N    MEAN    STDEV   SE MEAN     T  P VALUE
CO2diff   4   0.0500  0.1291   0.0645   0.77    0.50
```

Since the *p*-value is large (> 0.05) there is no evidence of any difference between the CO_2 emissions from the two types of converter.

Example 8.11

Use MINITAB to test whether a change in the method of treating effluent increased the level of dissolved oxygen in a lake into which the effluent was discharged (see Example 8.5). This requires a two-sample *t*-test. In the **2-Sample t** dialogue box, select the appropriate options and entries corresponding to the layout of your data (e.g. **Samples in different columns** if you have the data values in two columns). As the alternative hypothesis is directional we need to specify **less than** or **greater than** in the **Alternative** box. Which you choose depends on how you specified the samples in the **First:** and **Second:** or **Samples:** and **Subscripts:** boxes. Finally click on **Assume equal variances** and **OK**. The resulting output is:

```
TWOSAMPLE T FOR After VS Before

          N    MEAN   STDEV   SE MEAN
After     8  11.288   0.416    0.15
Before 9    10.733   0.339    0.11

95 PCT CI FOR MU After - MU Before: ( 0.16, 0.94)

TTEST MU After = MU Before (VS GT): T= 3.03 P=0.0042 DF= 15

POOLED SD = 0.377
```

The *p*-value indicates that there is strong evidence of an increase in dissolved O_2 following the change in method of treating effluent.

We note that the variances of the two samples are $(0.416)^2 = 0.173$ and $(0.339)^2 = 0.115$ and differ by a factor of less than 3. Thus our assumption of equality of population variances appears to be valid.

Had we not assumed equal variances the MINITAB output would have been:

```
TWOSAMPLE T FOR After VS Before

          N    MEAN   STDEV   SE MEAN
After     8  11.288   0.416    0.15
Before 9    10.733   0.339    0.11

95 PCT CI FOR MU After - MU Before: ( 0.15, 0.95)
TTEST MU After = MU Before (VS GT): T= 2.99 P=0.0052 DF= 13
```

Note the changes to the confidence interval, the *t*- and *p*-values and the adjustment to the degrees of freedom.

119

EXCEL offers both the paired samples and unpaired samples t-tests under the menu selection **Tools, Data Analysis...** For the paired t-test it is not necessary, as with MINITAB, to calculate the differences.

Example 8.12

Use EXCEL to test whether there is a mean difference between the mean CO_2 emissions of two types of catalytic converter (see Example 8.4).

From the **Data Analysis** window select **t-Test: Paired Two sample for Means** followed by **OK**. Enter the ranges containing the data values for the two samples in **Variable 1 Range:** and **Variable 2 Range:**. Click on labels if you have included column headings in the variable ranges. The **Hypothesized Mean Difference:** should equal 0 (zero). After selecting an appropriate **Output Range:** click on **OK** to get the following results:

```
t-Test: Paired Two Sample for Means

                          Cleanair  Nonox
Mean                        0.975   1.025
Variance                    0.076   0.129
Observations                    4       4
Pearson Correlation        0.9515
Hypothesized Mean Diff          0
df                              3
t Stat                    -0.7746
P(T<=t) one-tail           0.2475
t Critical one-tail        2.3534
P(T<=t) two-tail           0.4950
t Critical two-tail        3.1824
```

EXCEL performs both the one-tailed and two-tailed test, giving the critical values (at 5% level of significance by default or as specified next to **Alpha** in the dialogue box) and the p-values. Of course you should have decided on your alternative hypothesis (and therefore whether you are performing a one- or two-tailed test) before performing the analysis. In this example the two-tailed test is appropriate and gives a p-value of 0.4950 indicating that there is no significant difference between the CO_2 emissions of the two converters.

Example 8.13

Use EXCEL to test whether a change in the method of treating effluent increased the level of dissolved oxygen in a lake into which the effluent was discharged (see Example 8.5).

From the **Data Analysis** window, select **t-Test: Two-Sample Assuming Equal Variances**. The resulting dialogue box is exactly as for the paired t-test (see Example 8.12). On completion of this, click on **OK** to get the following results:

```
t-Test: Two-Sample Assuming Equal Variances
```

	Before	After
Mean	10.733	11.288
Variance	0.115	0.173
Observations	9	8
Pooled Variance	0.1419	
Hypothesized Mean Difference	0	
df	15	
t Stat	-3.0274	
P(T<=t) one-tail	0.0042	
t Critical one-tail	1.7531	
P(T<=t) two-tail	0.0085	
t Critical two-tail	2.1315	

As a one-tailed test is appropriate here the p-value is 0.0042, indicating that the new method of treating effluent has increased dissolved oxygen in the water.

Example 8.14

Use EXCEL to compare the variances of the following sets of data and perform the appropriate t-test to compare the population means from which the samples were taken.

Sample 1: 10, 12, 14, 13, 15
Sample 2: 14, 23, 12, 10, 16

Enter the data into two columns headed Sample1 and Sample2 and select **Tools, Data Analysis, F-Test Two-Sample for Variances, OK**. Enter the ranges of data for the two samples into the **Variable 1 Range** and **Variable 2 Range** boxes and click on **Output Range** and enter the top left cell of this range. Click on **OK** to get the following output:

	F-Test	Two-Sample for Variances
Means	12.8	15
Variances	3.7	25
Observations	5	5
df	4	4
F	6.756752	
P(F<=f) one-tail		0.045576
F Critical one-tail		0.156538

The F-ratio is 6.756752 and the p-value is 0.045576. Thus there is a significant difference between the variances of the two populations ($p = 0.046$).

To compare the two means we should therefore not assume that the two variances are equal. To perform this t-test in EXCEL we follow the procedure of Example 8.13 and select **t-Test: Two-Sample Assuming Unequal Variances**. Complete the dialogue box as before and click on **OK** to obtain:

```
t-Test: Two-Sample Assuming Unequal Variances
```

	Sample1	Sample2
Mean	12.8	15
Variance	3.7	25
Observations	5	5
Hypothesised Mean Difference	0	
df	5	
t Stat	-0.91826	
P(T<=t) one-tail	0.200305	
t Critical one-tail	2.015049	
P(T<=t) two-tail	0.400609	
t Critical two-tail	2.570578	

The *p*-values indicate that there is no significant difference between the two means.

Exercises 8

Exercise 8.1

The mean level of ozone in Oziland has been measured to be 15 ppb over the last 5 years. An environmental agency recently took samples of air from 16 randomly selected sites in Oziland with the following results:

20   23   15   12   25   14   13   15   20   25   17   17   18   24   19   16.

(a) Test the hypothesis that the level of ozone has *increased* from 15 ppb.
(b) What is the estimated increase? Calculate the 95% confidence interval for this increase.

Exercise 8.2

Maximum total phosphorus (mg/l) was determined in samples of water taken monthly from two sites in Chesapeake Bay from October to September in 1984/85 (Nagarj & Brunenmeister 1993). The results were as follows:

Month	Site 1	Site 2
Oct.	1.643	2.063
Nov.	1.575	1.951
Dec.	1.833	2.174
Jan.	1.837	3.269
Feb.	1.746	2.428
Mar.	2.931	5.531
Apr.	1.598	1.469
May	4.027	5.027
Jun.	4.608	5.334
Jul.	1.886	5.761
Aug.	3.105	5.440
Sep.	1.745	3.811

(a) A paired t-test is the appropriate statistical test to determine whether there is a significant difference in the level of maximum total phosphorus between the two sites. Why? State your null and alternative hypotheses.

(b) Perform a paired t-test on the data to determine whether there is a significant difference in the level of maximum total phosphorus between the two sites.

(c) Write a short summary of your results.

Exercise 8.3

Measurements of monthly maximum total phosphorus were taken again in 1987/88 with the following results:

Month	Site 1	Site 2
Oct.	1.616	2.058
Nov.	3.050	2.374
Dec.	1.683	2.556
Jan.	2.018	2.270
Feb.	1.395	1.666
Mar.	1.836	1.967
Apr.	3.602	4.023
May	3.873	3.876
Jun.	3.476	4.742
Jul.	2.903	3.606
Aug.	1.720	2.403
Sep.	2.068	2.526

(a) For each site test whether there has been any change in mean level of maximum total phosphorus from 1984/85 to 1987/88.

(b) Test whether Site 2 has a significantly *higher* mean level of maximum total phosphorus than Site 1 in 1987/88.

Exercise 8.4

Total suspended particulate (TSP) measurements ($\mu g/m^3$) were taken at random from a site on two months. The results are given below:

Month 1	Month 2	
18	25	
24	34	
25	29	
39	45	
21	52	
17	31	(Source: Gilbert 1987)

(a) Calculate the means and standard deviations of TSP for the two samples.

(b) Use an unpaired samples t-test to determine whether the mean TSP has significantly **increased** from Month 1 to Month 2.

(c) Write a sentence summarizing your results, including the mean TSPs and their standard error.

Exercise 8.5

Fifteen CO_2 measurements were taken from random points on each of two floors of a building (Sterling *et al.* 1987). A summary of the data appears below:

	Mean	SD
1st Floor	512.3	52.7
2nd Floor	442.0	43.4

Is there a significant difference between the mean CO_2 level on the two floors? If so, quote the level of significance.

9 Non-parametric tests

9.1 Introduction

The t-tests introduced in Chapter 8 are not strictly valid unless the population data is at least approximately normally distributed. When normality assumptions cannot be made, or there is evidence that the data is far from normal, these tests should not be used. The environmental scientist has two alternatives in this situation. The data may be transformed to a scale on which it is approximately normally distributed and the appropriate t-test performed on the transformed data. For example, positively skewed data can often be transformed to approximate normality by the use of the logarithmic transformation – see Section 6.6. Alternatively, use may be made of one of the many tests which make no assumptions about the form of the distribution of the population measurements. These are collectively known as non-parametric tests and in most cases the ranks of the data values are used rather than the measurements themselves. Hence non-parametric methods generally test hypotheses about the population median rather than the population mean. Use of ranks rather than the actual values clearly represents a loss of information and, consequently, non-parametric tests are not as efficient or powerful as their parametric counterparts when the data is normally distributed. However, t-tests are fairly insensitive to violations of the normality assumption and it is best to use these unless the normality assumption is clearly false.

   We shall consider three non-parametric tests corresponding to the three t-tests discussed in the previous chapter.

9.2 The sign test

The sign test can be used on single samples or paired samples. The sign test for a single sample from a population is used to test the null hypothesis that the population median, η, is equal to a specific value, η_0, against one of the possible directional ($\eta > \eta_0$ or $\eta < \eta_0$) or non-directional ($\eta \neq \eta_0$) alternatives. The test is simple to perform. Each data value is compared to the hypothesized population median; a minus sign is recorded if the value is below the median and a plus sign recorded if the value is above the median. Values equal to the median are ignored. A count is then made of the number of pluses (or minuses – it does not matter which). This is the test-statistic. Since each data value is allocated either a plus sign or a minus sign, the total number of pluses has a binomial distribution (Section 6.2). When the null hypothesis is true, it is equally likely that a sample value will be greater or less than η_0 and the probabilities of a plus sign and a minus sign are both equal to 0.5. Thus under the null hypothesis the test-statistic is an observation from a binomial distribution with $p = 0.5$ and n, the number of trials, equal to the sample size minus the number of ignored data values – i.e. those equal to η_0. The p-value for the test can be calculated from binomial probabilities. The following examples illustrate the use of this test.

Example 9.1

Data on the DDT levels in a random sample of 10 falcons nesting in a particular area were recorded as shown below. Test the hypothesis that the median level of DDT is 15 against the alternative that it is higher than 15.

Data:	19	17	16	16	13	15	74	25	20	12
Sign:	+	+	+	+	−		+	+	+	−

The null hypothesis is: H_0: $\eta_0 = 15$ and the alternative hypothesis is H_1: $\eta_0 > 15$.

The test-statistic is the number of plus signs (7) which, under the null hypothesis, represents an observation from a binomial distribution with $p = 0.5$ and $n = 9$ (since one data value equalled the hypothesized median of 15). As the alternative hypothesis is directional, the test is one-tailed and the p-value is the probability of getting 7 or more plus signs from this distribution.

$$P(7 \text{ or more plus signs}) = {}^9C_7(0.5)^9 + {}^9C_8(0.5)^9 + {}^9C_9(0.5)^9$$

$$= ({}^9C_7 + {}^9C_8 + {}^9C_9)(0.5)^9$$

$$= (36 + 9 + 1)0.001953125$$

$$= 0.090$$

As the p-value is greater than 0.05, we accept the null hypothesis and conclude that there is no evidence to suggest that the median level of DDT is not equal to 15. Note that the estimated value of the median DDT is 16.5.

Example 9.2

The marks of a random sample of 12 students from an exam in environmental statistics are given below. Use the sign test to determine whether the median mark is significantly different from 50.

Marks:	20	70	40	50	65	63	87	54	51	50	10	67
Sign:	−	+	−		+	+	+	+	+		−	+

The null hypothesis is H_0: $\eta_0 = 50$ and the alternative hypothesis is H_1: $\eta_0 \neq 50$.

The total number, S, of plus signs is 7 out of 10 (ignoring the two marks equal to 50). Since the alternative hypothesis is not directional, we employ a two-tailed test and the p-value is the probability of a result as (or more) extreme in either direction as that obtained.

The p-value is $P(S \geq 7) + P(S \leq 3)$. Because of the symmetry of the binomial distribution when $p = 0.5$ these two probabilities are equal and the p-value may be written as

$$2 \times P(S \geq 7) = 2(^{10}C_7 + {}^{10}C_8 + {}^{10}C_9 + {}^{10}C_{10})(0.5)^{10}$$

$$= 2(120 + 45 + 10 + 1)0.0009765625$$

$$= 0.344$$

Once again the p-value is greater than 0.05 and we accept the null hypothesis that the median mark is 50.

9.3 The Wilcoxon signed ranks test

The sign test can also be used to compare two paired samples in which the assumption of normality of the population cannot be justified. A plus or minus is allocated to each of the pairs of data depending on whether the value in the first sample is greater or less than the value in the second sample. Pairs where both values are the same are ignored. The test-statistic is, as before, the number of plus signs; and, under the null hypothesis of no difference in the medians of the two samples, the test-statistic represents an observation from a binomial distribution with $p = 0.5$ and $n =$ number of pairs less those with identical sample values. The calculation of the p-value and its interpretation is exactly as described in the previous section. The sign test uses information only about the direction of the difference between each pair of data values. However, the Wilcoxon signed ranks test takes into account the magnitude of the differences as well as their direction, making it a more powerful test that should be used instead of the sign test when the magnitudes of the differences are known.

As for the corresponding paired samples t-test, the first step is to calculate the difference between each pair of data values. The second step is to rank these differences without regard to their sign (i.e. whether the difference is positive or negative), assigning a rank of 1 to the smallest difference. Ignore all differences equal to zero and give tied differences the average of their ranks. The third step is to attach to each rank the sign of the corresponding difference, thus indicating which ranks arose from negative differences and which from positive differences. Finally sum the positively signed ranks (call this T^+) and sum the negatively signed ranks, T^-. The test-statistic is the smaller of T^+ and T^-.

The null hypothesis being tested in the Wilcoxon signed ranks test is that the medians of the two samples are equal. Under this hypothesis we would expect the sets of positive ranks and negative ranks to be similar and, therefore, the two rank sums to be similar. We would reject the null hypothesis if they were dissimilar. Since the test-statistic is the smaller of T^+ and T^-, we reject the null hypothesis when this value is small. Table B5 in Appendix B gives the critical values of this test-statistic. To illustrate the Wilcoxon signed ranks test consider the following example.

Example 9.3

Specimens of sediment were taken from eight sites along the edge of a river and the average particle size calculated. Six months later the same procedure was performed at the same eight sites. Use the Wilcoxon signed ranks test to determine whether the median particle size has changed over the six months. The data is given below.

Site:	1	2	3	4	5	6	7	8
1st Sample	5.7	5.6	4.5	6.7	6.9	7.8	8.0	4.9
2nd Sample	5.8	6.7	6.0	5.9	6.7	8.0	9.0	5.6
Difference	0.1	1.1	1.5	-0.8	-0.2	0.2	1.0	0.7
Rank	1	7	8	5	2.5	2.5	6	4
Signed Rank	1	7	8	-5	-2.5	2.5	6	4

The null hypothesis is H_0: $\eta_1 = \eta_2$ and the alternative hypothesis is H_1: $\eta \neq \eta_2$.

$$T^+ = 1 + 7 + 8 + 2.5 + 6 + 4 = 28.5 \quad \text{and} \quad T^- = 5 + 2.5 = 7.5.$$

Thus the test-statistic equals 7.5, and since the alternative hypothesis is not directional the test is a two-tailed test. From Table B5 the critical value at the 5% level of significance ($n = 8$) is 3 and as our test-statistic of 7.5 is greater than the critical value we accept the null hypothesis. There is no evidence in the sample to suggest that the median particle size has changed over the six-month period. The sample medians are 6.2 and 6.35.

9.4   The Mann–Whitney test

The Mann–Whitney test is used to compare the medians of two independent samples when the unpaired samples t-test (Section 8.4) is inappropriate because the assumption of normally distributed data cannot be justified.

To calculate the Mann–Whitney test-statistic we combine the data from the two samples (keeping note of the sample to which each value belongs) and rank all the values from smallest (rank 1) to largest. Tied values are given the average of the ranks for which they are tied. The sum of the ranks corresponding to the values from each sample (R_1 and R_2) are calculated. If the null hypothesis is true we would expect the average rank from each of the samples to be about equal. If one is very much smaller than the other we would have reason to reject the null hypothesis in favour of an alternative.

The Mann–Whitney U-statistic is the smaller of U_1 and U_2, where

$$U_1 = R_1 - \tfrac{1}{2}n_1(n_1 + 1)$$

and

$$U_2 = R_2 - \tfrac{1}{2}n_2(n_2 + 1)$$

in which n_1 and n_2 are the two sample sizes. Table B4 gives the critical values of U and the following examples illustrate the use of the Mann–Whitney test.

Example 9.4

Specimens of soil were taken from two sites and the pH levels of the specimens determined. The data is given below. Use the Mann–Whitney test to determine whether there is evidence of any difference in the median pH levels and the two sites.

Site 1:   5.8   6.0   6.2   6.6   7.1
Site 2:   6.5   7.0   7.5   7.6   7.7   7.8

The null hypothesis is H_0: $\eta_1 = \eta_2$ and the alternative hypothesis is H_1: $\eta_1 \neq \eta_2$.
The ranks of the combined data is shown below:

Site 1:   1   2   3   5   7
Site 2:   4   6   8   9   10   11

Therefore:

$$R_1 = 1 + 2 + 3 + 5 + 7 = 18 \quad \text{and} \quad R_2 = 4 + 6 + 8 + 9 + 10 + 11 = 48$$

So

$$U_1 = 18 - 15 = 3 \quad \text{and} \quad U_2 = 48 - 21 = 27$$

The test-statistic $U = 3$ and the critical value at the 5% level of significance (two-tailed test) is 3 (Table B4, Appendix B). Thus we reject the null hypothesis and conclude that there is a difference in the median pH levels at the two sites. From the data we estimate the median pH to be 6.2 at Site 1 and to be 7.55 at Site 2.

Example 9.5

Data on the DDT levels in a random sample of 10 falcons nesting in a particular area were recorded as shown in Table 9.1. On a second occasion 12 falcons were captured and DDT levels determined. Test the hypothesis that the median level of DDT is the same on both occasions against the alternative that it is less on the second occasion.

First occasion: 19 17 16 16 13 15 74 25 20 12
Second occasion: 28 14 15 18 10 10 22 54 19 21 15 34

The data has been combined in the table shown on the next page, ordered and their ranks shown. Adding the ranks of values from the first occasion we get $R_1 = 112.5$ and for the second occasion we get $R_2 = 140.5$. So

$$U_1 = 112.5 - \tfrac{1}{2}10 \times 11 = 57.5$$

and

$$U_2 = 140.5 - \tfrac{1}{2}12 \times 13 = 62.5$$

The critical value, at the 5% level of significance is found from Table B4 (Appendix B) to be 34 and we are obliged to accept the null hypothesis that the median DDT levels are not different on the two occasions.

Table 9.1   Ordered data from Example 9.5 with ranks

Occasion	DDT	Rank	Occasion	DDT	Rank
2	10	1.5	2	18	12
2	10	1.5	1	19	13.5
1	12	3	2	19	13.5
1	13	4	1	20	15
2	14	5	2	21	16
2	15	7	2	22	17
2	15	7	1	25	18
1	15	7	2	28	19
1	16	9.5	2	34	20
1	16	9.5	2	54	21
1	17	11	1	74	22

9.5   Using MINITAB

All the tests described in this chapter are available in MINITAB by selecting

Stat, Nonparametrics

from the menus and then choosing from

1-Sample Sign,
1-Sample Wilcoxon,

or

Mann–Whitney

To perform the sign test on paired data it is necessary, as for the paired t-test (see Section 8.6), to calculate the differences between the pairs of data values as the first step and use the **1-Sample Sign** option on these.

Example 9.6

To use MINITAB to analyze the data from Exercise 9.1, enter the data into a column of a MINITAB worksheet and name the column, say, DDT. Click on **Stat, Nonparametrics, 1-Sample Sign** and enter the name of the column (DDT) into the **Variables:** box of the resulting dialogue box. To perform the test, click on **Test median:** and enter the median associated with the null hypothesis (15 in our example) and change the **Alternative:** to the appropriate alternative hypothesis (in this example it is '**greater than**'). Finally click on **OK** to get the following output:

```
SIGN TEST OF MEDIAN = 15.00 VERSUS G.T. 15.00

        N   BELOW  EQUAL  ABOVE  P-VALUE  MEDIAN
DDT    10     2      1      7    0.0898   16.50
```

The output gives the number of data values (N) and how many of those are below, equal to, and above the hypothesized median. The p-value of the test is given, as is the estimated median.

Example 9.7

As an example of the use of MINITAB to perform the Wilcoxon signed ranks test consider the data from Example 9.3. Assuming that the data values from the two samples have been entered into columns labelled Samp1 and Samp2, the first step is to calculate the differences between the two sets of values by using **Calc, Mathematical Expressions...** placing the results in a new column (Diff). Then select **Stat, Nonparametrics, 1-Sample Wilcoxon** and enter the name of the differences column (Diff) into the **Variables:** box. To perform the test, click on **Test median:** and enter zero and change the **Alternative:** to the appropriate alternative hypothesis (in this example it is '**not equal to**'). Click on **OK** to get the following output:

```
TEST OF MEDIAN = 0.000000 VERSUS MEDIAN N.E. 0.000000

             N FOR   WILCOXON              ESTIMATED
        N    TEST   STATISTIC  P-VALUE      MEDIAN
Diff    8     8       28.5      0.161       0.4500
```

The output shows the full sample size (N) and how many of these were used in the test (remember that zero differences are ignored – there are none in this example). The Wilcoxon statistic is the number of positive differences. The p-value and difference between the sample medians are also displayed. Since the p-value is greater than 0.05 we accept the null hypothesis.

Example 9.8

Finally, we use the data from Example 9.4 to illustrate the use of MINITAB to perform a Mann–Whitney test on two independent samples. We shall assume that the data from the two samples has been entered into two columns of a MINITAB worksheet labelled Site1 and Site2. Select **Stat, Nonparametrics, Mann-Whitney** and enter the names of the two columns into the **First Sample:** and **Second Sample:** boxes. To perform the test, change the **Alternative:** to the appropriate alternative hypothesis (in this example it is '**not equal to**'). Click on **OK** to get the following:

```
Mann-Whitney Confidence Interval and Test
Site1     N =   5      Median =   6.200
Site2     N =   6      Median =   7.550
Point estimate for ETA1-ETA2 is   -1.050
96.4 Percent C.I. for ETA1-ETA2 is (-1.800,-0.300)
W = 18.0
Test of ETA1 = ETA2 vs. ETA1 N.E. ETA2 is significant at 0.0358
```

The output gives the sample size (N) and estimated medians (ETA1, ETA2) for both samples and the estimate of the difference between the medians. An approximate 95% confidence interval for this difference is shown followed by the value of W which equals the sum of the ranks for the first sample. Note that MINITAB does not give the value of the U-statistic, giving the value of R_1, called W, instead! The last line of the output gives the p-value for the test, which in this case is less than 0.05 so that we reject the null hypothesis in favour of the alternative that there is a difference between the median pH values at the two sites.

Exercises 9

Exercise 9.1

The sulphur dioxide levels given below were obtained from 12 sites in Cardiff. Calculate the p-value for the sign test to test the hypothesis that the median sulphur dioxide level in Cardiff is 5 ppb versus the alternative hypothesis that it is not equal to 5 ppm.

SO$_2$ levels: 6   0   5   0   0   1   9   4   0   4   2   0

Give reasons why a non-parametric test is appropriate for this data.

Exercise 9.2

Twelve randomly selected members of the public of South Rankem were asked which of two proposals (P or Q) they preferred for a new town centre in order to determine whether a majority of the public preferred P or Q. The results were as follows:

Preference: P Q P P P P P P P Q P P

Using the sign test, calculate the p-value to test the hypothesis that there is no overall preference for either scheme. What are your conclusions?

Exercise 9.3

The Greenup Britain Party claimed that the data below from 10 cities in Britain provide strong evidence that hydrocarbon levels have increased from 1991 to 1995. Does the Wilcoxon signed ranks test confirm this claim?

Site:	1	2	3	4	5	6	7	8	9	10
1991	0.0	1.3	2.1	0.0	1.5	1.7	0.0	0.6	0.2	1.0
1995	0.2	1.3	2.7	0.4	1.7	1.9	1.1	0.7	0.0	0.5

Exercise 9.4

Maximum total phosphorus (mg/l) was determined in samples of water taken monthly from two sites in Chesapeake Bay from October to September in 1984/85 (Nagarj and Brunenmeister 1993).

The results were as follows:

Month	Site 1	Site 2
Oct.	1.643	2.063
Nov.	1.575	1.951
Dec.	1.833	2.174
Jan.	1.837	3.269
Feb.	1.746	2.428
Mar.	2.931	5.531
Apr.	1.598	1.469
May	4.027	5.027
Jun.	4.608	5.334
Jul.	1.886	5.761
Aug.	3.105	5.440
Sep.	1.745	3.811

(a) Which of the non-parametric tests would be appropriate to analyze the data above?
(b) Use MINITAB to analyze this data. What is the p-value? Use this to draw your conclusions.

Exercise 9.5

On one summer's day a randomly selected sample of eight houses with roof insulation and eight without roof insulation were used in a study to estimate the effect of roof insulation in the summer. The temperature (°C) at the centre of the downstairs of each house was measured at 3 pm and the values are shown below. Use the Mann–Whitney test to test the hypothesis that roof insulation does not affect this temperature against the alternative claim that insulation gives rise to higher downstairs summer temperatures.

No insulation:	20	18	15	20	19	18	16	22
With insulation:	23	20	22	22	21	25	17	24

Exercise 9.6

Assume that the data in 9.3 was collected from randomly selected sites around Britain in both years. Use the appropriate non-parametric test to test the hypothesis that there is no difference between the median level of hydrocarbons in the two years.

Analysis of variance

10.1 Introduction

The data shown in Table 10.1 was collected by an environmental studies student at UWE, Bristol. The objective was to determine whether the water quality of a river in Dorset deteriorates along its course as it passes through intensively farmed agricultural areas, villages and small towns.

It would be illuminating to determine whether the mean pH values for any of the three sites differ from any of the others. That is, have we any evidence to suggest that the river is any more acidic at some locations than at others? If the reader has studied Chapter 3 it will be recognized that the data comes from a *completely randomized study* (the sample locations at each site were chosen randomly), with *3 treatments* (this is the generalized statistical term for the different groups/samples of interest), and that each treatment has *10 replicates*.

If we had just two sites of interest, we could of course carry out a *t*-test to determine whether there were any significant differences between the sample means. Here, however, we have three samples. The reader may well be thinking that this is not a problem, and why can we not carry out three *t*-tests as follows:

Site 1 v Site 2; Site 1 v Site 3; and Site 2 v Site 3?

There are two good reasons why this is not, in general, a good strategy:

Table 10.1   The pH of 10 water specimens taken from each of three sites on the river Brid in Dorset

	Site 1	Site 2	Site 3
	7.00	7.85	8.30
	7.00	8.00	8.45
	7.10	8.15	8.00
	7.10	8.15	8.00
	7.05	8.00	8.20
	7.50	7.65	7.85
	7.40	7.70	8.05
	7.05	7.20	8.00
	7.70	7.75	7.70
	7.70	7.80	7.65
Means	7.26	7.825	8.02

Note: Site 1 – Source of the river
Site 2 – 10 miles downstream of the source
Site 3 – 18 miles downstream of the source

1. A series of *t*-tests could be time consuming. In this example the three sample sites would require a manageable number of *t*-tests (three of them). However, if we had sampled the river at five sites we would require 10 *t*-tests, and if we had 10 sample sites no fewer than 45 *t*-tests would be required!
2. When we carry out a *t*-test at say the 5% level of significance, we willingly accept the fact that if no differences exist between the two sample means, there is still a 5% chance that an erroneous conclusion will be made suggesting that a difference does exist.

If we now conduct three different *t*-tests for a set of data, the chance of incorrectly stating that differences exist between at least two of the three samples is approximately 15%. (*If the three tests were independent, the precise figure would be* $(1 - 0.95^3) \times 100\% = 14.26\%$.)

A 15% chance of making a mistake of this type is not acceptable, and, of course, if there are more than three samples the risk of finding 'bogus differences' is higher (indeed with six samples there is approximately a 50% chance of finding 'bogus differences').

The most used techniques for determining whether the means for a number of treatments differ significantly from each other are called **analysis of variance techniques** (usually shortened to ANOVA). In this chapter we shall look at ANOVA techniques for the analysis of data from completely randomized design surveys and experiments, and also for the analysis of data from randomized block design surveys and experiments.

10.2   The analysis of completely randomized design surveys and experiments: one-way ANOVA

An inspection of Table 10.1 reveals that the mean pH readings for samples from each of the three sites vary from 7.26 to 8.02. The question is: Are these differing means due to real differences in the water acidity at the three sites, or could they reasonably be this varied purely as a result of random variation?

10.2.1 The null hypothesis

We begin our testing procedure by assuming that the differences are merely the result of random variation and that the population means of the pH values are the same at each site. That is, we test the hypothesis

$$H_0: \quad \mu_1 = \mu_2 = \mu_3$$

As with any hypothesis test we only reject this working hypothesis if we have significant evidence to suggest that it is unreasonable.

10.2.2 Estimating variation in the population

If our null hypothesis is true, the three samples (treatments) all come from the same population with a mean pH level of μ, and a variance in pH levels of σ^2. When the null hypothesis is true, σ^2 can be equally well approximated by two different variance estimates. These are the **within treatment variance** and the **between treatment variance**.

In order to verify that this is true, and to show how the two variance estimates can be calculated, consider Example 10.1 below.

Note: *In this text, hand calculations will only be considered for the simplest case where we have equal numbers of replicates for each treatment.*

Example 10.1

The data below was generated artificially by computer. All three samples are random samples taken from a normal distribution with a mean of 7.0 and a variance of 0.02. (These values might describe the pH values of a stretch of water.)

When there are equal numbers of replicates for each treatment the calculations of the **within treatment variance** and the **between treatment variance** are straightforward.

Sample 1	Sample 2	Sample 3	
6.8	7.2	6.9	
7.1	7.0	7.1	
7.0	6.8	7.0	
6.9	7.0	6.9	
6.8	7.1	7.2	
$\bar{x}_1 = 6.92$	$\bar{x}_2 = 7.02$	$\bar{x}_3 = 7.02$	Overall mean $\bar{x} = 6.9867$

The within treatment variance

As the three samples all come from the same population, the variation within each sample should be approximately equal to the variation in the population. We could thus estimate the variance of the population by:

1. Estimating the variance from each of three samples separately.
2. Pooling these three estimates to obtain one pooled estimate.

This estimate is known as the **within treatment variance**. In this example, where we have equal replication, the within treatment variance is simply the average of the three sample variances.

$$s_p^2 = \frac{0.017 + 0.022 + 0.017}{3} = 0.0187$$

As we might hope this estimate is pretty close to the known population variance of 0.02.

The between treatment variance

We could find the sample variance between the three treatments means as follows:

$$s_{\bar{x}}^2 = \frac{(\bar{x}_1 - \bar{x})^2 + (\bar{x}_2 - \bar{x})^2 + (\bar{x}_3 - \bar{x})^2}{3 - 1}$$

$$s_{\bar{x}}^2 = \frac{(6.92 - 6.9867)^2 + (7.02 - 6.9867)^2 + (7.02 - 6.9867)^2}{2}$$

$$s_{\bar{x}}^2 = 0.0033$$

The reader might remember from Chapter 7 that the variance between the sample means is related to the variance of the population by the following expression:

$$s_{\bar{x}}^2 \approx \frac{\sigma^2}{n}$$

We can rearrange the above expression to obtain another estimate of the population variance, σ^2, namely the **between treatment variance**.

$$\sigma^2 \approx n s_{\bar{x}}^2$$

For this example, the between treatment estimate of the variance is:

$$n s_{\bar{x}}^2 = 5 \times 0.0033 = 0.017$$

Once again, this estimate is reasonably close to the known population variance of 0.02.

Example summary

It has been shown that when all the observations from a completely randomized experiment come from the same population, the between treatment variance and the within treatment variance produce very similar estimates of the population variance σ^2. As we shall see below, this is not the case when the treatments have differing population means.

The variance calculations for the river Brid pH example

Let us now return to the real-life data collected from the river Brid. The reader can verify that the required summary statistics for each site are as shown below:

Site 1	Site 2	Site 3
$\bar{x}_1 = 7.26$	$\bar{x}_2 = 7.825$	$\bar{x}_3 = 8.02$
$s_1^2 = 0.0821$	$s_2^2 = 0.0796$	$s_3^2 = 0.0629$

Overall mean $\bar{x} = 7.7017$; Sample size, $n = 10$

We can now find the *within treatment variance* and the *between treatment variance* as was shown in Example 10.1.

Within treatment variance

$$s_p^2 = \frac{0.0821 + 0.0796 + 0.0629}{3} = 0.0749$$

Between treatment variance
Variance of sample means is:

$$s_{\bar{x}}^2 = \frac{(7.26 - 7.7017)^2 + (7.825 - 7.7017)^2 + (8.02 - 7.7017)^2}{2}$$

$$= 0.1558$$

The between treatment variance is thus:

$$ns_{\bar{x}}^2 = 10 \times 0.1558 = 1.558$$

Unlike Example 10.1, the between treatment variance, and the within treatment variance are not at all similar here. The between treatment variance is far higher than the within treatment variance.

In general, if no differences exist between the population means for each treatment, then the variability between the treatments is roughly equal to the variability within the treatments.

If, however, the population means for each treatment differs, this has the effect of increasing the variability between the treatments, so the between treatment variability is higher than the within treatment variability.

For our data then, there is far more variability in the pH values between the three sites than there is in the pH values within the sites. This may well suggest that the acidity of the water may vary significantly between the three sites. In order to determine whether this is the case we need to test whether the between treatment variance is significantly higher than the within treatment variance using an *F*-test.

10.2.3 The ANOVA F-test

In order to test the null hypothesis

$$H_0: \quad \mu_1 = \mu_2 = \mu_3$$

we simply test whether the between treatment variance is significantly greater than the within treatment variance using an F-test. (The F-test was explained in Chapter 8.)

The test-statistic

The F-statistic we calculate is

$$F = \frac{\text{Between treatment variance}}{\text{Within treatment variance}} \qquad \textbf{(Equation 10.1)}$$

When all treatments have equal replication this can be written as:

$$F = \frac{ns_{\bar{x}}^2}{s_p^2} \qquad \textbf{(Equation 10.2)}$$

The degrees of freedom for the F-test

For an F-test for a one-way ANOVA, the degrees of freedom are as follows:

Let $\quad N = $ total number of observations

$\qquad k = $ number of treatments

Between treatment degrees of freedom: $\quad k - 1$
Within treatment degrees of freedom: $\quad (N - 1) - (k - 1)$

In our example we have

$$F = \frac{ns_{\bar{x}}^2}{s_p^2} = \frac{1.558}{0.0749} = 20.8$$

Between treatment degrees of freedom are:

$$3 - 1 = 2$$

Within treatment degrees of freedom are:

$$(30 - 1) - (3 - 1) = 27$$

and by inspection of Table B3 in Appendix B we can see that $F_{2, 27, 0.01\%} \approx 9.0$.

As our test-statistic is greater than the critical value, we have shown that the null hypothesis

$$H_0: \quad \mu_1 = \mu_2 = \mu_3$$

can be rejected at the 0.1% significance level. This tells us that the pH of the river varies at different sites. (The reader may well have noticed that we have not yet explored which sites differ from which others in terms of the pH of the water. This will be the focus of Section 10.3.)

10.2.4 One-way ANOVA for data with unequal sample sizes

Wherever possible it is desirable to have equal replication for each treatment, as this is the most efficient way to obtain information from a given volume of data. However, if this is not possible it is still not a problem to carry out a one-way ANOVA on the data. The general idea is exactly the same, with the possibility of differing treatment means being tested via an F-test of the between treatment variance/ within treatment variance ratio. The reader is reminded, however, that the calculations of the required variances are a little more complicated than they are in the simpler case of a balanced design with equal replication. In this text the emphasis is on the understanding of principles and the applicability of techniques, hence the majority of the remainder of this chapter will rely on MINITAB carrying out the calculations.

10.2.5 One-way ANOVA with MINITAB

Exhibit 10.1 shows some MINITAB one-way ANOVA output for the river Brid pH data. The data should be entered into two MINITAB columns as follows:

Row	c1 (site)	c2 (pH)
1	1	7.00
2	2	7.85
3	3	8.30
4	1	7.00
5	2	8.00
6	3	8.45
..	..	..
..	..	..
28	1	7.70
29	2	7.80
30	3	7.65

where Site 1 is the source of river, Site 2 is 10 miles downstream of the source and Site 3 is 18 miles downstream of the source

Notes:

1. MINITAB treatment labels should be integers starting at 1.
2. It is possible to carry out a one-way ANOVA with MINITAB by having the data for each treatment in separate columns. However, as more complex ANOVA calculations require a similar data format to that shown, it makes sense to become accustomed to this format of data input.

Once the data has been entered as shown above, the menu sequence

S̲tat, A̲NOVA, O̲neway

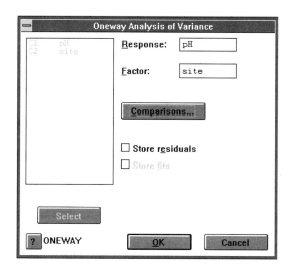

```
Analysis of Variance on pH
Source    DF      SS       MS      F       p
site       2   3.1162  1.5581  20.81  0.000
Error     27   2.0212  0.0749
Total     29   5.1374
                              Individual 95% CIs For Mean
                              Based on Pooled StDev
Level   N    Mean    StDev   --------+---------+---------+--------
  1    10  7.2600   0.2866  (----*-----)
  2    10  7.8250   0.2821                (-----*----)
  3    10  8.0200   0.2508                      (----*----)
                              --------+---------+---------+--------
Pooled StDev=0.2736              7.35      7.70      8.05
```

Exhibit 10.1 MINITAB output relating to a one-way ANOVA of the river Brid pH data introduced in Table 10.1.

produces the menu shown at the top of Exhibit 10.1. If the pH is selected as the response variable, and site is selected as the factor, the output shown is produced.

The ANOVA table

MINITAB presents the ANOVA results in the form of an ANOVA table. This is common practice when carrying out an ANOVA.

The **Source** column shows the source of the variation. The site variation is the between treatment variation, and the error variation is the within site variation.

The **DF** column shows the degrees of freedom for each of the sources of variation. As we saw earlier, the between treatment variation and the within treatment variation have 2 and 27 degrees of freedom respectively.

The **MS** (standing for mean square) column shows the between treatment and within treatment variances. As we calculated earlier, these are 1.5581 and 0.0749 respectively.

The **SS** (sum of squares) column shows a measure of variability for each source of variability that we did not use in this chapter. The SS for each source of variation is equal to the variance for the source times the degrees of freedom for the source.

The **F** column shows the F-ratio test-statistic which is

$$F = \frac{\text{Between treatment variance}}{\text{Within treatment variance}} \left(\text{or} \; \frac{\text{Treatment MS}}{\text{Error MS}} \right)$$

The final column **p**, is very useful. It allows the user to determine whether the F-ratio is significant or not, without having to look up critical values from a set of F tables. The p-value is the probability of obtaining an F-ratio as large as we have (or larger), if the treatment means are all the same. So the smaller p is, the more evidence we have to reject the null hypothesis of equal means.

In this example the p-value of 0.000 (to 3 decimal places) means that if the pH of the river Brid was the same at all three sites, the chance of obtaining an F-ratio as large as 20.8 is 0.000 (to 3 decimal places). Hence there is very little chance that the pH is the same for all three sites.

10.2.6 The assumptions of the one-way ANOVA

In order for a one-way ANOVA to be valid, certain assumptions are made. The reader is advised to check whether the assumptions in Box 10.1 are reasonable for any data that may be dealt with before proceeding with an ANOVA.

BOX 10.1 ▶ **The assumptions for a one-way ANOVA**

1. The samples for each treatment are random samples from the populations of interest.

2. All treatment populations are approximately normally distributed. (Hence all observations must be continuous, or at least covering a very wide discrete scale.)

3. All treatment populations have a common variance, σ^2.

Notes

1. If assumption 1 is not valid because observations from each treatment are **matched** to particular observations from the other treatments, a two-way ANOVA should be used. (See Section 10.4.)

2. If assumptions 2 or 3 are in doubt, a non-parametric test might be more appropriate. The Kruskal–Wallis test will perform a similar job to a one-way ANOVA without making assumptions 2 or 3. (See, for example, Chapter 7 of Hampton 1994.)

10.3   Comparisons between treatment means

An analysis of variance is useful for determining whether or not all the treatment (sample) means are equal or not. However, if differences in the treatment means are found to exist we need to know where the differences lie; i.e. which treatments have means different to the others.

There are a wide range of methods available for conducting these multiple comparisons; we shall consider three methods which are readily available in MINITAB and many other statistical packages.

10.3.1 Visual inspection of the treatment means

In many situations, an ANOVA followed by a visual inspection of the treatment means is sufficient to determine the differences of interest.

With MINITAB 10 Xtra the menu sequence

Stat, ANOVA, Main Effects Plot

allows for a visual inspection of the treatment means. For example, the mean pH value for samples from each of the three sites on the river Brid have been plotted using this facility, as is shown in Figure 10.1.

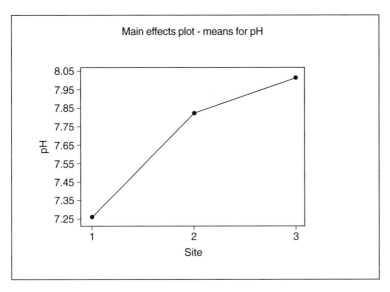

Figure 10.1 A visual representation of the mean pH values for each of three sites on the river Brid, as produced by MINITAB.

It would appear from this graph that there is a tendency for the acidity of the water to decrease as the distance from the source increases. In particular, the acidity at the source (site 1), appears to be greater than at the other two sites further downstream. The plot, in conjunction with the ANOVA carried out earlier, tell us for certain that the mean pH level at site 3 is significantly higher than at site 1 (we know this because as the ANOVA results are significant, the highest and lowest sample means must differ significantly).

This conclusion may well be precise enough for answering the question of interest. However, we might need a slightly more precise conclusion so as to determine whether site 2 has a pH level significantly different from the two extremes observed at sites 1 and 3.

10.3.2 Confidence intervals for treatment means

When a one-way ANOVA is carried out with MINITAB, 95% confidence intervals for the mean response for each treatment are shown diagrammatically underneath the ANOVA table (see Exhibit 10.1). These plots are not as attractive as the graphs discussed above, but they are in fact more illuminating.

Clearly, if the 95% confidence intervals for two treatments do not overlap, then the differences between the two treatment means must be significant at the 5% significance level. Conversely, if the 95% confidence intervals for two treatment means overlap over almost all of their ranges, it is unlikely that the two treatment means differ significantly from each other. It is only when a small overlap exists between the two confidence intervals that any doubt exists as to whether the means of two treatments differ significantly.

Referring back to Exhibit 10.1, we can see that the 95% confidence interval for the mean pH value at site 1 (the source of the river) does not overlap with the confidence intervals for sites 2 or 3. We thus know that the pH of the river Brid at the source is significantly lower than at either of the other two sites. Whether or not the pH differs significantly between sites 2 and 3 is still rather unclear, as the degree of overlap is neither minimal nor almost total.

How are the confidence intervals for the treatment means calculated?

A 95% confidence interval for the mean response for treatment i, μ_i, is given by:

$$\bar{x}_i \pm t_{0.025} \sqrt{\frac{s_p^2}{n_i}}$$

This will look familiar from Section 7.4, but there are some differences:

1. The variance used is the within treatment variance (the error variance), **not** the sample variance for treatment i.
2. The degrees of freedom for the t-value are the degrees of freedom for the within treatment variance.

For the river Brid example we have:

Site 1	*Site 2*	*Site 3*
$\bar{x}_1 = 7.26$	$\bar{x}_2 = 7.825$	$\bar{x}_3 = 8.02$
$s_p^2 = 0.0749$	$n_1 = n_2 = n_3 = 10$	

So the 95% confidence interval for the mean pH value of water specimens at the source of the river Brid (site 1) is:

$$7.26 \pm 2.2622 \times \sqrt{\frac{0.0749}{10}}$$

that is:

$$7.26 \pm 0.196$$

As all three sites had equal replication, the 95% confidence intervals for the three sites are:

Site 1: 7.26 ± 0.196 or   7.064 to 7.456
Site 2: 7.825 ± 0.196 or   7.629 to 8.020
Site 3: 8.02 ± 0.196 or   7.824 to 8.216

10.3.3 Confidence intervals for $\mu_i - \mu_j$

Another way to examining significant differences is to find 95% confidence intervals for the differences between each treatment mean, and to conclude that a difference is real if the confidence interval does not contain zero – similar to the approach taken in Section 7.5. This approach would allow us to determine whether the mean pH values differ between sites 2 and 3. (The confidence intervals above cannot do this as they overlap.)

The trouble with this approach is that each comparison has a 5% chance of incorrectly finding a 'bogus difference'. As was discussed in the introduction to this chapter, when a number of treatment comparisons are made this way the chance of making incorrect statements grows large. This was the problem that we used ANOVA to overcome! One solution is to use Tukey's simultaneous confidence intervals instead.

Tukey's simultaneous confidence intervals for $\mu_i - \mu_j$

MINITAB and many other statistical packages will calculate a set of simultaneous confidence intervals for the differences between all possible pairs of treatment means. A set of Tukey's 95% confidence intervals is arrived at such that there is only a 5% chance of one or more of the confidence intervals not containing the true difference in treatment means. As a result, Tukey's confidence intervals tend to be conservative (wide), and any apparent differences found can be confidently taken as 'real'.

Tukey's simultaneous confidence intervals for the differences between the treatment means for the river Brid example are shown below. They confirm our conclusion that the river Brid is significantly more acidic at the source than at the other two locations, and that the acidity does not differ significantly between sites 2 and 3 (or at least we do not have enough data to show any difference that exists).

Using MINITAB Tukey's confidence intervals are available by selecting **C**omparisons from the one-way ANOVA menu.

Tukey's confidence intervals for the river Brid example as produced by MINITAB 10 Xtra

Tukey's pairwise comparisons

Family error rate = 0.0500

Individual error rate = 0.0196

Critical value = 3.51

Intervals for (column level mean) – (row level mean)

	1	2
2	−0.8687	
	−0.2613	
3	−1.0637	−0.4987
	−0.4563	0.1087

Summarized information

Comparison	Confidence interval	Significance
Mean for site 1		
– Mean for site 2 $(\mu_1 - \mu_2)$	−0.8687 to −0.2613	Significant
Mean for site 1		
– Mean for site 3 $(\mu_1 - \mu_3)$	−1.0637 to −0.4563	Significant
Mean for site 2		
– Mean for site 3 $(\mu_2 - \mu_3)$	−0.4987 to 0.1087	Not significant

---

BOX 10.2 ▶ **Recap of methods for determining significant differences**

A common sense approach to take is as follows:

1. If the 95% confidence intervals for two treatments do not overlap, then take the two treatment means as differing significantly. (The chance of the difference not being real must be well under 5%.)

2. If the 95% confidence intervals for two treatment means overlap for anything more than the extreme tails of the interval, take the two treatment means as not offering any significant evidence of any differences in the means.

3. If the 95% confidence intervals are inconclusive, or if a large number of treatments are being used, it is safest to consider using Tukey's simultaneous confidence intervals for $\mu_i - \mu_j$.

4. Differences between treatment means are best relayed to non-statisticians by the use of a simple plot of the treatment means.

10.4   The analysis of randomized block design surveys and experiments: two-way ANOVA

The data shown in Table 10.2 was collected as part of the same study referred to previously in this chapter. It shows the nitrate concentrations of water specimens collected from three different sites on the river Brid. The question of interest is: Does the nitrate concentration of the river water change as the distance from the source changes? (We might expect the nitrate concentration to increase as the distance from the source increases.)

If the readers have studied Chapter 3 they will recognize that the data comes from a **randomized block study**, which has **3 treatments** (the three river sites), and **4 blocks** (each week's measurements are a block of observations).

10.4.1 Why not carry out a one-way ANOVA?

We could carry out a one-way ANOVA on this data, much like the example seen earlier. The results of such an ANOVA are shown in Exhibit 10.2.

Using this approach, the ANOVA F-ratio and accompanying p-value suggest that there are no significant differences in the mean nitrate concentrations between the three river sites. But is this really the case?

When data comes from a **completely randomized design** study, the variability in the data is assumed to come from **two** sources:

1. Variability due to the different treatments.
2. Unexplained variability.

The significance or not of the treatment effect is determined by carrying out a one-way ANOVA which compares the relative sizes of the treatment and unexplained variability.

Table 10.2   The nitrate concentrations (mg/l) of three water specimens taken from each of three sites on the river Brid in Dorset

	Site 1	Site 2	Site 3
Week 1	0.36	1.10	1.88
Week 2	1.10	4.00	7.40
Week 3	4.00	4.80	6.00
Week 4	4.20	4.80	6.50

Note: Site 1 – Source of the river
　　　 Site 2 – 10 miles downstream of the source
　　　 Site 3 – 18 miles downstream of the source

```
ANALYSIS OF VARIANCE ON Nitrate
SOURCE  DF    SS     MS     F      p
Site     2   18.54  9.27   2.15   0.173
ERROR    9   38.87  4.32
TOTAL   11   57.41
                         INDIVIDUAL 95% CI'S FOR MEAN
                         BASED ON POOLED STDEV
   LEVEL   N   MEAN   STDEV  ----------+---------+---------+------
     1     4   2.415  1.971  (---------*--------)
     2     4   3.675  1.758       (---------*--------)
     3     4   5.445  2.446           (---------*--------)
                             ----------+---------+---------+------
POOLED STDEV = 2.078               2.5       5.0       7.5
```

Exhibit 10.2 MINITAB output relating to a one-way ANOVA of the river Brid nitrate data shown in Table 10.2.

When data comes from a **randomized block design** study, as it does in Table 10.2, the variability could come from **three** sources:

1. Variability due to the different treatments.
2. Variability due to the different blocks.
3. Unexplained variability.

We should thus allow for the fact that, apart from our data possessing variability due to differences between the river sites, it will also contain some variability which is due to differing nitrate concentrations between the weeks. (If it rains a lot in any week, the nitrate concentrations are likely to be lower.)

If the block effects of a randomized block design study are ignored, there is a strong possibility that interesting differences between treatment means will be obscured. The analysis that caters for this extra source of variability is called a **two-way ANOVA**.

10.4.2 Two-way ANOVA with MINITAB

A two-way ANOVA of the data in Table 10.2 can easily be carried out if the data is entered into a MINITAB spreadsheet as shown below:

Row	c1 (site)	c2 (block)	c3 (nitrate)
1	1	1	0.36
2	2	1	1.10
3	3	1	1.88
4	1	2	1.10
5	2	2	4.00

Row	c1 (site)	c2 (block)	c3 (nitrate)
6	3	2	7.40
7	1	3	4.00
8	2	3	4.80
9	3	3	6.00
10	1	4	4.20
11	2	4	4.80
12	3	4	6.50

Output similar to that shown in Exhibit 10.2 is produced by using the menu sequence

Stat, ANOVA, Twoway

10.4.3 What does Exhibit 10.3 show?

The ANOVA table shown in Exhibit 10.3 is interpreted in a very similar way to the one-way tables seen previously, the only difference being that an additional source of variation is listed.

```
Analysis of Variance for Nitrate
Source  DF     SS       MS      F      P
Site     2   18.535   9.268   7.53  0.023
Week     3   31.490  10.497   8.53  0.014
Error    6    7.380   1.230
Total   11   57.406

                  Individual 95% CI
Week  Mean   ---+---------+---------+---------+--------
  1   1.11   (-------*------)
  2   4.17               (-------*-------)
  3   4.93                 (-------*-------)
  4   5.17                  (-------*-------)
             ---+---------+---------+---------+--------
             0.00      2.00      4.00      6.00

                  Individual 95% CI
Site  Mean   ---+---------+---------+---------+--------
  1   2.41   (--------*--------)
  2   3.68        (---------*--------)
  3   5.45                (--------*--------)
             ---+---------+---------+---------+--------
             1.50      3.00      4.50      6.00
```

Exhibit 10.3 MINITAB output relating to a two-way ANOVA of the river Brid nitrate data shown in Table 10.2.

The reader will notice:

1. The between site variance is 9.27, exactly as is shown in Exhibit 10.2.
2. The unexplained variability when carrying out a two-way ANOVA is 1.23, which is much lower than the unexplained variability of 4.32 seen in Exhibit 10.2. This is because most of the previously unexplained variability in nitrate concentrations can be explained by differences between the weeks.
3. As the unexplained variability is lower in Exhibit 10.3, the F-ratio

$$F = \frac{\text{Between treatment variance}}{\text{Unexplained variance}}$$

is now significant, suggesting that the nitrate concentrations of water specimens do differ significantly between at least two of the river sites.
4. The F-ratio

$$F = \frac{\text{Between block variance}}{\text{Unexplained variance}}$$

is significant. This suggests that the nitrate concentrations of specimens varied significantly between the different weeks of the study.

10.4.4 Summarizing the results of the study

Now that the correct analysis has been carried out on this data we can summarize the results as follows (see Figure 10.2):

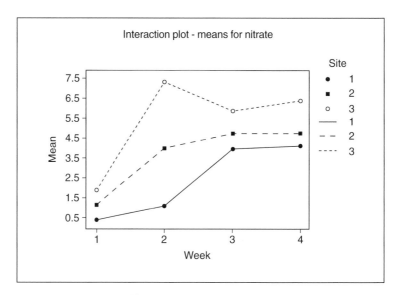

Figure 10.2 Interaction plot.

There is graphical evidence to suggest that the nitrate concentrations of the river Brid progressively rise as the distance from the source increases. Due to the small size of the study, we can only state that the nitrate concentration is significantly higher at site 3 (18 miles from the source) than it is at site 1 (the source of the river).

It might also be useful to add:

It was found that the blocking factor (week) was significant; this reinforces the necessity of treating weeks as a blocking factor in any future studies.

10.4.5 A note regarding interactions

An important assumption regarding the two-way ANOVA for randomized block design experiments/surveys, is that the treatments effects are the same for all the blocks. In the example covered in this section this assumption is valid. This can be seen by considering Figure 10.2, where the treatment means for each block are approximately parallel.

Figure 10.3 below shows a situation relating to another part of the river Brid study. Here it was found that for some weeks one site had a higher pH than the other, but for other weeks the situation was reversed. This is a classic case of **inter-action**. If you meet this type of data you will need to use a **factorial design ANOVA** which is beyond the scope of this text. (Readers will find Chapter 7 of Hampton 1994 to be a readable introduction to this topic.)

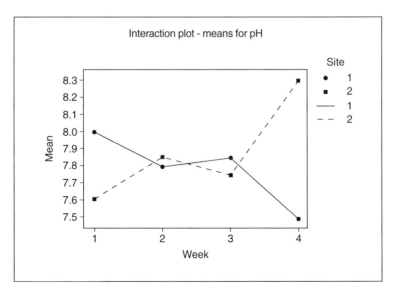

Figure 10.3 A typical case of interaction.

10.4.6 The assumptions of the two-way ANOVA

A two-way ANOVA for a randomized block design experiment/survey is only valid if the assumptions listed in Box 10.3 are valid.

BOX 10.3 ▶ **The assumptions for a two-way ANOVA**

1. The samples for each treatment, from each block, are random samples from the populations of interest.

2. The responses for each treatment, from each block, have equal variances, σ^2.

3. The responses for each treatment, from each block, are approximately normally distributed.

4. There should be no interaction between the treatments and the blocks.

Notes

1. If normality of the data, or the equivalence of variances, is doubtful, a non-parametric test such as Friedman's test should be used. (See, for example, Hampton 1994, Chapter 7.)

2. If interaction is a possibility, a factorial design ANOVA should be used. (See, for example, Hampton 1994, Chapter 7.)

Exercises 10

Exercise 10.1

A study of a woodland was carried out in the summer of 1996. Nine transects of 100 metres were taken, three from each of three areas of the woodland.

The numbers of tree species recorded from each of the nine transects are shown below:

Area 1	Area 2	Area 3
5	2	4
6	3	3
7	4	1

(a) Find the between treatment (area) variance, and the between treatment degrees of freedom.
(b) Find the within treatment (area) variance, and the within treatment degrees of freedom.
(c) Carry out an F-test to determine whether the mean number of tree species differs significantly between the three woodland areas.
(d) Calculate 95% confidence intervals for the mean number of tree species per 100 metre transect for each woodland area. Hence determine which areas are more/less diverse in terms of tree species than the others.

Exercise 10.2

The pH of soil in the vicinity of Carob trees

Distance 1	Distance 2	Distance 3
10.0	9.6	9.8
10.0	9.9	9.9
9.8	9.8	9.7
10.0	9.8	9.8
10.0	9.8	9.9

The data above is shown by kind permission of Paul Knuckle. It comes from his final year thesis *'An evaluation of the effect of native and exotic tree species upon the soil fertility of a semi-arid soil and its ability to accommodate land use change'* (BSc Environmental Quality and Resource Management degree, UWE, Bristol, 1996).

The table above shows the pH of soil specimens taken at three distances around Carob tree in the Almeria region of south-east Spain. Measurements were taken at the following distances from the tree trunks:

Distance 1: Around the trunk of the tree
Distance 2: Edge of tree canopy
Distance 3: Twice (Distance 2 – Distance 1) beyond the influence of the tree

Using hand calculations:

(a) Find the between treatment (distance) variance, and the between treatment degrees of freedom.
(b) Find the within treatment (distance) variance, and the within treatment degrees of freedom.
(c) Carry out an F-test to determine whether the mean pH level differs significantly between the three measurement distances.
(d) Calculate 95% confidence intervals for the mean pH level for each distance. Hence determine which distances have significantly higher/lower pH values than the others.

Exercise 10.3

Repeat Exercise 10.2, but this time use a computer package such as MINITAB to carry out the ANOVA calculations.

Also, use Tukey's simultaneous confidence intervals to determine which distances from Carob trees are associated with higher/lower acidity than the others.

Exercise 10.4

The nitrate concentration (mg/l) of 18 soil specimens from the Wetmoor Nature Reserve (Lower Woods), Gloucestershire

LAST COPPICING

1929	1982	1995
2.9	3.8	5.7
3.8	2.9	5.3
5.3	3.2	7.7
2.7	4.3	6.9
4.3	4.4	5.1
4.4		
4.1		
2.9		

The data above is shown by kind permission of Marcus Wright. It comes from his final year thesis *'Can repeated coppicing lead to a decline in the available nitrate and phosphate status in a coppiced woodland soil?'* (BSc Environmental Quality and Resource Management degree, UWE, Bristol, 1996).

The above table shows the nitrate concentrations (mg/l soil) of 18 soil specimens from a coppiced woodland, collected at a depth of 30 cm. It would be interesting to carry out an ANOVA to determine whether the nitrate concentration of soil is higher in the more recently coppiced woodland areas.

The reader will notice that there are more soil specimens from the area coppiced in 1929 than from the other areas. The hand calculations for examples such as this have not been covered in this chapter, so a computer package such as MINITAB should be used.

(a) Carry out an ANOVA to determine whether the mean nitrate concentrations differ according to the year of last coppicing.
(b) Using appropriate methods, determine what (if any) significant differences exist between the treatment (year of coppicing) means.

Exercise 10.5

Rice yields (tons per acre) for six identical plots of land.

	Fertilizer formula		
Rice variety	Formula 1	Formula 2	Formula 3
A	7	7	9
B	3	4	6

An experiment was carried out to determine which of three fertilizer formulae produced the best rice yield (tons per acre) on six virtually identical plots of land.

(a) Carry out a one-way ANOVA, and hence test whether there are significant differences between the mean yields according to the formula of fertilizer used.
(b) Now carry out a two-way ANOVA using the rice varieties as blocks.
(c) Compare your conclusions from (b) with those from (a). Explain why these differing conclusions were reached.

Exercise 10.6

The data below shows the ammonia concentration of water specimens collected at three different sites along a river. It might be expected that the nitrate contamination is highest at the sites furthest from the river source.

Using the weeks of data collection as blocks, carry out an ANOVA to determine how the distance from the river source affects the nitrate contamination of the river.

Ammonia concentration (mg/l) of specimens from three sites on a river

	Site 1	Site 2	Site 3
Week 1	0.00	0.03	0.07
Week 2	0.02	0.10	0.30
Week 3	0.01	0.15	0.24
Week 4	0.05	0.26	0.40

Note: Site 1 – Source of the river
      Site 2 – 15 miles downstream of source
      Site 3 – 30 miles downstream of source

Exercise 10.7

The MINITAB example file 'poplar.mtw' contains data relating to the heights of poplar trees of two ages, which were treated in four different ways.

It would be possible to carry out a two-way ANOVA on this data using the ages of the trees as blocks. By studying this diagram, explain why this would not be a good idea.

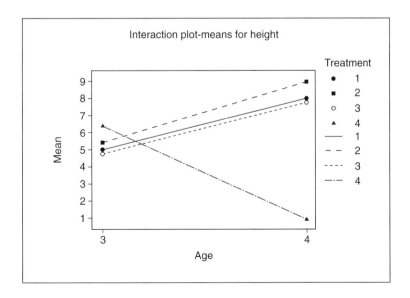

157

Exercise 10.8

Try and think of some situations from your field work and laboratory work where interactions occurred.

11 The chi-squared test

11.1 Introduction

In this chapter we shall consider the chi-squared test (chi is a Greek letter written as χ, and pronounced 'kie'). This test is one of the most widely used hypothesis tests of all, as it is versatile and easy to apply.

The two major applications of the chi-squared test are for the **analysis of contingency tables** and for assessing the **goodness of fit** of observed data to a theoretical distribution. Both of these application areas will be covered in this chapter.

11.2 Contingency tables

Before considering the mechanics of the chi-squared test as applied to contingency tables, it is worth while briefly discussing where the test is appropriate, and why chi-squared tests are so widely used.

Supposing we were to investigate the ages and salaries of the employees of a large waste management company. Having sampled 250 employees we could produce a table something like Table 11.1. The measured variables, age and wage, are represented by the columns and rows, and the contents of each cell are **counts**. This is an example of a **two-way contingency table**.

Table 11.1   Salaries by age, for 250 workers from a large waste management company

Salary (£000s)	Age		
	20 to under 30	30 to under 50	≤ 50
10 to under 15	35	20	5
15 to under 20	32	31	32
20 or over	10	40	45

A chi-squared test could now be used to determine whether there is any relationship between the ages and salaries of the employees.

Similarly, Table 11.2 shows salaries tabulated by sex for the same 250 employees of the waste management company. Here a chi-squared test could be used to answer the question 'Are the salary distributions of males and females the same?'.

Some readers might have noticed that Table 11.1 relates to two quantitative variables (salary and age), while Table 11.2 shows a quantitative variable (salary), tabulated against a qualitative variable (sex). The beauty of the chi-squared test is that it can be used for tables where the variables are of **any type**. Furthermore, a chi-squared test for Table 11.1 or 11.2 would assume **nothing** about the distribution of the salaries, or ages, or sex distribution of the workforce.

Some readers may also have noticed that if the raw data tabulated in Tables 11.1 and 11.2 is available, then the data from both tables could be analyzed by methods discussed elsewhere in this textbook. In the case of Table 11.1 a correlation coefficient could be used (see Chapter 12), while the data shown in Table 11.2 could be examined by using a *t*-test or Mann–Whitney test (see Chapters 8 and 9). It is a measure of how far the readers have progressed, that they are now spoilt for choice! The particular strengths of the chi-squared test are that it can be used on tables even when the raw data is not available, and also that the test can be used on tables concerning purely qualitative variables where other tests cannot be used.

11.3   The analysis of one-way contingency tables

The rationale behind the chi-squared test, and the method of execution, are best explained by consideration of a simple example.

Table 11.2   Salaries by sex, for 250 employees from a large waste management company

Salary (£000s)	Sex	
	Males	Females
10 to under 15	30	30
15 to under 20	55	40
20 or over	65	30

11.3.1 A simple example

An environmental pressure group opposed to a new airport have amassed a large list of signatures to a petition. The pressure group asked the local university to test their belief that their support comes from a politically representative cross-section of the community.

A university team established that the community consists of Conservative voters, Labour voters, and other voters in the proportions $1:1:1$. A sample of the petition signatories was taken, and, after further investigation, the voting habits (at the last general election) of each of the signatories in the sample were established. The voting patterns of the signatories in the sample were as follows:

Political allegiance (at last general election)

Conservative	Labour	Other	Total
53	46	60	159

Does this data support the beliefs of the environmental pressure group?

The first step is to clearly state the null hypothesis, H_0. In this case a suitable null hypothesis is:

H_0: Proportions of signatories falling into each of the three political categories are in the ratios 1:1:1 (i.e. the pressure groups support comes from a politically representative cross-section of the local community).

Now, if the above hypothesis is true, of the 159 signatories sampled, we would expect one-third of them (i.e. 53) to be Conservative supporters. Similarly, we would expect 53 signatories to be Labour supporters, and a further 53 signatories to be supporters of other parties. These frequencies suggested by the null hypothesis are known as **expected frequencies**.

To determine whether H_0 is reasonable or not we compare the **observed frequencies** with the **expected frequencies** for each category. In essence, if the observed and expected values are in close agreement then the hypothesis H_0 seems reasonable, but if the observed and expected values differ substantially then the hypothesis seems somewhat dubious.

The degree of agreement between the observed and expected values is determined by calculating the statistic:

$$\chi^2 = \sum \frac{(O - E)^2}{E} \qquad \textbf{(Equation 11.1)}$$

where O denotes the observed frequencies and E the expected frequencies.

This statistic is in effect a weighted sum of the squared deviations between the observed and the expected values. The larger χ^2 is, the more we doubt the null hypothesis. To understand why the statistic deals with weighted squared deviations it is necessary to consider the following tableau:

Observed value, O	Expected value, E	O − E	(O − E)²	(O − E)²/E
505	500	5	25	0.05
0	5	−5	25	1.00

Here we see a hypothetical situation where the observed and expected values differ by 5. The first point to notice is that the sum of the differences $(O - E)$ comes to zero. This is always the case when carrying out analyses of contingency tables (verify that this is the case for the tableau shown below). This problem is much the same as the one discussed in Chapter 5 when defining a measure of variability; the solution here, as it was then, is to square the differences and use $(O - E)^2$ as a measure of deviation. The second point to notice is the relative size of the squared deviations. In the first case, a squared deviation of just 25 when the expected frequency is 500 indicates a good deal of agreement between the observed and expected frequencies. The second case again has a squared deviation of 5; in this case, however, that represents a pretty poor agreement. In each case the degree of fit is shown better by the weighted squared deviation shown in the final column.

Returning to our example, we can calculate the X^2 statistic as follows:

Political loyalty	Observed frequency, O	Expected frequency, E	O − E	(O − E)²	(O − E)²/E
Con	53	53	0	0	0.0000
Lab	46	53	−7	49	0.9245
Other	60	53	7	49	0.9245
					$X^2 = 1.8490$

The way we calculated the X^2 statistic it is clear that if the observed values are in broad agreement with the expected values, then X^2 will be small; but if the observed values and expected values differ greatly, then X^2 will be large. The question is: How large does the X^2 statistic need to be before we decide that the null hypothesis H_0 is unreasonable and reject it?

11.3.2 Testing the null hypothesis H_0

In Chapters 7 and 8 the idea of sampling distributions was discussed. It can be shown that the sampling distribution of the statistic X^2, is a χ^2-distribution (chi-squared distribution). This is a continuous distribution, a little like a normal distribution, but it is asymmetric. A typical χ^2 distribution is shown in Figure 11.1.

As with the normal distribution, there are in fact an infinite number of χ^2-distributions. In each case the general form is much as shown in Figure 11.1, but the mean can differ. The parameter that determines the shape of the χ^2-distribution is known as the **degrees of freedom** (d.f.),where the degrees of freedom are in fact the mean of the distribution.

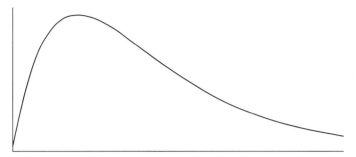

Figure 11.1 A typical chi-squared distribution.

When carrying out a chi-squared test on a one-way table, as in this section, the degrees of freedom (d.f.) can be written as:

d.f. = Number of categories − 1

Tables of critical values are now used to determine whether a calculated value of X^2 provides evidence of the null hypothesis, H_0, being unreasonable or not. Table B6 in Appendix B provides critical values of the chi-squared distribution.

In our example we have:

X^2 = 1.8490 degrees of freedom

= Number of categories − 1 = 3 − 1 = 2

The critical value for a chi-squared distribution with 2 degrees of freedom, for a 5% significance test, is 5.99. This means that if H_0 is true, the chance of obtaining a X^2 value of 5.99 or greater is 5% (this is shown diagrammatically in Figure 11.2). Any calculated X^2 statistic of 5.99 or greater would cast reasonable doubt upon H_0 causing us to reject H_0 in favour of the alternative hypothesis H_1. In our calculated example the X^2 value of 1.849 is well below the 5% critical value so we **do not reject H_0**. The claims of the pressure group, that their support comes from a politically representative cross-section of the local community, seem valid.

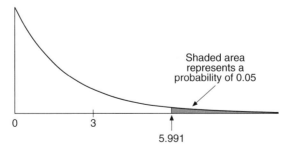

Shaded area represents a probability of 0.05

0

3

5.991

Figure 11.2 The rejection region for a chi-squared test at the 5% significance level, with 2 degrees of freedom.

The chi-squared test procedure for one-way tables is in essence very simple. As we shall soon see in the remainder of this chapter, the procedure is very similar for all chi-squared tests. The recap listed in Box 11.1 will help reinforce what we have covered so far.

BOX 11.1 ▶ **Recap of the method for a chi-squared test on a one-way contingency table**

1. State the null hypothesis H_0 (where H_0 counts follow a stated ratio).

2. Assuming H_0 is true, find the expected counts for each cell in the contingency table.

3. Calculate the statistic: $x^2 = \sum[(O - E)^2/E]$.

4. Determine the degrees of freedom (d.f.) for the test. This is the number of categories -1.

5. Look up the critical value for a chi-squared distribution with the appropriate degrees of freedom.

6. If $x^2 >$ critical value, reject H_0.

11.4   The analysis of two-way contingency tables

The chi-squared test can be a useful tool when analyzing two-way contingency tables. As an example, consider Table 11.3. This shows the pH levels of a total of 39 water specimens taken from the rivers Dee and Taff during the summer of 1993.

If we are interested in testing whether this table shows evidence of differences in the pH levels between the two rivers, a chi-squared test will do this for us.

11.4.1 The null hypothesis

When carrying out a chi-squared test on a two-way contingency table, we are testing whether the rows and columns are independent. In this example this means that we

Table 11.3   pH levels of 39 water specimens from the rivers Dee and Taff

pH	Dee	Taff	Total
Under 1.5	3	10	13
1.5 to under 1.7	6	6	12
1.7 or over	10	4	14
Total	19	20	39

are testing whether or not the pH levels of the water specimens are independent of the rivers. This is equivalent to testing the hypothesis:

H_0: The proportions of water specimens in each of the three pH categories are the same for both rivers

against

H_1: The proportions of water specimens in each of the three pH categories differ for the two rivers.

11.4.2 The expected values

In Table 11.3 we see that, in all, 13 of the 39 water samples registered pH levels of under 1.5. If the null hypothesis, H_0, is true, we would expect 13/39 of the samples from each river to have pH levels under 1.5. Hence we would expect $(13 \times 19)/39 = 6.3333$ samples from the river Dee to have pH levels under 1.5.

Similarly, 12/39 of all the samples were in the 1.5 to under 1.7 pH category, so we would expect 12/39 of the 20 samples from the river Taff to be in this category, so the expected frequency is $(12/39) \times 20 = 6.1538$.

In general, the expected frequency for the cell position in row i, and column j of a two-way contingency table is:

$$\text{Expected frequency (cell}_{ij}) = \frac{\text{Total of row } i \times \text{Total of column } j}{\text{Grand total}}$$

Using this formula the expected values can be worked out as follows:

Observed frequency, O	Expected frequency, E
3	$(13 \times 19) \div 39 = 6.3333$
10	$(13 \times 20) \div 39 = 6.6667$
6	$(12 \times 19) \div 39 = 5.8462$
6	$(12 \times 20) \div 39 = 6.1538$
10	$(14 \times 19) \div 39 = 6.8205$
4	$(14 \times 20) \div 39 = 7.1795$

We can now calculate the statistic X^2 just as we did for the one-way contingency table:

O	E	O − E	$(O - E)^2$	$(O - E)^2/E$
3	6.3333	−3.3333	11.1111	1.7544
10	6.6667	3.3333	11.1111	1.6667
6	5.8462	0.1538	0.0237	0.0040
6	6.1538	−0.1538	0.0237	0.0038
10	6.8205	3.1795	10.1092	1.4822
4	7.1795	−3.1795	10.1092	1.4081

$$X^2 = 6.3192$$

11.4.3 The degrees of freedom for a two-way contingency table

For two-way contingency tables such as this, the degrees of freedom (d.f.) are:

d.f. = (Number of rows − 1) × (Number of columns − 1)

So, in our example we have $(3 − 1) \times (2 − 1) = 2$ degrees of freedom.

11.4.4 Testing the null hypothesis

The critical values for a 5% significance test is 5.99; as our test-statistic is 6.319 we **reject H_0 at the 5% level of significance**. There is evidence to suggest that the proportion of samples in each of the pH categories differs between the two samples.

One drawback of the chi-squared test is that when a hypothesis is rejected it does not tell us in what way the hypothesis is violated. The way to spot any violation is to look closely at your calculations, noting the largest $(O − E)^2/E$ values. These are the values primarily responsible for rejecting H_0 so this is where the most important differences between the observed and expected frequencies occur.

In our example such an examination reveals that the river Dee produced fewer specimens with a low pH than we would expect if H_0 were true, and more specimens with a pH of over 1.7. The reverse picture is evident from the river Taff. This would suggest that the river Dee is more acidic than the river Taff.

Example 11.1

A Chi-squared test with MINITAB

Chi-squared tests on contingency tables can be easily carried out with the MINITAB statistical package as the following example will illustrate.

Goodman and Kruskal (1954) published an interesting set of results relating to the hair colour and eye colour of a large sample of German men. The results are shown in Table 11.4.

We can use a chi-squared test to determine whether or not there is any association between the hair colours and eye colours of German men in 1954. The appropriate null and alternative hypotheses are:

Table 11.4   The hair colour and eye colour of 6,800 German men

Eye colour	Hair colour			
	Brown	Black	Fair	Red
Brown	438	288	115	16
Grey or green	1,387	746	946	53
Blue	807	189	1,768	47

(Source: Goodman and Kruskal 1954)

H_0: The eye colours and hair colours of the men are independent of each other.
H_1: The eye colours and hair colours of the men are not independent of each other.

To carry out a chi-squared test the data first needs to be read into a MINITAB worksheet in the following form:

c1	c2	c3	c4
438	288	115	16
1,387	746	946	53
807	189	1,768	47

The menu selections **Stat, Tables, Chisquare Test** are now made. The resulting chi-squared menu, and the subsequent output produced by MINITAB are shown in Exhibit 11.1.

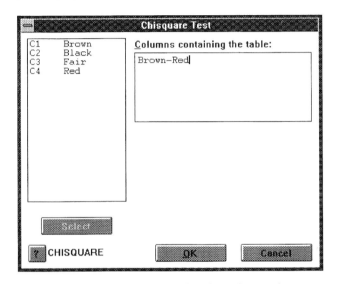

Expected counts are printed below observed counts

	C1	C2	C3	C4	Total
1	438	288	115	16	857
	331.71	154.13	356.54	14.62	
2	1387	746	946	53	3132
	1212.27	563.30	1303.00	53.43	
3	807	189	1768	47	2811
	1088.02	505.57	1169.46	47.95	
Total	2632	1223	2829	116	6800

ChiSq = 34.059 +116.263 +163.630 + 0.130 +
        25.185 + 59.257 + 97.814 + 0.003 +
        72.584 +198.222 +306.340 + 0.019 = 1073.508

df = 6

Exhibit 11.1 MINITAB chi-squared test menu, and the output from a chi-squared test of the data from Table 11.4.

We can see that the chi-squared statistic is 1,073.508 and that the test has six degrees of freedom. This statistic is so large that it provides extremely strong evidence that the null hypothesis is not true. Thus it seems almost certain that the hair colours and eye colours of the German men are indeed related. Inspection of the observed and expected values shows the following:

1. Men with fair hair tend to have blue eyes.
2. Men with black hair usually have grey or green eyes, with blue eyes being rare.
3. Men with brown hair rarely have blue eyes.
4. Red-haired males do not tend to show any tendency for or against having eyes of any colour.

11.4.5 An important note regarding the chi-squared test

The important result that the sampling distribution of the test-statistic

$$X^2 = \sum \frac{(O - E)^2}{E}$$

is a chi-squared distribution is only true when all the **expected values** are sufficiently large. The usual interpretation of this necessity being that all expected values should be **5 or greater**. If any expected values are smaller than 5 it does not usually mean that a chi-squared test cannot be used at all, it just means that some row or column categories need to be merged. As an example, consider Table 11.5. This shows the hourly SO_2 concentrations recorded in the atmosphere at two sites in the Bristol area on 1 February 1994.

A chi-squared test on this table would test the following hypothesis:

H_0: The proportions of samples falling into each of the six SO_2 concentration categories are the same for the city centre and the rural outskirts site.

Assuming this hypothesis is true, the expected values for the contingency table would be as shown by the figures in parentheses in Table 11.5. Here only two of the expected

Table 11.5 A table of the SO_2 recorded at two sites in the Bristol area on 1 February 1994

Atmospheric SO_2 concentration (ppm)	Site		Total
	City centre site	Rural outskirts site	
10 to under 20	0 (4)	8 (4)	8
20 to under 30	9 (9.5)	10 (9.5)	19
30 to under 40	8 (6)	4 (6)	12
40 to under 50	4 (3)	2 (3)	6
50 to under 60	1 (0.5)	0 (0.5)	1
60 or over	2 (1)	0 (1)	2
Total	24 (24)	24 (24)	48

Note: The figures in parentheses are expected values.

Table 11.6   The reduced table of SO_2 concentrations recorded at two sites in the Bristol area

Atmospheric SO_2 concentration (ppm)	Site		Total
	City centre site	Rural outskirts site	
Under 30	9 (*13.5*)	18 (*13.5*)	8
30 or over	15 (*10.5*)	6 (*10.5*)	19
Total	24 (*24*)	24 (*24*)	48

values for the table are greater than the required threshold of 5, so proceeding with the usual chi-squared calculations and hypothesis test would be misleading. The solution here is to combine some of the SO_2 categories together such that the resulting expected values from the new categories are all greater than 5. In this example, reducing the six original categories to just two categories is required. This has been done in Table 11.6 (as before, the expected counts are shown in parentheses).

In general, having merged categories such that all expected values are greater than 5, a standard chi-squared analysis can be performed on the reduced contingency table. However, in this case we now have a **two by two contingency table** which is a special case. Such tables should be analyzed by using **Yates' correction** (see the next section).

11.5   The analysis of two by two tables

Two by two contingency tables occur frequently. A typical (hypothetical) example is shown in Table 11.7

It can be shown that if a standard chi-squared test procedure is applied to such tables the null hypothesis is rejected more often than it should be. That is, significant relationships between the row categories and the column categories tend to be suggested when no such relationship really exists. The solution is to calculate a modified chi-squared statistic which uses **Yates' correction**. This modified statistic is

$$X^2 = \sum \frac{(|O - E| - \frac{1}{2})^2}{E}$$

Table 11.7   A typical (hypothetical) two by two contingency table

Smoker	Sex	
	Male	Female
Yes	20	25
No	15	10

This modified test statistic is simpler to calculate than it appears. The easiest way to see how the calculation is performed is to study a step-by-step example.

11.5.1 An example of a chi-squared test on a two by two table

Table 11.6 shows the number of atmospheric specimens from two sites where SO_2 concentrations were less than 30 ppm and 30 ppm or more. A chi-squared test on this two by two contingency table will test the hypotheses:

H_0: The ratios of samples with SO_2 concentrations falling into each of the SO_2 categories are the same for both sites.

H_1: The ratios of samples with SO_2 concentrations falling into each of the SO_2 categories are not the same for both sites.

As with previous examples the first step is to calculate the **expected values**, assuming H_0 is true. This step is carried out in an identical fashion to previous examples. For this example the expected values are already provided in Table 11.6, so we can immediately list the observed and expected frequencies and find the differences between the two as follows.

Observed frequencies, O	Expected frequencies, E	Difference $(O - E)$
9	13.5	−4.5
18	13.5	4.5
15	10.5	4.5
6	10.5	−4.5

The modified chi-squared statistic requires us to find $|O - E| - \frac{1}{2}$. This merely means you find the absolute size of the difference, $O - E$, and then subtract $\frac{1}{2}$ from it. This has been done below.

O	E	$|O - E|$	$|O - E| - \frac{1}{2}$
9	13.5	4.5	4.0
18	13.5	4.5	4.0
15	10.5	4.5	4.0
6	10.5	4.5	4.0

Finally the $|O - E| - \frac{1}{2}$ values are now squared and divided by the expected values, as shown below:

O	E	$|O - E| - \frac{1}{2}$	$(|O - E| - \frac{1}{2})^2$	$(|O - E| - \frac{1}{2})^2/E$
9	13.5	4	16	1.1852
18	13.5	4	16	1.1852
15	10.5	4	16	1.5238
6	10.5	4	16	1.5238

$$X^2 = 5.4180$$

The reader will notice that all the $|O - E|$, $|O - E| - \frac{1}{2}$ and $(|O - E| - \frac{1}{2})^2$ values are identical. As this is always the case with two by two tables, calculation can be saved by directly calculating just one $(|O - E| - \frac{1}{2})^2$ value, although it is prudent to calculate two values as a check.

The calculation is now complete. The test procedure is identical to that for any other chi-squared test of a contingency table. In this example the test-statistic is 5.418. The critical value for a test at the 5% level of significance when there is just one degree of freedom is 3.84. Therefore we **reject H_0 at the 5% level of significance**. There is evidence to suggest that the atmospheric concentration of SO_2 differs between the two sites. Not surprisingly, the city centre site produced a higher proportion of specimens showing high levels of SO_2 than the site on the rural outskirts.

11.6 Chi-squared goodness of fit tests

In previous chapters some probability distributions that commonly occur in the environmental sciences were introduced, namely the Poisson distribution and the normal distribution. It is frequently useful to be able to test whether a set of data collected in the field follows a well-known distribution, for if a variable is shown to follow a well-known distribution it often illuminates the environmentalist about the nature of the variable in question, and it allows for the easy construction of confidence intervals and probabilistic statements.

The chi-squared test provides an excellent way of testing whether data collected in the field does indeed follow a particular theoretical probability distribution. The method for conducting such tests is illustrated by the following example.

11.6.1 A goodness of fit example

In a Ministry of Agriculture study in an area of a well-known national park, 78 hectares of woodland were inspected and the number of fox lairs in each hectare was recorded. The results of the study are shown in Table 11.8.

Table 11.8   The distribution of fox lairs over a 78 hectare area of an English national park

Number of lairs	Number of hectares
0	16
1	46
2	12
3	2
4	2
Total	78

At a glance the number of lairs per hectare can be seen to follow a skewed distribution, which may well be a **Poisson distribution**, but is this the case? This example is interesting because, as was discussed in Chapter 6, a Poisson distribution occurs where events happen at random over time or space. The practical interpretation of this for our example is that if the number of lairs per hectare follows a Poisson distribution here, it would suggest that foxes choose the sites for their lairs with no regard for other fox lairs in the area. Let us test this interesting hypothesis.

The null hypothesis and the alternative hypothesis are as follows:

H_0: The number of fox lairs per hectare follows a Poisson distribution (i.e. foxes choose sites for their lairs without considering the proximity of other fox lairs).

H_1: The number of fox lairs per hectare does not follow a Poisson distribution.

We now need to estimate the parameter(s) of the distribution assumed true in H_0.

In our example we are testing for a Poisson distribution. This distribution is defined as

$$P(r) = \frac{e^{-\mu} \mu^r}{r!}$$

where there is just one parameter, μ, the mean. In our example the mean number of fox lairs per hectare is **1.0769**, so the particular Poisson distribution we are testing for is defined as

$$P(r) = \frac{e^{-1.0769} 1.0769^r}{r!}$$

Assuming H_0 to be true, we now calculate the **expected** number of hectares with $0, 1, 2$, etc. fox lairs. This requires a familiarity with the Poisson distribution, so readers who do not fully understand how this is done should consult Chapter 6.

As a reminder, if H_0 is true, the probability of a hectare containing exactly 0 fox lairs is:

$$P(0 \text{ lairs}) = \frac{e^{-1.0769} 1.0769^0}{0!} = 0.3406$$

so the expected number of hectares containing exactly 0 lairs is $0.3406 \times 78 = 26.5668$ hectares (because our study involved 78 hectares). Similarly the probability of a hectare containing exactly 1 fox lair is

$$P(1 \text{ lair}) = \frac{e^{-1.0769} 1.0769^1}{1!} = 0.3668$$

so the expected number of hectares containing exactly one lair is $0.3668 \times 78 = 28.6104$ hectares. In a similar fashion the theoretical Poisson probabilities and expected values shown below can be obtained.

Number of lairs	Theoretical Poisson probability	Theoretical Poisson frequency
0	0.3406	$0.3406 \times 78 = 26.5668$
1	0.3668	$0.3668 \times 78 = 28.6104$
2	0.1975	$0.1975 \times 78 = 15.4050$
3 or more	0.0951	$0.0951 \times 78 = 7.4178$

We now need to determine whether the observed field frequencies are sufficiently close to the frequencies we would expect if the null hypothesis is true. To do this we carry out a chi-squared test using the field counts as the observed values, O, and the theoretical Poisson frequencies as the expected frequencies, E.

Number of fox lairs	Observed number of hectares, O	Theoretical Poisson frequency, E	$O - E$	$(O - E)^2 / E$
0	16	26.5668	-10.5668	4.2029
1	46	28.6104	17.3896	10.5695
2	12	15.4050	-3.4050	0.7526
3 or more	4	7.4178	-3.4178	1.5748
				$X^2 = 17.0998$

For any chi-squared goodness of fit test, the degrees of freedom, d.f. are given by:

d.f. = Number of categories − Number of estimated parameters − 1

In this example we had to estimate the **arithmetic mean** in order to find the theoretical frequencies from a Poisson distribution, so we estimated **one parameter**. (This is always the case when carrying out a goodness of fit test for a Poisson distribution.) We had **four** categories, namely 0, 1, 2 and 3 or more, so we have $4 - 1 - 1 = 2$ **degrees of freedom**.

From the tables of critical values provided in Appendix B we can see that our test-statistic of 17.0998 is larger than every value provided for 2 degrees of freedom, including the 0.1% critical value. Therefore we can **reject H_0 at the 0.1% significance level**.

We have very strong evidence to reject the null hypothesis, meaning that the number of fox lairs per hectare is very unlikely to follow a Poisson distribution. Looking at the observed and expected values it is clear that there are far more hectares containing exactly one fox lair than a Poisson distribution would suggest. Similarly, there are fewer hectares with either no lairs, or multiple lairs than we would expect if a Poisson distribution was appropriate. These results show that foxes do not choose the sites of their lairs at random. Instead, being territorial creatures, they tend to space themselves out. Typically a fox will find a territory that does not impinge on the territories of existing fox families, and will build the lair close to the centre of this territory. Hence it is rare for more than one or two lairs to lie within the same hectare. It is also rare for a hectare to be completely free of fox lairs unless, of course, the land is unsuitable.

Goodness of fit tests can, of course, be carried out to determine whether a set of data follows **any** probability distribution, not just a Poisson distribution. Example 11.2 shows a goodness of fit test for a **normal distribution**.

A recap of the chi-squared goodness of fit test is given in Box 11.2.

BOX 11.2 ▶ **Recap of the method for a chi-squared 'goodness of fit' test**

1. State the null hypothesis, H_0 (where H_0 data follows a specified probability distribution).

2. Estimate the parameters of the probability distribution being tested for. For example, if testing for a Poisson distribution the **mean** needs to be estimated. If testing for a normal distribution the **mean** and **standard deviation** need to be estimated.

3. Assuming that H_0 is true, find the expected frequencies for each category.

4. Calculate the usual chi-squared test-statistic:

$$x^2 = \sum [(O - E)^2 / E]$$

5. Determine the appropriate degrees of freedom for the test, given by:

   Degrees of freedom = Number of categories

   $-$ Number of estimated parameters $- 1$

   so when testing for a Poisson distribution there are

   Number of categories $- 2$ degrees of freedom.

   and when testing for a Normal distribution there are

   Number of categories $- 3$ degrees of freedom.

6. Look up the critical value for a chi-squared distribution with the appropriate degrees of freedom.

Example 11.2

When considering the ecology of an estuarine environment, it is important to consider the nature of the sediment in the estuary. One important feature of the sediment is its size, as the particle size partly determines the speed at which erosion and deposition take place.

The following data relates to the particle sizes (μm) of 37 grains from a sample of sediment from the Severn estuary (by kind permission of Dr D. Case, University of the West of England). It would be interesting to know whether the particles in the Severn estuary silt can be taken as following a normal distribution or not.

Particle size (μm)	Number of particles
3.0 to under 5.0	14
5.0 to under 6.0	10
6.0 to under 7.0	7
7.0 to under 9.0	6
Total	37

The arithmetic mean and standard deviation of the particle sizes can be estimated from the particle size distribution above as being:

sample mean $= 5.5270 \, \mu$m

sample standard deviation $= 1.4527 \, \mu$m

(re-read Chapter 5 if you can't remember how to do this!)

For the purposes of carrying out a chi-squared test, the above table is presented more accurately below, because the categories used should cover every possible particle size that could be found.

Particle size (μm)	Number of particles
Under 5.0	14
5.0 to under 6.0	10
6.0 to under 7.0	7
7.0 or over	6
Total	37

We can now test whether the 37 particles in our sample could come from sediment with normally distributed diameters with a mean of 5.5270 μm and a standard deviation of 1.4527 μm. Assuming that our 37 particles constitute a representative sample of particles from the Severn estuary, we can test

H_0: The diameters of particles from the silt of the Severn estuary are normally distributed with a mean of 5.527 μm and a standard deviation of 1.4527 μm.

The next step is to find the probabilities of randomly selected particles collected from the Severn estuary falling into each of the four particle size groupings shown in the above table, assuming that H_0 is true. For example, if H_0 is true the probability of a randomly selected particle having a diameter of under 5.0 μm is given by:

$$Pr(\text{diameter} < 5.0 \, \mu\text{m}) = Pr\left(Z < \frac{5.0 - 5.527}{1.4527}\right) = Pr(Z < -0.3628) = 0.358$$

Similarly, if H_0 is true, the probability of a randomly selected particle having a diameter in the range 5.0 μm to under 6.0 μm is given by:

$$Pr(5.0 \, \mu\text{m} < \text{diameter} \le 6.0 \, \mu\text{m}) = Pr\left(\frac{5.0 - 5.527}{1.4527} < Z \le \frac{6.0 - 5.527}{1.4527}\right)$$

$$= Pr(-0.3628 < Z \le 0.3256) = 0.27$$

A completed table showing the theoretical probabilities, and the expected frequencies of particles falling into each particle size category is shown below.

Particle size (μm)	Observed number of particles, O	Theoretical normal probabilities	Theoretical normal frequencies, E
Under 5.0	14	0.358	$0.358 \times 37 = 13.246$
5.0 to under 6.0	10	0.270	$0.270 \times 37 = 9.990$
6.0 to under 7.0	7	0.217	$0.217 \times 37 = 8.029$
7.0 or over	6	0.155	$0.155 \times 37 = 5.735$
Totals	37	1.000	37.000

A quick scan at the above table would seem to suggest that the observed frequencies of particles in each size category are very close to the frequencies we would expect if the particle sizes do indeed follow a normal distribution. This view is borne out with the following chi-squared calculations and test.

Observed frequencies, O	Theoretical normal frequencies, E	$O - E$	$(O - E)^2$	$(O - E)^2/E$
14	13.246	0.754	0.5685	0.0429
10	9.990	0.010	0.0001	0.0000
7	8.029	−1.029	1.0588	0.1319
6	5.735	0.265	0.0702	0.0122
				$x^2 = 0.187$

For this test we have four categories of particle sizes, and we estimated two parameters (the mean and the standard deviation). This means there are $4 - 2 - 1 = 1$ degree of freedom. To reject H_0 at the 5% level of significance a test-statistic of 3.84 or higher would be needed. Our test-statistic of 0.187 is very low so we have no reason to doubt H_0. The hypothesis that the particle sizes follow a normal distribution seems entirely reasonable. This backs up our original thoughts when we saw how similar the observed and expected values were.

11.7 Summary

Because of their simplicity and versatility, chi-squared tests are very widely used. However, they are also widely misused. This section provides some brief guidelines as to the correct use of the chi-squared test.

Tests for contingency tables

1. Chi-squared tests are only appropriate when cells contain **counts**.
   A typical misuse of the chi-squared test often occurs when tables of percentages are treated as contingency tables. Chi-squared tests **are not** applicable for tables such as:

Wage	Male (%)	Female (%)	Total
10 to under 15	12	8	20
15 to under 20	30	30	60
20 to under 30	18	2	20
Total	60	40	100

2. A **clearly worded, precise** null hypothesis H_0 must be stated.
   In general this is:

   H_0: The rows and columns of the contingency table are independent.

3. The categories of the table must cover the entire range of observed values without any of the categories overlapping.

4. Two by two tables are a special case and **Yates' correction** should be used.
5. For a one-way contingency table the degrees of freedom are:

   Number of categories −1.

6. For a contingency table with r rows and c columns, the degrees of freedom are $(r-1) \times (c-1)$.

Goodness of fit tests

1. The listed categories of the possible values of the variable being dealt with must cover **the entire range** of possible values.
2. In general, the degrees of freedom are:

   Number of categories – Number of estimated parameters −1

   (a) If a Poisson distribution is being tested for this means there are

      Number of categories – 2 degrees of freedom.

   (b) If a normal distribution is being tested for this means there are

      Number of categories – 3 degrees of freedom.

Chi-squared tests in general

1. **All expected values must be at least 5.**

Exercises 11

Exercise 11.1

Supposing an experiment to determine whether radiation exposure of workers in the nuclear industry can lead to cancer in the workers' offspring. A table with the following totals might result.

Cancer in child?	Radiation exposure of father				
	None	Low	Medium	High	Total
Yes					40
No					160
Total	30	100	50	20	200

(a) Assuming the hypothesis 'H_0: *the ratio of children who develop cancer is independent of the degree of exposure to radiation of their fathers*' is true, find the expected counts for the table above.

(b) If the observed cell counts for the above table were available, how and why would you reorganize the table to ensure that a chi-squared test was safe to use?

Exercise 11.2

The table below shows a breakdown of the wages received by a random sample of the employees of Enviro Products Ltd (all figures are percentages).

Wage (£000s)	Male	Female	Total
10 to under 15	12	8	20
15 to under 20	30	30	60
Over 20	18	2	20
Total	60	40	100

The union representing the workforce are interested in testing the hypotheses

H_0: The proportion of employees within each of the three wage categories is the same for both male and female employees.

H_1: The proportion of employees within each of the three wage categories differs between male and female employees.

(a) Is it appropriate to carry out a chi-squared test on this table as it stands? Give reasons for your answer.
(b) It is later found that the sample from which the table was based consisted of 200 employees.
   (i) Form a contingency table which could be analyzed using a chi-squared test.
   (ii) Carry out a chi-squared test of the hypotheses stated earlier. Comment upon your results.

Exercise 11.3

During 1902 and 1903 Britain had its last serious epidemic of the severe 'Variola Major' strain of smallpox. Although vaccinations were widely available, it has been estimated that around 29% of infants had not been vaccinated.

The following table shows the mortality resulting from vaccinated and unvaccinated cases of 'Variola Major' treated by the London hospitals from 1901 to 1904.

	Survived	Died	Total
Unvaccinated	2,042	942	2,984
Vaccinated	6,997	752	7,749
Total	9,039	1,694	10,733

(Source: Parish 1968.)

Assuming that the mortality statistics for the London hospitals constitute a representative sample of all hospitals in England at the time, test the following hypothesis using a chi-squared test:

H_0: The ratio of smallpox (Variola Major) patients who died in hospitals between 1901 to 1904 was the same for both vaccinated and unvaccinated patients.

Comment upon your results.

Exercise 11.4

Part 1

The environmental officer of a large water treatment plant in southern England keeps a close eye on any contamination the plant might cause to the surrounding water system. Over the last 10 years the environmental officer has recorded every incident where the nearby river Thames has been contaminated with pollution levels exceeding the EEC limits. The number of contamination incidents from the plant over the last 10 years can be summarized as follows:

Number of pollution incidents:	0	1	2	3	4
Number of months:	55	42	16	6	1

The environmental officer believes that the number of pollution incidents each month may follow a Poisson distribution. Carry out a suitable hypothesis test to determine if this is the case.

Part 2

Day:	Mon.	Tues.	Wed.	Thur.	Fri.	Sat.	Sun.
Number of pollution incidents:	14	13	13	11	12	15	18

The same officer has produced the breakdown above of how many incidents have taken place on different days of the week. He's worried because more incidents (18) have taken place on Sundays than on any other day of the week. This is when staffing levels are at their lowest. Test whether this is due to chance, or whether accidents are indeed more likely to happen on certain days.

Exercise 11.5

During a recent field trip, students at UWE in Bristol collected 400 random soil samples from an area of the Mendip Hills. At a later date the concentrations of lead and zinc, among other metals, were measured. The lead and zinc concentrations of the 400 samples are summarized in the following table:

	Zinc concentration (mg/kg)			
Lead concentration (mg/kg)	<50	50 to <100	100 to <200	≥ 200
Under 200	115	60	21	8
200 to under 500	32	63	18	3
500 or over	20	12	32	16

Carry out a significance test to determine whether there is any association between the concentrations of lead and of zinc in the soil of the Mendip area.

Exercise 11.6

The MINITAB example data file **'lakes.mtw'** contains information pertaining to 71 lakes from the state of Wisconsin in the USA. Among the information provided is the pH of each of the lakes. The pH levels of the lakes are summarized below. (All measurements were made between 1959 to 1963, so the current pH levels may be significantly different.)

pH Level	Number of lakes
Under 6.2	10
6.2 to under 6.6	9
6.6 to under 7.0	15
7.0 to under 7.4	21
7.4 to under 7.8	9
7.8 or over	7

Using MINITAB, the sample mean and sample standard deviations of the pH levels can be found to be 6.9479 and 0.6805 respectively.

Use a chi-squared test to determine whether the pH levels can be taken as following a normal distribution.

Exercise 11.7

With reference to Table 11.1 (see p. 160), test the hypothesis

H_0: The salaries of the employees of the large waste management company are independent of their ages.

Exercise 11.8

With reference to Table 11.7 (see p. 169), assuming the table was the result of a random survey of environmental studies students in England and Wales, test the hypothesis

H_0: The proportion of environmental studies students in England and Wales who smoke is the same for males and females.

12 Relationships between variables

12.1 Introduction

The environmentalist is often interested in exploring relationships which might exist between two or more variables. For example, an understanding of the relationship between the cross-sectional area of a river and its flow rate could prove invaluable when trying to determine the environmental implications of altering the natural course of a river.

In this chapter we shall consider some techniques which are available to explore such relationships between variables. The bulk of the chapter concerns relationships between pairs of variables, although extensions to these ideas will be presented in Section 12.7.

12.1.1 A topical example: the effect of CFC-12 on the ozone column

Ozone in the atmosphere has a profound effect upon all forms of life, as it acts as a filter of the sun's ultraviolet radiation. Some 90% of the ozone in the atmosphere lies in a band of the stratosphere at an altitude of around 20–35 km, this is the so called 'ozone layer'.

In the 1930s man-made gases called chlorofluorocarbons (CFCs) were developed. These gases are non-inflammable and non-toxic, hence they seemed ideal for use as

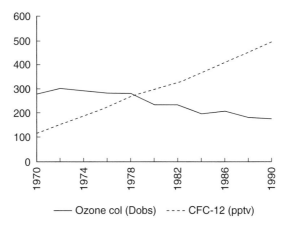

Figure 12.1 Global concentrations of CFC-12 (pptv), and the ozone column (Dobson units) over Antarctica, 1970–90. (Source: *The UK Environment*, p. 38. HMSO, 1992.)

aerosol propellants, refrigerants and solvents. The use of CFCs accelerated quickly from the 1950s onwards, levelling off only from the early 1980s as it was realized that these CFCs might be contributing towards a depletion of the ozone layer.

Figure 12.1 shows the global concentrations of CFC-12, and the ozone column in Antarctica, from 1970 to 1990. It would appear that as levels of CFC-12 have risen, the ozone column has been depleted.

In this chapter we will use a range of techniques to determine whether the relationship is significant, the form it takes, and how the relationship can be described mathematically.

12.1.2 Dependent and independent variables

Throughout this chapter, the primary aim is to determine how the values of one or more **independent** or **predictor** variables, $x_1, x_2, \ldots$, relate to the values of a **dependent** variable y.

In the case of the CFC-12/ozone data, we want to determine how values of the independent variable, **CFC-12 concentration**, relate to the dependent variable **ozone column thickness**.

12.2 The scatter plot

A simple first approach to analyzing the relationship between concentrations of CFC-12 and the ozone column is to draw a **scatter plot** of the data presented in Table 12.1.

Table 12.1 Global concentrations of CFC-12, and the ozone column over Antarctica, 1970–90

Year	CFC-12 concentration (pptv)	Ozone column (Dobson units)
1970	120	281
1972	150	302
1974	185	295
1976	225	282
1978	270	280
1980	295	235
1982	320	233
1984	365	196
1986	405	208
1988	450	182
1990	490	178

(Source: *The UK Environment*, Figs 3.17 and 3.18, p. 38. HMSO, 1992.)

The scatter plot is a simple graph where the horizontal axis represents the independent, *x*, variable (in this case the CFC-12 concentrations), and the vertical axis represents the dependent, *y*, variable (in this case the ozone column readings). A single point is plotted to represent each pair of *x*, *y* data observations. For example, the scatter plot for the ozone/CFC-12 data, includes a point $x = 120, y = 281$, which represents the data for 1970. This point is shown as an asterisk in Figure 12.2, the scatter plot.

We can immediately see from this figure that the ozone column has been eroded, as levels of CFC-12 have risen, and that this relationship appears to be approximately linear.

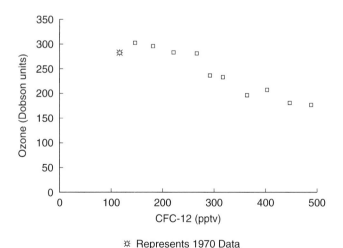

☆ Represents 1970 Data

Figure 12.2 A scatter plot of ozone column against CFC-12 concentrations.

Scatter plots like Figure 12.2 are a very simple yet effective method of examining relationships between two variables. Indeed, often the existence or not of a relationship can be spotted without carrying out any complicated calculations. Furthermore, interesting non-linear relationships can be spotted quickly with a scatter plot, whereas most mathematical measures of association can miss such relationships. Hence, it is always wise to use the scatter plot as a preliminary tool when investigating relationships between variables.

12.3 Pearson's sample correlation coefficient

Whereas the scatter plot provides a visual image of the form of a relationship between two variables, Pearson's sample correlation coefficient provides a numerical measure of the strength of a relationship. Pearson's sample correlation coefficient, r, can be defined as:

$$r = \frac{S_{xy}}{\sqrt{(S_{xx} \cdot S_{yy})}}$$

(Equation 12.1)

where

$$S_{xy} = \sum xy - \left(\frac{\sum x \sum y}{n} \right)$$

(Equation 12.2)

$$S_{xx} = \sum x^2 - \left(\frac{(\sum x)^2}{n} \right)$$

(Equation 12.3)

$$S_{yy} = \sum y^2 - \left(\frac{(\sum y)^2}{n} \right)$$

(Equation 12.4)

Note: *Pearson's sample correlation coefficient is often called* **the product moment correlation coefficient**, *or sometimes* **the correlation coefficient**. *A number of different but equivalent formulae are also used. The terminology used here will be beneficial when simple linear regression is introduced in Section 12.5.*

The use of Pearson's correlation coefficient is demonstrated by the example that follows.

Example 12.1

The calculation of a Pearson's correlation coefficient

Calculate Pearson's sample correlation coefficient, for the CFC-12/ozone column data shown in Table 12.1.

Solution

The tableau below provides a simple method of calculating r.

CFC-12	OZONE			
x	y	x^2	y^2	xy
120	281	14,400	78,961	33,720
150	302	22,500	91,204	45,300
185	295	34,225	87,025	54,575
225	282	50,625	79,524	63,450
270	280	72,900	78,400	75,600
295	235	87,025	55,225	69,325
320	233	102,400	54,289	74,560
365	196	133,225	38,416	71,540
405	208	164,025	43,264	84,240
450	182	202,500	33,124	81,900
490	178	240,100	31,684	87,220
Total 3,275	2,672	1,123,925	671,116	741,430
$\left(\sum x\right)$	$\left(\sum y\right)$	$\left(\sum x^2\right)$	$\left(\sum y^2\right)$	$\left(\sum xy\right)$

Pearson's correlation coefficient can now be calculated by using Equations 12.1-12.4.

$$S_{xy} = \sum xy - \left(\frac{\sum x \sum y}{n}\right) = 741,430 - \left(\frac{3275 \times 2672}{11}\right) = -54,097.273$$

$$S_{xx} = \sum x^2 - \frac{(\sum x)^2}{n} = 1,123,925 - \frac{(3275)^2}{11} = 148,868.18$$

$$S_{yy} = \sum y^2 - \frac{(\sum y)^2}{n} = 671,116 - \frac{(2672)^2}{11} = 22,062.909$$

$$r = \frac{S_{xy}}{\sqrt{(S_{xx} \cdot S_{yy})}} = \frac{-54,097.273}{\sqrt{(148,868.18 \times 22,062.909)}} = -0.9439$$

12.3.1 Calculating Pearson's correlation coefficient with a calculator, or by computer

Scientific calculators capable of calculating the summations $\sum x$, $\sum y$, $\sum x^2$, $\sum y^2$, and often $\sum xy$, are now available at around £10. This removes much of the drudgery from the calculations shown above.

It is also possible to obtain Pearson's correlation coefficient directly from a number of statistical software packages. With the MINITAB for Windows package Pearson's correlation coefficient between pairs of variables can be calculated by using the menu selection sequence Stat, Basic Statistics, Correlation.

12.3.2 What does a calculated coefficient mean?

Pearson's sample correlation coefficient will always lie between −1 and +1. A negative coefficient means that as one variable increases the other tends to decrease.

185

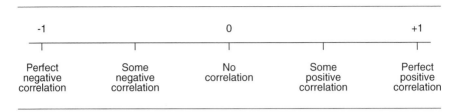

Figure 12.3 The range of possible values for Pearson's correlation coefficient.

A positive coefficient means that as one variable increases the other variable also tends to increase. In general, the closer the coefficient is to either −1 or +1, the stronger the linear relationship between the two variables. Coefficients close to zero suggest little or no linear association between the variables.

In Example 12.1 the Pearson's coefficient of -0.9439 is indicative of a very strong negative relationship; that is, high levels of CFC-12 tend to be associated with low levels of atmospheric ozone.

12.3.3 How significant is a calculated Pearson's correlation coefficient?

Students often ask how large a calculated correlation coefficient needs to be to provide evidence of an association. Unfortunately no single value answer exists. A coefficient of, say, 0.4 would provide no evidence of association from a sample of 10 pairs of x, y data; but if 100 pairs of data resulted in a coefficient of 0.4, this would provide extremely strong evidence of an association.

Table B7 in Appendix B provides critical values to enable probabilistic statements to be made regarding a calculated Pearson's correlation coefficient for a given number of data pairs. Looking at the table for the row $n = 11$, we see 0.6021 in the 5% column. This means that the chance of obtaining a coefficient as extreme as 0.6021, if no relationship exists between the two variables, is 5%. Similarly, the chance of obtaining a coefficient of 0.7348 or larger is 1%.

For a calculated coefficient based upon 11 pairs of data, a value of less than 0.6021 offers **no meaningful evidence** of any association. A coefficient between 0.6021 and 0.7348 would provide **some evidence** of a relationship. A coefficient between 0.7348 and 0.8471 would provide **strong evidence** of a relationship between the two variables.

In our CFC-12/ozone example, our coefficient was −0.9439. Ignoring the minus sign, which tells us about the form of the relationship, this provides **very strong evidence** of an association between levels of CFC-12 and the ozone column. This is the result we might expect from this set of data.

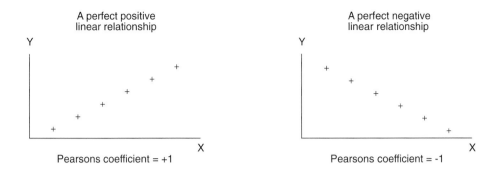

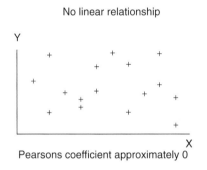

Figure 12.4 Scatter plots of data that would result in Pearson's correlation coefficients of +1, −1, and 0.

Words of warning

There are a number of potential traps to avoid when using Pearson's correlation coefficient.

The first point to note is that Pearson's coefficient measures the strength of **linear relationships** only. It is quite possible to have a strong relationship between two variables, which results in a coefficient close to zero, because the relationship is non-linear (see Figure 12.5). As non-linear relationships are not always identified with Pearson's correlation coefficient, it is always a good idea to draw a scatter plot as well as calculating a correlation coefficient when investigating relationships between variables. We should also note that Pearson's correlation coefficient assumes that both the variables being considered are approximately normally distributed. In practice, this assumption is not too restrictive, as Pearson's coefficient is safe unless the data is plainly asymmetric, discrete or in the form of ranks. In cases such as these an alternative coefficient called **Spearman's rank correlation coefficient** should be used.

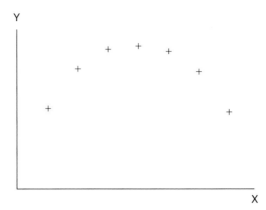

Figure 12.5 A strong non-linear relationship where Pearson's correlation coefficient would be close to zero.

There are other traps the user can fall into when using correlation coefficients. These are discussed in Box 12.1 (page 193) as they relate to all correlation coefficients. The reader is advised to read this section even if Spearman's rank correlation coefficient is not to be studied.

12.4 Spearman's rank correlation coefficient

Spearman's rank correlation coefficient is defined as:

$$r_S = 1 - \left(\frac{6 \sum d^2}{n(n^2 - 1)} \right)$$ (**Equation 12.5**)

where d = rank x – rank y (this will be clearer when we study an example).

This coefficient is normally used when Pearson's correlation coefficient is not valid due to data being clearly non-normal, or where data is provided in the form of ranks rather than in the form of measurements. Spearman's rank correlation coefficient is also sometimes used even when Pearson's coefficient would be valid, due to the simplicity of the required calculations.

Although the formula for Spearman's rank correlation coefficient does not look at all like the formula for Pearson's coefficient, the two are closely related. In fact if we have x, y data in a ranked form, with no tied ranks, Pearson's and Spearman's coefficients for the data would be identical. (If ties exist, the two measures will be approximately equal, but not identical.)

As with Pearson's correlation coefficient, Spearman's rank correlation coefficient ranges from −1 to +1, with the same general interpretation. A slight difference, however, does exist in that a perfect (i.e. +1 or −1) coefficient does not necessarily indicate a perfect linear relationship, but it does mean that every time one variable

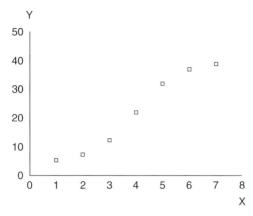

Figure 12.6 A non-linear relationship which would result in a Spearman's rank correlation coefficient of +1.

increases or decreases, then so too does the other. As an example, the data shown in Figure 12.6 would result in a Spearman's coefficient of exactly +1. Pearson's coefficient, on the other hand, would be high, but not exactly +1.

It is also possible to make probabilistic statements regarding calculated coefficients, as we considered for Pearson's correlation coefficient. The table necessary to make such statements is presented as Table B8 in Appendix B.

Example 12.2

The calculation of a Spearman's rank correlation coefficient

Between 1986 and 1987, a survey was carried out by the Department of the Environment in order to determine the effects of lead from motor car emissions, on the citizens of the UK. Part of the results from this survey are shown in Table 12.2.

Table 12.2   Mean blood lead concentrations (µg/100 ml) for females of different ages, GB

Age, x	Blood lead conc. (µg/100ml), y	Age, x	Blood lead conc. (µg/100ml), y
18–20	4.9	41–45	5.7
21–25	5.1	46–50	6.1
26–30	5.2	51–55	7.5
31–35	5.3	56–60	7.4
36–40	5.6	61–64	7.5

(Source: *The UK Environment*, Fig. 14.4, p. 200. HMSO, 1992.)

Determine whether there is a relationship between the age of females, and their blood lead concentrations.

Solution

We carry out the necessary calculations by constructing the following tableau:

Age, x	Lead, y	Rank x	Rank y	d (Rank x − Rank y)	d²
18–20	4.9	1	1	0	0
21–25	5.1	2	2	0	0
26–30	5.2	3	3	0	0
31–35	5.3	4	4	0	0
36–40	5.6	5	5	0	0
41–45	5.7	6	6	0	0
46–50	6.1	7	7	0	0
51–55	7.5	8	9.5	−1.5	2.25
56–60	7.4	9	8	1	1
61–64	7.5	10	9.5	0.5	0.25

$$\sum d^2 = 3.5$$

Note: In general, if k cases tie for ranks, each is allocated the average of the k ranks they occupy. For example, where there was a tie for the 9th and 10th ranks for the lead concentrations, each case was allocated the rank of 9.5.

$$r_S = 1 - \left(\frac{6 \sum d^2}{n(n^2 - 1)} \right)$$

$$r_S = 1 - \left(\frac{6 \times 3.5}{10(10^2 - 1)} \right) = 1 - 0.0212 = 0.9798$$

Spearman's rank correlation coefficient suggests a very strong positive relationship between age and blood lead concentrations, which is significant at the 0.1% significance level. This is the result we might expect; indeed it has been suggested that the build up of lead concentrations over the years might contribute towards senile dementia.

12.4.1 The relative merits of Pearson's, and Spearman's rank correlation coefficients

When a valid choice of correlation coefficients exists, Pearson's correlation coefficient is to be preferred as it is more **powerful**. This means it is more likely to indicate that a relationship exists, if one does indeed exist.

If the normality of the data being considered is in doubt, then Spearman's correlation coefficient is the safest choice.

> **BOX 12.1** **A note of caution**
>
> A note of caution should be sounded regarding a popular but dangerous misconception when interpreting correlation coefficients. If a significant correlation is found to exist between two variables, it **does not** mean that changes in one variable **cause** changes in the other. This may be true, but usually, especially in the environmental sciences, the cause and effect structure in operation is far more complicated than this. It is usually the case that a number of unmeasured variables influence the variables that were measured.
>
> For example, when looking at Pearson's correlation coefficient earlier, we did not prove that high CFC-12 levels destroy the ozone column, but we did find a relationship worthy of further investigation. In fact the true situation is that CFC-12 **does** destroy ozone, but is only responsible for about 40% of the destruction, the remainder of the damage being caused largely by other CFCs and methyl chloroform.

12.5 Simple linear regression

In Sections 12.2 and 12.3 we showed that, as atmospheric concentrations of CFC-12 increase, the thickness of the ozone column over Antarctica decreases. This is an interesting relationship worthy of further examination.

Rather than merely show that a relationship exists, it is more useful to express the form of the relationship in terms of a mathematical equation. In our example, this equation could then be used to predict the thickness of the ozone column over Antarctica, for any given concentration of CFC-12.

12.5.1 Fitting a straight line

Stated simply, if we plot the data of interest in the form of a scatter plot, expressing the form of the relationship mathematically involves finding the *best* straight line through the points.

If a linear relationship exists between two variables, x and y, the equation of the relationship can be expressed as:

$$y = a + bx$$

where a is the point where the line crosses the y axis, i.e. when $x = 0$, and b is the gradient (slope) of the line (i.e. b measures the change in y for every 1 unit change in x).

Figure 12.7 shows the form of a linear relationship diagrammatically.

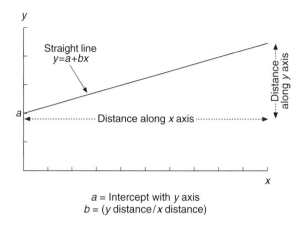

a = Intercept with y axis
b = (y distance/x distance)

Figure 12.7 The form of a linear relationship.

Our requirement is to fit a straight line to best fit a set of sample data. This involves estimating the form of the true underlying relationship, by an equation of the form:

$$\hat{y} = \hat{a} + \hat{b}x \qquad \textbf{(Equation 12.6)}$$

where $\hat{a}$ and $\hat{b}$ are estimates of the true constants a and b.

Sometimes a line of best fit is drawn by hand for guidance purposes. However, this approach is rather rough and ready. If we look at Figure 12.8, it is not easy to say which of the lines through the data is the *best*. Furthermore, we could draw any number of similar lines, each looking as accurate as the others. So how do we decide which is the best line? One answer is to use the *method of least squares*.

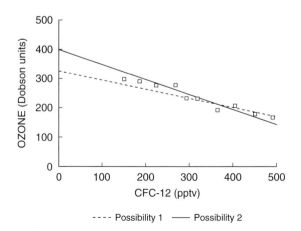

Figure 12.8 Two possible lines of 'best fit' for the CFC-12/ozone data.

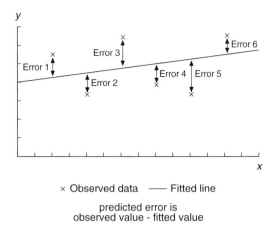

× Observed data ——— Fitted line

predicted error is
observed value - fitted value

Figure 12.9 The errors when fitting a straight line to a set of data.

The method of least squares

If we wanted to fit a straight line through the data shown in Figure 12.8, it would be impossible for a line to pass exactly through all the points. For each observed data value there would be a difference between the observed data value and the fitted line; this is known as a **prediction error**.

These errors are measured in the y direction as we are trying to find the best equation to predict y from x (see Figure 12.9).

Clearly, we want to make these prediction errors as small as possible. It can be shown that no unique line can minimize the sum of these prediction errors. It is though possible to obtain a unique straight line equation which minimizes the sum of the squared prediction errors.

In mathematical terminology, we minimize

$$\sum (y - \hat{y})^2$$

– where y is the observed values of the dependent variable and
$\hat{y}$ is the prediction of the dependent variable –

to obtain **the least squares regression line of y on x**, or a **simple linear regression equation of y on x** (SLR equation).

Finding the least squares regression line

It can be shown that the least squares regression line of y on x, of the form

$$\hat{y} = \hat{a} + \hat{b}x,$$

193

is obtained from the formulae

$$\hat{b} = \frac{S_{xy}}{S_{xx}}$$

(Equation 12.7)

and

$$\hat{a} = \bar{y} - \hat{b}\bar{x}$$

(Equation 12.8)

where, we remember from Section 12.3,

$$S_{xx} = \sum x^2 - \frac{\left(\sum x\right)^2}{n}$$

and

$$S_{xy} = \sum xy - \left(\frac{\sum x \sum y}{n}\right)$$

Example 12.3

The calculation of a simple linear regression equation

Obtain the simple linear regression equation of ozone column (Dobson units) on CFC-12 (pptv) for the data introduced in Section 12.3.

Solution

We are asked to fit an equation of the form:

$$\hat{y} = \hat{a} + \hat{b}x$$

where

$$S_{xx} = \sum x^2 - \frac{\left(\sum x\right)^2}{n}$$

and

$$S_{xy} = \sum xy - \left(\frac{\sum x \sum y}{n}\right)$$

The tableau that follows can be used, although many of the terms required can be calculated more quickly by use of a calculator.

CFC-12	Ozone			
x	y	x^2	y^2	xy
120	281	14,400	78,961	33,720
150	302	22,500	91,204	45,300
185	295	34,225	87,025	54,575
225	282	50,625	79,524	63,450
270	280	72,900	78,400	75,600

CFC-12	Ozone			
x	y	x^2	y^2	xy
295	235	87,025	55,225	69,325
320	233	102,400	54,289	74,560
365	196	133,225	38,416	71,540
405	208	164,025	43,264	84,240
450	182	202,500	33,124	81,900
490	178	240,100	31,684	87,220
Total 3,275	2,672	1,123,925	671,116	741,430
$(\sum x)$	$(\sum y)$	$(\sum x^2)$	$(\sum y^2)$	$(\sum xy)$

$$\bar{x} = 297.7272 \qquad \bar{y} = 242.9091$$

$$S_{xx} = \sum x^2 - \frac{(\sum x)^2}{n} = 1,123,925 - \frac{(3,275)^2}{11} = 148,868.18$$

$$S_{xy} = \sum xy - \frac{(\sum x)(\sum y)}{n} = 741,430 - \frac{3,275 \times 2,672}{11} = -54,097.273$$

so

$$\hat{b} = \frac{S_{xy}}{S_{xx}} = \frac{-54,097.273}{148,868.18} = -0.3634$$

and

$$\hat{a} = \bar{y} - \hat{\beta}\bar{x} = 242.9091 - (-0.3634 \times 297.7273) = 351.10$$

so our fitted regression equation is

$$\hat{y} = 351.1 - 0.3634x$$

or

Ozone column (Dobson units) $= 351.1 - 0.3634$ CFC-12 (pptv)

to four significant figures.

12.5.2 Interpretation of the regression equation

Remembering that the constants $\hat{a}$ and $\hat{b}$ represent the intercept and slope of a fitted regression line, useful interpretations of these constants can often be made. For instance, in Example 12.3 the regression equation was found to be:

Ozone column (Dobson units) $= 351.1 - 0.3634$ CFC-12 (pptv)

This equation suggests that on average, each 1 unit increase in the concentration of CFC-12 in the atmosphere is associated with a reduction of 0.3634 Dobson units of ozone.

The intercept constant of 351.1 suggests that if no CFC-12 was present in the atmosphere, the ozone column would be 351.1 Dobson units. This estimate is not unreasonable. In 1956, when global concentrations of CFC-12 were low, the ozone column in Antarctica measured 330 Dobson units. Unfortunately ozone levels for the pre-CFC era are not readily available to check our estimate.

The most useful aspect of a regression equation is the ability to predict values for the dependent variable, for any given value of the independent variables. This is demonstrated in Example 12.4.

Example 12.4

A simple linear regression prediction

Using the regression equation

Ozone column (Dobson units) = 351.1 − 0.363 CFC-12 (pptv)

predict the ozone column for when the atmospheric concentration of CFC-12 was 400 pptv.

Solution

We substitute the value 400 for the CFC-12 term in the regression equation to produce the prediction

$$\text{Ozone column} = 351.1 - (0.3634 \times 400)$$
$$= 351.1 - 145.36$$
$$= 205.7 \text{ Dobson units}$$

This prediction is shown diagrammatically in Figure 12.10.

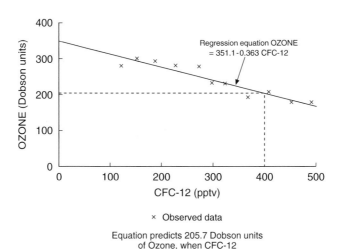

× Observed data

Equation predicts 205.7 Dobson units
of Ozone, when CFC-12
concentration is 400 pptv

Figure 12.10 The regression equation as fitted to the CFC-12/ozone data.

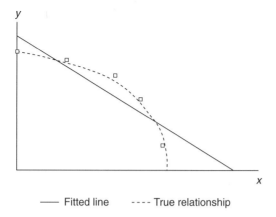

—— Fitted line   ---- True relationship

Figure 12.11 A graph showing how a relationship may only be approximately linear over a particular range.

A few notes regarding predictions

It is dangerous to predict the value of the dependent y variable, from the independent x variable, for values outside the range of x values included in the original data set. This is because the relationship between the two variables may only be approximately linearly related within a certain range. This situation is shown in Figure 12.11.

There are, of course, times when such predictions are exactly what is required. For instance, you might want to predict what further increases in CFC-12 concentrations might do to the ozone layer. If you must do so, limit yourself to predictions only fractionally outside the scope of your sampled data, and bear in mind that your predictions might not be as accurate as you think. A student who did not appreciate this fact once informed me that if 10 supermarket checkouts were operating, the average customer queuing time would be −1.6 minutes!

A further point worth remembering is that the regression equation, and hence any predictions made from it, are only estimates based upon a sample. So if, in Example 12.3, we had used data from 30 different years rather than 11, the resulting regression equation and predictions would be different. In fact, the resulting estimates would be more accurate due to the larger data set. Section 12.6 deals with this uncertainty a little further by considering the likely margins of error for regression predictions.

12.6   Further regression analysis with the aid of statistical packages

A whole host of statistical packages, including MINITAB, SPSS and GENSTAT, will fit a regression equation in seconds, as will some spreadsheet packages such as

EXCEL. In this section we shall concentrate on results obtained from the MINITAB for Windows package, although the same results could be obtained from any major statistical software package.

12.6.1 Regression with MINITAB for Windows

> **Scatter plots** can be obtained by selecting **Graph, Plot.**
> **Regression equations** are most easily fitted by selecting **Stat, Regression, Regression.**

Let us consider the CFC-12/ozone data that was used in Example 12.3. Exhibit 12.1 shows the resulting output when MINITAB was instructed (a) to draw a scatter plot and (b) to carry out a regression analysis of ozone on CFC-12, using the above menu selections. The items marked in **bold text** are particularly worthy of mention, and will be discussed in this section. The remainder of the output is also useful, but beyond the scope of this text.

12.6.2 The regression equation

The regression equation of ozone on CFC-12 for our example data is shown at the top of the printout in Exhibit 12.1. The equation is shown to be

Ozone $= 351 - 0.363$ CFC-12

This is identical to the equation we calculated by hand in Example 12.3. The interpretation of this equation was discussed in Section 12.5.2.

The predictor p-*values*

We remember that a fitted equation is only an estimate of the true underlying linear relationship of the form:

$$y = a + bx$$

If the true relationship is such that either $a = 0$, or $b = 0$, then fitting a simple linear regression line of the form

$$\hat{y} = \hat{a} + \hat{b}x$$

is not really appropriate. The p-values provide the probabilities of a and b taking values as extreme as they do, given that the true values of a and b are actually zero. Generally, statisticians like to be sure that an equation is suitable, so they like all p-values to be <0.05.

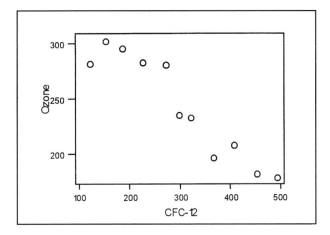

(a) A Scatter plot

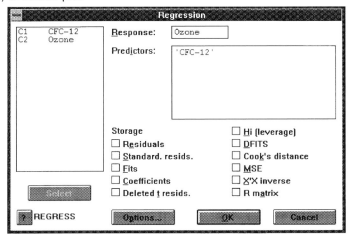

(b) The MINITAB regression menu

```
The regression equation is
ozone = 351 - 0.363 CFC-12
```

Predictor	Coef	Stdev	t-ratio	p
Constant	351.10	13.54	25.93	0.000
CFC-12	-0.36339	0.04236	-8.58	0.000

s = 16.35   **R-sq = 89.1%**   R-sq(adj) = 87.9%

Analysis of Variance

SOURCE	DF	SS	MS	F	p
Regression	1	19658	19658	73.58	0.000
Error	9	2404	267		
Total	10	22063			

Exhibit 12.1 MINITAB regression output for the CFC-12/ozone data.

In our example the p-values for both a and b (labelled as constant and CFC-12 on the printout), are both 0.000 to 3 d.p.s. This means that it is virtually certain that neither a nor b should really be zero.

The analysis of variance p-value

Regression analysis of variance (regression ANOVA) could provide the subject for a whole section of this book, and is hence largely beyond our scope. However, some understanding of the ANOVA p-value is useful.

Put simply, the p-value is the probability of obtaining a fit as good as we do, simply by chance, if no linear relationship really exists. So the lower the p-value, the more evidence we have that our equation is useful.

In our example the p-value of 0.000 suggests that our equation is almost certainly useful, as a linear relationship almost certainly exists.

R-squared (R^2)

The ANOVA p-value mentioned earlier tells us *whether* a regression equation is useful or not. The R-squared value on the output provides a measure of *how well* the regression equation fits our sample data. The closer R-squared is to 100%, the better the fit, where an R-squared of 100% would mean that the regression line passes exactly through all the data points.

In our example, the R-squared value of 89.1% suggests that our equation fits the data very well, and is hence likely to provide good predictions.

R-squared is in fact (Pearson's correlation coefficient)^2, expressed as a percentage. So from our output we know that Pearson's correlation coefficient for our data would be $\sqrt{0.891} = \pm 0.9439$, which agrees with our calculations from Section 12.3 where we showed that the coefficient is in fact -0.9439.

The importance of this relationship is that it highlights the close link between correlation and regression. If two variables are highly correlated a regression equation is useful, whereas if no significant correlation exists a simple linear regression equation will prove to be of limited value.

12.6.3 Predictions with MINITAB

In Example 12.4 we showed how a prediction could be made from a regression equation. We should remember that the prediction obtained is only an estimate based upon the available data. MINITAB allows us to provide predictions in the form of **confidence intervals** and **prediction intervals**.

The **95% confidence interval** provides a range of values which will contain the **mean value for** y for a given value of x, on 95% of occasions.

The **95% prediction interval** provides a range of values which will contain the **true value of** y **for an individual**, for a given value of x, on 95% of occasions.

Prediction intervals are always wider than confidence intervals. This makes intuitive sense because a mean is always less variable than a single observation (for example, it would be easier to predict the mean daily rainfall over a period of time than it would be to predict the rainfall for one particular day).

Both prediction intervals and confidence intervals are very useful to the environmentalist. In this particular example only the prediction interval makes any sense. It is meaningless to consider the mean global ozone concentration for the occasions when the mean global CFC-12 concentration is/was 400 pptv, as the global CFC-12 concentration was only 400 pptv at one point in history.

The **95% prediction interval** (95% P.I) shown in **bold type** in Exhibit 12.2 tells us that we can be 95% certain that when the global CFC-12 concentration was 400 pptv,

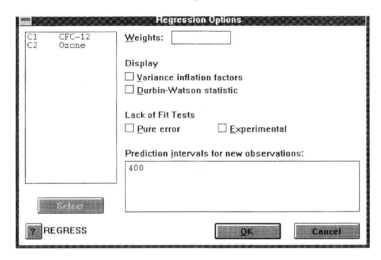

```
The regression equation is
ozone = 351 - 0.363 CFC-12

Predictor        Coef       Stdev      t-ratio        p
Constant        351.10      13.54        25.93      0.000
CFC-12         -0.36339     0.04236      -8.58      0.000

s = 16.35        R-sq = 89.1%        R-sq(adj) = 87.9%

Analysis of Variance
SOURCE          DF        SS         MS          F         p
Regression       1      19658      19658      73.58      0.000
Error            9       2404       267
Total           10      22063

  Fit      Stdev.Fit     95% C.I.              95% P.I.
205.74       6.56     ( 190.90, 220.59) (  165.89,  245.60)
```

Exhibit 12.2 Making a regression prediction using MINITAB.

the ozone column over Antarctica measured somewhere between 165.89 and 245.6 Dobson units. This range is quite large. In order to produce a smaller range and hence a better estimate, we would need to increase our sample to include more than the 11 years of data currently included.

12.7 Multiple linear regression

In many practical areas of statistical application, including the environmental sciences, a dependent variable of interest might not be influenced by a single independent variable, but only by a number of independent (predictor) variables. The least squares fitting ideas of simple linear regression can be extended to incorporate any number of predictor variables, and when this is done the technique is known as **multiple linear regression** (MLR).

The general form of a MLR equation is

$$\hat{y} = \hat{a} + \hat{b}_1 x_1 + \hat{b}_2 x_2 + \cdots + \hat{b}_p x_p$$

where $x_1, x_2, \ldots, x_p$ are the p independent (predictor) variables.

Multiple linear regression is a large topic, and hand calculations are complicated and time consuming. In this section the reader will be given just a taster of the technique by considering a practical example where most calculations are carried out with the MINITAB statistical package.

12.7.1 A practical example: predicting atmospheric concentrations of carbon dioxide (CO_2)

In recent years much has been written about the problem of **global warming**. In simple terms, radiation from the Sun is reflected from the Earth in the form of infrared radiation. Some of this infrared is trapped by **greenhouse gases** in the atmosphere, which keep the heat in. Over the years the levels of the greenhouse gases have been increased through human activity, raising global temperatures.

A key greenhouse gas is carbon dioxide (CO_2); in fact it is estimated that CO_2 is responsible for around 72% of the global warming effect. Much of the CO_2 in the atmosphere is the result of activities by mankind since the industrial revolution. Given the importance of CO_2 to global warming, the prediction of atmospheric concentrations of CO_2 is obviously an important task.

Table 12.3 shows the CO_2 levels in the atmosphere (ppmv), alongside the global CO_2 emissions (million tonnes of carbon – mtc) through two anthropogenic sources, from 1960 to 1984.

Having entered the CO_2 concentrations, natural gas emissions and solids emissions into the first three columns of a MINITAB spreadsheet, we can produce a multiple regression equation by using the usual MINITAB selections **S̲tat, R̲egression,**

Table 12.3 CO_2 levels in the atmosphere (ppmv) and anthropogenic CO_2 emissions by natural gas and solids (million tonnes carbon), 1960–84

Year	CO_2 concentration	Natural gas	Solids
1960	316.6	235	1,419
1962	318.2	277	1,358
1964	319.1	328	1,442
1966	320.7	380	1,485
1968	322.3	445	1,455
1970	325.5	516	1,595
1972	327.6	582	1,612
1974	330.4	616	1,620
1976	332.0	645	1,754
1978	335.4	673	1,828
1980	338.7	724	1,924
1982	341.2	734	1,983
1984	344.2	784	2,103

(Source: *UNEP Environmental Data Report*, Table 1.1, p. 9. Basil Blackwell, 1987.)

Regression. The menu selections from the regression menu, and the resulting output, are shown in Exhibit 12.3.

12.7.2 The multiple linear regression equation for the CO_2 data

The output shown in Exhibit 12.3 tells us that the best equation for predicting CO_2 levels from emissions by natural gas and solids is

CO_2 (ppmv) $= 278 + 0.0191$ natural gas (mtc) $+ 0.0243$ solids (mtc)

This equation tells us that if CO_2 emissions by solids remain steady, then each million tonne of carbon emitted by natural gas leads to a 0.0191 ppmv increase in global CO_2 concentrations. Similarly, if emissions by natural gas remain steady, then each million tonne of carbon emitted by solids leads to a 0.0243 ppmv increase in global CO_2 concentrations.

The two constants 0.0191 and 0.0243 are, of course, estimates based upon our sample of 13 years. Given the closeness of these constants, it is quite possible that in reality they should be equal. If this is the case it would imply that the CO_2 concentrations were related to the sum of the two forms of emission, in which case a simple linear regression equation of CO_2 concentrations on total emissions would suffice. If, however, the two coefficients really do differ, then it would imply that emissions from solids increase CO_2 concentrations more than emissions from natural gas. More data would be necessary to investigate these possible alternatives more thoroughly.

In this example it would be unwise to make too much of the constant term 278. This implies that the global CO_2 concentration would have been 278 ppmv before anthropogenic emissions from natural gas and solids began. This interpretation would assume that our fitted relationship held true for values well outside the range of our data. It is interesting to note, however, that the global concentration

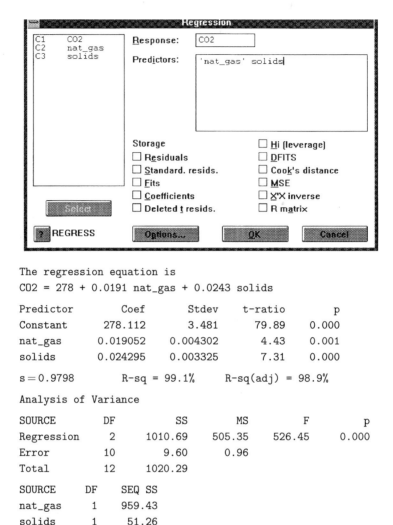

The regression equation is
$CO2 = 278 + 0.0191$ nat_gas $+ 0.0243$ solids

Predictor	Coef	Stdev	t-ratio	p
Constant	278.112	3.481	79.89	0.000
nat_gas	0.019052	0.004302	4.43	0.001
solids	0.024295	0.003325	7.31	0.000

$s = 0.9798$ R-sq = 99.1%   R-sq(adj) = 98.9%

Analysis of Variance

SOURCE	DF	SS	MS	F	p
Regression	2	1010.69	505.35	526.45	0.000
Error	10	9.60	0.96		
Total	12	1020.29			

SOURCE	DF	SEQ SS
nat_gas	1	959.43
solids	1	51.26

Exhibit 12.3 MINITAB regression analysis menu, and resulting out, for the CO_2 data example.

of CO_2 in 1750, before the industrial revolution, has been estimated by experts as being 278 ppmv! (*The UK Environment*, p. 32, HMSO, 1992.)

How good is the equation?

The *R*-squared of 99.1% suggests that this equation is very accurate indeed. The usefulness and appropriateness of the equation is reinforced further by the small predictor p-values, and the very small regression ANOVA p-value. All in all, the equation seems very successful, despite our ignoring other useful predictor variables including emissions from liquid fuels, gas flaring, and the manufacture of cement.

Making predictions

As with simple linear regression, we can use this equation to predict CO_2 levels, given particular levels of emissions from natural gas and solids.

Example 12.5

Predict the global CO_2 concentration for when emissions by natural gas and solids are 600 and 1600 million tonnes of carbon respectively, using the MLR equation

CO_2 (ppmv) $= 278 + 0.0191$ natural gas (mtc) $+ 0.0243$ solids (mtc)

Solution

By hand: We simply substitute the values 600 and 1600 into the regression equation as follows:

$$CO_2 \text{ (ppmv)} = 278 + (0.019 \times 600) + (0.0243 \times 1600)$$
$$= 278 + 11.5 + 38.9 = 328.4 \text{ (ppmv)}$$

By computer: We could use a computer package such as MINITAB to provide the prediction, and to also provide a confidence interval for the mean CO_2 concentration for when natural gas emissions and solids emissions are 600 and 1600 mtc respectively. The appropriate output from the MINITAB package is shown below.

```
CO2 = 278 + 0.0191 nat_gas + 0.0243 solids
```

Predictor	Coef	Stdev	t-ratio	p
Constant	278.112	3.481	79.89	0.000
nat_gas	0.019052	0.004302	4.43	0.001
solids	0.024295	0.003325	7.31	0.000

s = 0.9798   R-sq = 99.1%   R-sq(adj) = 98.9%

Analysis of Variance

SOURCE	DF	SS	MS	F	p
Regression	2	1010.69	505.35	526.45	0.000
Error	10	9.60	0.96		
Total	12	1020.29			

SOURCE	DF	SEQ SS
nat_gas	1	959.43
solids	1	51.26

Fit	Stdev.Fit	95% C.I.	95% P.I.
328.416	0.548	(327.194,329.637)	(325.913,330.918)

From this output we can see that the best single prediction is for 328.4 ppmv of CO_2, and we can be 95% sure that the mean concentration would lie between 327.2 ppmv and 329.6 ppmv.

12.8 Non-linear relationships

It is often the case that relationships between variables are non-linear. This is particularly true in the environmental sciences. Fortunately the ideas behind regression analysis can often be extended to cater for such relationships.

When a non-linear relationship exists between two or more variables, there are two approaches that can be taken: either

(1) transform one or more of the variables so that the relationship becomes linear, then fit a linear regression equation; or
(2) fit a curve (usually a quadratic or sometimes a cubic function) to the data.

In this introductory text a detailed account of these approaches is not possible. Instead a brief example follows.

Example 12.6

The following data and scatter plot show the percentage of mud found in core samples at varying depths from 10 to 200 metres. Fit a regression equation to the data and hence predict the percentage of mud to be found in a core sample from a depth of 200 metres.

Depth (m)	Percentage mud	Depth (m)	Percentage mud
10	31.91	110	8.08
20	36.23	120	5.52
30	34.61	130	3.37
40	26.85	140	5.44
50	21.64	150	3.91
60	18.26	160	3.95
70	14.50	170	4.43
80	12.52	180	2.85
90	7.88	190	4.98
100	7.73	200	4.27

Solution

Through examining the above scatter plot it is clear that a relationship exists between the depth of the core samples and the percentage of mud in the samples, but there is a suggestion that the data in the plot follows more of a curve than a straight line. We shall look at three possible approaches to finding a prediction equation from this data.

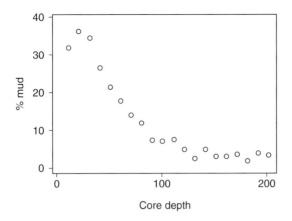

Approach 1: Fitting a standard regression equation

If we fit a standard regression equation to the data using MINITAB we obtain the following output:

```
The regression equation is
%mud = 30.8 - 0.170 depth

Predictor          Coef        Stdev      t-ratio          p
Constant         30.819        2.447        12.59      0.000
depth          -0.17022      0.02043        -8.33      0.000

s = 5.268          R-sq = 79.4%      R-sq(adj) = 78.3%

Analysis of Variance

SOURCE             DF           SS           MS          F          p
Regression          1       1926.8       1926.8      69.43      0.000
Error              18        499.5         27.8
Total              19       2426.3

      Fit    Stdev.Fit         95% C.I.            95% P.I.
    -3.22         2.27   ( -8.00,    1.55)   ( -15.28,    8.83)
```

This suggests that the equation shown in bold is a useful prediction equation because the p-values are all small and R^2 takes the encouraging value of 79.4%, **but** is this a sensible equation? The answer is **NO**; we have in fact fitted a straight line through a curve here. An undesirable result of this is that the equation predicts **negative percentage mud contents** for depths above 181 metres. That is why the predicted mud content for a depth of 200 metres is shown in bold as an impossible −3.22%.

Approach 2: Linearizing the data by transforming a variable

The above scatter plot suggests a possibility of a curved relationship existing between the depth and the mud content of the core samples. One approach to fitting a prediction equation would be to linearize the relationship by transforming a variable. In many environmental situations **logarithmic** relationships exist between pairs of variables. This seems to be a possibility for this data set, so an equation of the form

$$\log_{10} (\text{percentage mud}) = a + b \ (\text{depth in metres})$$

is worth fitting. An initial MINITAB worksheet containing values for the depths and percentages mud found in the core samples in columns 1 and 2 was set up. Values for $\log_{10}$(percentage mud) were then created in column 3 by using the command:

MTB > let c3 = logten(c2)

This produced the following worksheet:

ROW	depth	%mud	$\log_{10}$mud
1	10	31.91	1.50393
2	20	36.23	1.55907
3	30	34.61	1.53920
4	40	26.85	1.42894
5	50	21.64	1.33526
6	60	18.26	1.26150
7	70	14.50	1.16137
8	80	12.52	1.09760
9	90	7.88	0.89653
10	100	7.73	0.88818
11	110	8.08	0.90741
12	120	5.52	0.74194
13	130	3.37	0.52763
14	140	5.44	0.73560
15	150	3.91	0.59218
16	160	3.95	0.59660
17	170	4.43	0.64640
18	180	2.85	0.45484
19	190	4.98	0.69723
20	200	4.27	0.63043

The hope now is that the new **$\log_{10}$mud** variable might show a more linear relationship with the depth than the original **%mud** variable. This in fact is the case. This can be verified numerically by looking at the correlations below. Whereas the correlation between **%mud** and **depth** was -0.891, the correlation between **$\log_{10}$mud** and **depth** is an even better -0.940.

	Depth	%mud
%mud	−0.891	
$\log_{10}$mud	−0.940	0.960

Furthermore, the scatter plot of **$\log_{10}$mud** against **depth** is much more linear than the scatter plot seen earlier of **%mud** against **depth**.

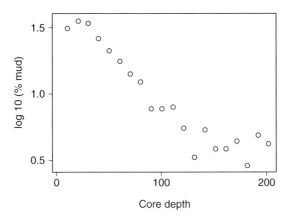

MINITAB can now be used to obtain the output that follows.

```
The regression equation is
log10mud = 1.58 - 0.00587 depth

Predictor             Coef         Stdev      t-ratio          p
Constant           1.57675       0.06027        26.16      0.000
depth            -0.0058729     0.0005031       -11.67      0.000

s = 0.1297           R-sq = 88.3%        R-sq(adj) = 87.7%

Analysis of Variance

SOURCE            DF          SS          MS           F          p
Regression         1      2.2937      2.2937      136.26      0.000
Error             18      0.3030      0.0168
Total             19      2.5967

Unusual Observations
Obs.    depth    log10mud        Fit Stdev.Fit     Residual    St.Resid
13        130      0.5276     0.8133    0.0316       -0.2856       -2.27R

R denotes an obs. with a large st. resid.

    Fit    Stdev.Fit         95% C.I.            95% P.I.
  0.4022      0.0559    ( 0.2847, 0.5197)    (0.1053, 0.6990)
```

The fitted equation

$\log_{10} \text{mud} = 1.58 - 0.00587 \text{ depth}$

is better than the previous equation because:

(1) the R^2 value is higher while the p-values are still low;
(2) all prediction estimates are now sensible, i.e. no impossible negative estimates for the mud content can be obtained.

The reader should note that the predictions made from this equation are for **log₁₀mud** and not **%mud**. Hence, the procedure for predicting the percentage mud in a core sample from 200 metres would be as follows:

$$\log_{10} \text{mud} = 1.58 - (0.00587 \times \text{depth})$$
$$= 1.58 - (0.00587 \times 200)$$
$$= 0.40$$

This prediction is shown highlighted on the MINITAB output above.

The prediction for the percentage of mud in a sample at a depth of 200 metres is now found as follows:

Percentage of mud in a sample at 200 metres $= 10^{0.4} = $ **2.5%**

This prediction is a lot more sensible than the negative prediction obtained from the standard regression equation earlier.

Approach 3: Fitting a quadratic equation to the data

An alternative approach to coping with this data is to fit a quadratic equation of the form:

$$\%\text{mud} = a + b(\text{depth}) + c(\text{depth}^2)$$

To fit this equation a new variable **depth²** was created. A multiple regression model to predict the **%mud** was then fitted using **depth** and **depth²** as the predictor variables.

Using this approach the results are very pleasing. The R-squared value is a very encouraging 96.1% and all the p-values are very small. Furthermore when a prediction is made for the percentage of mud in a sample at a depth of 200 metres the prediction of 5.4% looks intuitively sensible given the observed data at this depth. It seems as though this model provides realistic predictions throughout the range of observed data. All in all, this seems to be the most satisfactory of the fitted models.

```
The regression equation is
%mud = 42.5 - 0.489 depth + 0.00152 depthsq
```

Predictor	Coef	Stdev	t-ratio	p
Constant	42.498	1.765	24.08	0.000
depth	-0.48872	0.03871	-12.62	0.000
depthsq	0.0015167	0.0001791	8.47	0.000

```
s = 2.373        R-sq = 96.1%      R-sq(adj) = 95.6%
```

Analysis of Variance

SOURCE	DF	SS	MS	F	p
Regression	2	2330.6	1165.3	207.00	0.000
Error	17	95.7	5.6		
Total	19	2426.3			

SOURCE	DF	SEQ SS
depth	1	1926.8
depthsq	1	403.8

Fit	Stdev.Fit	95% C.I.	95% P.I.
5.421	1.445	(2.372, 8.470)	(-0.442, 11.283)

12.8.1 Summary

The methods covered in this section worked because **a non-linear function of** x (depth) could be expressed in the form of a **linear equation of a redefined variable** (such as x^2, or $\log_{10} x$). So linear regression could still be used to model non-linear data.

Sometimes data follows a relationship which is **non-linear in terms of the coefficients**. For example, data may follow relationships such as

$$y = a + e^{bx}$$

Relationships such as these cannot be modelled using linear regression. Instead, a more advanced method known as **non-linear regression** is required.

The modelling of non-linear relationships could provide the basis for a text on its own. It is hoped, however, that this short section at least suggests some of the approaches that the environmentalist can take. The reader who requires a more detailed regression text is recommended to consult Wonnacott and Wonnacott (1981).

Exercises 12

The following exercises are based on Sections 12.1 to 12.4

Exercise 12.1

The scatter plots below resulted from some field experiments. For each of the plots estimate what values Pearson's correlation coefficient, and Spearman's rank correlation coefficient, would take.

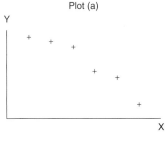

Plot (a)

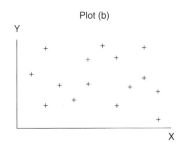

Plot (b)

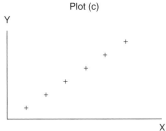

Plot (c)

Exercise 12.2

The following data relates to the Gross Domestic Product (GDP) per capita, and the percentage of energy produced by wood burning, for 16 selected countries. The countries are listed in order of wealth (as measured by the GDP), with the poorest countries at the top of the list.

Country	Percentage of energy through wood burning
Ethiopia	93
Mali	97
B.Faso	94
Niger	87
Tanzania	94
Burundi	89
Somalia	90
Benin	86
Rwanda	96
Kenya	74
Guinea	74
Ghana	74
Sri Lanka	54
Senegal	63
Ivory Coast	46
Honduras	45

(Source: Foley 1987, p. 199.)

(a) Calculate, and interpret Spearman's rank correlation coefficient.
(b) Does your calculated coefficient provide statistically significant evidence of a relationship between the two measured variables.

Exercise 12.3

The following table shows the monthly averages of smoke, and sulphur dioxide (SO_2), from April 1991 until March 1992, for the town of Kirkby.

Month	Smoke (ppm), y	SO_2 (ppm), x
April	5.3	24.5
May	15.0	61.6
June	4.0	17.6
July	8.3	34.3
August	6.5	20.4
September	11.0	38.5
October	11.8	43.0
November	11.3	28.2
December	21.9	40.4
January	32.7	42.9
February	12.7	28.4
March	6.5	17.7

(a) Plot the data in the form of a scatter plot, and comment upon the nature of the relationship between concentrations of smoke, and SO_2.
(b) Calculate Pearson's correlation coefficient, and hence determine whether there is a significant relationship between concentrations of smoke, and concentrations of SO_2.

Exercise 12.4

The data below shows the number of pairs of breeding adults, and the number of Fledglings per breeding pair, for Great Tits in Marley Wood, Oxfordshire.

Year	Number of pairs of breeding adults, x	Fledglings per pair, y
1947	13	9.2
1948	41	10.0
1949	59	8.8
1950	63	6.2
1951	67	5.0
1952	38	7.6
1953	40	8.8
1954	61	8.6
1955	52	6.9
1956	48	8.0
1957	99	3.6
1958	53	5.8
1959	80	7.0
1960	103	5.6
1961	169	2.4
1962	84	5.3
1963	76	6.8

(Source: Solomon 1976.)

(a) Plot the data in the form of a scatter plot, and comment upon the relationship shown.
(b) What are the likely reasons for this relationship?
(c) Calculate Pearson's correlation coefficient, and hence test whether the relationship is statistically significant.
(d) Repeat part (c) using Spearman's rank correlation coefficient.

The following exercises are based on Sections 12.5 to 12.8

Exercise 12.5

A simple linear regression equation

$$y = 10 + 4x$$

was fitted to a set of environmental data.

(a) Using the equation above, predict y for $x = 0$.
(b) Using the equation above, predict y for $x = 5$.
(c) Sketch the form of this relationship.

Exercise 12.6

During a field trip, the cross-sectional area (m²), and average velocity (m/s) of the river Brew in Somerset were measured at nine different sites. The resulting measurements are shown below:

Site	Cross-sectional area (m²)	Average velocity (m/s)
1	0.556	0.138
2	1.282	0.398
3	1.368	0.160
4	0.838	0.230
5	0.708	0.209
6	1.805	0.318
7	2.002	0.604
8	2.086	0.597
9	2.034	0.236

(a) Fit a simple linear regression equation of the form

Average velocity $= a + b$ cross-sectional area

(b) What is the practical interpretation of the constants a and b in your equation?
(c) Use your equation to predict the average velocity of a section of the river Brew where the cross-sectional area is 1 m².

Exercise 12.7

The following table shows the acreage (expressed in thousands of acres) of agricultural land used for the production of wheat and barley in the UK from 1980 until 1989.

Year	Wheat	Barley
1980	1441	2330
1981	1491	2327
1982	1663	2222
1983	1693	2143
1984	1939	1978
1985	1902	1965
1986	1997	1916
1987	1994	1830
1988	1886	1878
1989	2083	1652

(Source: *Annual Abstract of Statistics*, HMSO (1991).)

(a) Fit a regression equation of the form

Wheat (000s acres) $= a + b$ Barley (000s acres)

(b) Use your equation to predict the amount of land used for wheat production when 2 million acres of land are used for barley production.

Exercise 12.8

Referring to the data from Exercise 12.7, use an appropriate statistical package to carry out the following:

(a) Find the SLR equation of the form

Wheat (000s acres) $= a + b$ Barley (000s acres)

(b) Discuss the practical interpretation of the constants a and b.

(c) Examine the regression ANOVA p-value, and hence determine whether the fitted regression equation is useful.

(d) Provide a 95% prediction interval for the amount of land used for wheat production when 2 million acres are used for barley production.

(e) Using the value of R-squared, determine Pearson's correlation coefficient between the wheat and barley acreages.

Exercise 12.9

A multiple linear regression equation

$$y = 10 + 25x_1 + 15x_2$$

was fitted to a set of data.

(a) On average, how much will y increase for every 1 unit change in x_1 if x_2 is held fixed?

(b) On average, how much will y increase for every 1 unit change in x_2 if x_1 is held fixed?

(c) Predict the average value of y when $x_1 = 10$ and $x_2 = 5$.

Exercise 12.10

In a sample of cherry trees, the heights, diameters, and volumes of 20 trees were measured. These measurements are shown below.

Volume (ft^3)	Height (ft)	Diameter (in.)
18.2	75	11.0
16.4	72	10.5
24.9	64	13.8
21.3	69	11.7
34.5	78	14.0
77.0	87	20.6
51.0	80	18.0
22.6	80	11.1
15.6	66	11.0
58.3	80	17.9
55.4	81	17.3
19.9	75	11.2
31.7	80	14.2
24.2	79	11.3
19.7	83	10.8
27.4	86	13.3
21.4	76	11.4
10.2	63	8.8
38.3	72	16.0
42.6	77	16.3

(Source: MINITAB example file 'trees'.)

(a) Use an appropriate statistical package to find the MLR equation of the form

$$\text{volume} = a + b \text{ (height)} + c \text{ diameter)}$$

(b) What is the practical interpretation of the constants a, b, and c?
(c) Determine whether the equation is useful.
(d) Find a 95% prediction interval for the volume of a tree which has a height of 85 inches and a diameter of 13 inches.

Appendix A:
Solutions to exercises

Exercises 3

Exercise 3.1

Definitions all available to the reader in Chapter 3.

Exercise 3.2

(a) Examples include time, and weights.
(b) Examples include the number of tree species observed in a transect study.
(c) Degree classification is an example, i.e. 1, 2(a), 2(b), 3.
(d) An example would be the variable 'sex'.

Exercise 3.3

(a) If random digits from 00 to 19 are allocated to the 20 staff, the sample consists of:
Wiseman, Hughes, Patel, Thomas, Rhodes, Gallier, Lawes, Oliver, Storey.
(b) Two systematic samples are possible:
either Abrahams, Cornwall, Dixon, Hughes...
or Barnes, Davies, Gallier, Khimji...
(c) Staff of all grades and sexes will be represented equally. Numbers in each category are:

	Male	Female
SO	1	3
HSO	2	2
SSO	1	1

Exercise 3.4

Computer exercise.

Exercises 3.5 to 3.9

These are discussion questions with no right or wrong answers as such. Read the chapter, and discuss these problems with colleagues and/or your tutor. (You may wish to combine ideas from more than one methodology discussed in this chapter.)

Exercises 4

Exercise 4.1

(a)

Number of vehicles	Frequency
0	8
1	12
2	6
3	3
4	0
5	1

(b)

The number of vehicles passing in
30 one-minute intervals

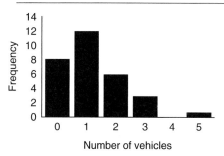

Exercise 4.2

(a) The sum of the average radiation concentrations for all three species of fish has no useful interpretation.
(b) It would be better to produce a multiple bar chart as shown below.

Average concentration of beta radiation in 3 species
of fish in the Sellafield (off-shore) area

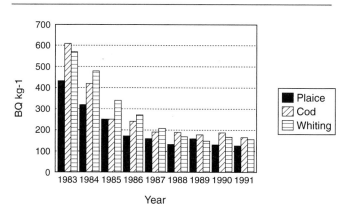

Exercise 4.3

(a)

Water quality	Sub-region		
	North	*South*	*Total*
Good	6	9	15
Fair	4	4	8
Poor	1	1	2
Bad	1	0	1
Total	12	14	26

(b)

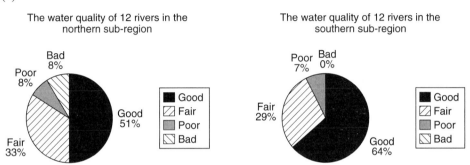

The water quality of 12 rivers in the northern sub-region

The water quality of 12 rivers in the southern sub-region

(c)

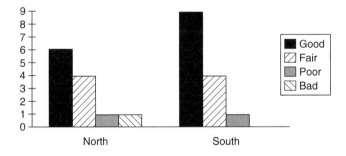

The water quality of specimens from rivers in the northern and southern areas of Westshire water

219

Exercise 4.4

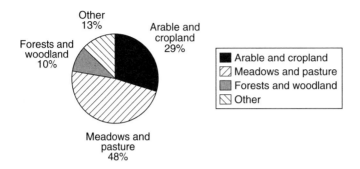

Land use in the UK (1988)

Other 13%

Forests and woodland 10%

Arable and cropland 29%

Meadows and pasture 48%

- Arable and cropland
- Meadows and pasture
- Forests and woodland
- Other

Exercise 4.5

(a) Nitrate concentrations (mg/1 N) for water samples taken from the rivers Dee and Taff

Dee					Taff							
			1.2	0								
7	5	2	**1.3**	3	4							
			1.4	0	1	2	4	5	8	8		
	8	3	**1.5**	0	2	7						
9	8	6	5	**1.6**	3	5	7					
	9	4	**1.7**	1	3							
	8	6	**1.8**									
8	6	4	1	**1.9**	0	3						
		4	**2.0**									
		1	**2.1**									

(b) **River Dee**

Nitrate level	Frequency	Relative frequency
1.3 to under 1.5	3	3
1.5 to under 1.7	6	6
1.7 to under 1.9	4	4
1.9 to under 2.2	6	4

River Taff

Nitrate level	Frequency	Relative frequency
1.2 to under 1.4	3	3
1.4 to under 1.6	10	10
1.6 to under 1.8	5	5
1.8 to under 2.0	2	2

(c) The histograms below suggest that the nitrate concentration tends to be a little lower in the river Taff than the river Dee. The concentrations also seem to be more variable in the river Dee.

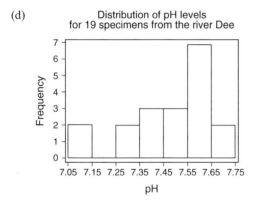

Distribution of nitrate levels (mg/l N)
for 19 specimens from the river Dee

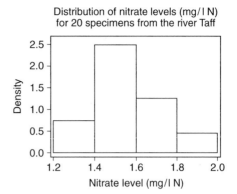

Distribution of nitrate levels (mg/l N)
for 20 specimens from the river Taff

(d)

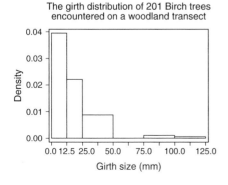

Distribution of pH levels
for 19 specimens from the river Dee

Exercise 4.6

The histograms show that for this transect, the most common scenario is for both Birch and Rowan trees to be small with a girth of under 12.5 mm. The distribution of trees larger than this is much scarcer for Rowan trees than it is for Birch trees.

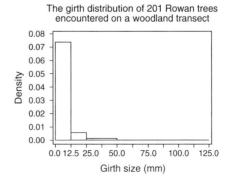

The girth distribution of 201 Birch trees
encountered on a woodland transect

The girth distribution of 201 Rowan trees
encountered on a woodland transect

Exercise 4.7

(a) The rise in share values is quite modest (up 30p from £1.70 to £2.00), however the graph makes the rise look dramatic. The reason is that the vertical axis starts at £1.70. The vertical axis should start at £0.00.

(b) This is supposed to be a histogram as the salary is a continuous variable. To draw the graph correctly:

    (i) The width of each bar should represent the width of each class interval.

    (ii) There should be no spaces between the bars.

Exercises 4.8–4.11

Solutions as for hand-drawn exercises.

Exercises 5

Exercise 5.1

The reader should read the chapter again if they are not sure of the advantages and disadvantages of the various measures.

Exercise 5.2

(a) Mean = £477.14; sample standard deviation = £672.05

(b) Median = £240; Q1 = £200, Q3 = £260, so IQR = £260 − £200 = £60

(c) Mean (£200), and sample standard deviation (£28.28) drop substantially.
Median (£220) and IQR (£40) are not reduced anywhere near so much. This shows that the median and IQR are not influenced by extreme values as much as the mean or the standard deviation.

Exercise 5.3

Overall, SO_2 levels tend to be higher in town 2 than in town 1. They are also less variable. Because the mean SO_2 level is higher than the median SO_2 level for both towns, we know that the SO_2 levels for both towns follow a positively skewed distribution. (Particularly true for the levels in town 1.)

Exercise 5.4

(a) pH levels: mean = 7.9474; sample s.d. = 0.0964

(b) Nitrate concentrations: mean = 1.5411 mg/l N; sample s.d. = 0.1913 mg/l N

(c) The sample standard deviations are based upon measurements made on completely different measurement scales, so they cannot be compared.

(d) Coefficients of variation: pH, 1.21%; nitrate, 12.42%. Neither the pH nor the nitrate concentrations vary greatly, but the pH levels are certainly far more constant than the nitrate concentrations.

Exercise 5.5

(a) Using a frequency distribution, the correct midpoints (µm) are 3.45, 4.45, 5.45 etc. The resulting estimates are then: mean = 5.5851 µm; sample standard deviation = 1.2945 µm.
(b) From an ogive, the median estimate should be around 5.45 µm.
(c) (i) Fine silt; (ii) around 35%.
(d) Sample mean = 5.47 µm; sample standard deviation = 1.2494 µm.

Exercise 5.6

Computer exercises.

Exercises 6

Exercise 6.1

(a) 0.2461   (b) 0.0439   (c) 0.0439
(d) 0.0010   (e) 0.0547   (f) 0.6563

Exercise 6.2

(a) 0.0473   (b) 5.9×10^{-6} (c) 0.0282   (d) 0.1029
(e) Assumes that the tutorial group is a random sample of students and their opinions are independent.

Exercise 6.3

(a) We can assume a Poisson distribution is a good approximation to the binomial distribution since n is large (200) and $p = 0.001$ is small with $np = 2$. We are also assuming that the chances of individuals getting an ear infection are independent.
(b) 0.1353
(c) 0.4060

Exercise 6.4

(a) 0.5   (b) 0.74857   (c) 0.90824   (d) 0.74857
(e) 0.25143   (f) 0.15866   (g) 0.37787

Exercise 6.5

(a) −2.040, 0.113, −0.799, 0.182, −0.511, 0.319, −0.274, 0.525, 0.049, 0.723
(b) Mean = −0.1717; SD = 0.8019
(c) −1.74 to 1.40
(d) 0.175 to 4.055

Exercises 7

Exercise 7.1

(a) Mean is 1.043, standard error is 0.1842
(b) 0.626 to 1.460
(c) 0.445 to 1.641

Exercise 7.2

(a) 5.52 to 7.48
(b) (a) 0.3085
    (b) 0.1587

Exercise 7.3

(a) 330.2 to 767.4
(b) That there is a probability of 0.95 that the range from 330.2 to 767.4 g/100 miles contains the average emission of CO from all vehicles.
(c) 12

Exercise 7.4

(a) 0.17 to −0.85
(b) The reduction was 0.34 ppm and this is 33% of 1.043 but is only an estimate based on a sample of 10 in the first year and 20 in the second year. The 95% confidence interval for the **true** reduction ranges from an increase of 0.17 ppm to a decrease of 0.85 ppm. This range contains zero, thus there is no evidence of a decrease in mercury levels.

Exercise 7.5

(a) (i) 76.924 ppb to 82.076 ppb   (ii) 70.212 ppb to 78.188 ppb
(b) 1.60 ppb to 9.00 ppb

Exercise 7.6

$P = 55\%$, s.e.$(p) = 3.518\%$, 48.1% to 61.9%

Exercise 7.7

−0.56% to 16.56%. As this range includes zero, the difference is not quite statistically significant.

Exercises 8

Exercise 8.1

(a) There is a significant difference at the 1% level.
(b) 1.063 to 5.562

Exercise 8.2

(a) A paired t-test is appropriate as the readings are taken from the same months at each site.

H_0: There is no difference in the average maximum total phosphorus at the two sites.
H_1: There is a difference in the average maximum total phosphorus at the two sites.

(b) $t = 3.838$. Reject H_0 at the 1% significance level.
(*N.B.* Using MINITAB or EXCEL gives an exact p-value of 0.0028.)

Exercise 8.3

(a) One-tailed, paired t-test for each site.

Site 1: $t = 0.20$. No significant change.
Site 2: $t = 1.79$. No significant change.

(b) One-tailed, paired t-test. $t = 2.88$. Site 2 has a significantly higher level in 1987/88 ($p < 0.01$).
(*N.B.* Using MINITAB or EXCEL gives an exact p-value of 0.0075.)

Exercise 8.4

(a) Means $= 24.00$ and 32.67; standard deviations $= 8.00$ and 13.78
(b) One-tailed unpaired t-test. $t = 2.25$. There has been a significant increase from Month 1 to Month 2 ($p < 0.05$).
(*N.B.* Using MINITAB or EXCEL gives an the exact p-value of 0.024.)
(c) s.e. $= 3.776$

Exercise 8.5

Two-tailed unpaired t-test. $t = 3.988$. There is a significant difference between the CO^2 levels on the two floors ($p < 0.001$).

Exercises 9

Exercise 9.1

$p = 0.065$, so we accept the null hypothesis that the median level is 15. A non-parametric test is appropriate as the data appears to be skewed with many zero values and a few high values.

Exercise 9.2

$p = 0.039$. Therefore we reject the null hypothesis that there is no overall preference for either proposal. Note, it is estimated that 2 in 12, or 83%, prefer P.

Exercise 9.3

$T^- = 10.5$ and $T^+ = 34.5$. Thus the test-statistic is 10.5. The critical value (one-tailed test) is 8 ($n = 9$). Hence we accept the null hypothesis that there has been no change in the levels of hydrocarbons between 1991 and 1995.

Exercise 9.4

(a) Wilcoxon signed ranks test.
(b) p-value $= 0.003$. We thus conclude that there is a significant difference ($p = 0.003$) between the medians of the maximum total phosphorus levels at the two sites. Note that the difference between the two medians is estimated to be 1.228 mg/l.

Exercise 9.5

$U_1 = 10$ and $U_2 = 54$, so the test-statistic is 10. The critical values (one-tailed test) are 15 (5% level) and 9 (1% level). Therefore reject null hypothesis at 5% level.

Exercise 9.6

$U_1 = 42$ and $U_2 = 58$. Test-statistic is 42. Critical value (one-tailed test) is 27 (5% level). Therefore we accept the null hypothesis of no change in the levels of hydrocarbons between 1991 and 1995.

Exercises 10

Exercise 10.1

(a) Between treatment variance is 10.11 with 2 degrees of freedom.
(b) Within treatment variance is 1.44 with 6 degrees of freedom.
(c) F-ratio is 7.0. This is significant at the 5% significance level.

(d) Area 1: 4.30 to 7.70
     Area 2: 1.30 to 4.70
     Area 3: 0.97 to 4.37

The confidence intervals are not totally conclusive as they overlap somewhat. However it is suggested that area 1 is more diverse. (This is the conclusion reached by Tukey's confidence intervals.)

Exercise 10.2

(a) Between treatment variance is 0.045 with 2 degrees of freedom.
(b) Within treatment variance is 0.009 with 12 degrees of freedom.
(c) F-ratio is 5.0 (or precisely 4.96). This is significant at the 5% significance level.

(d) Distance 1: 9.87 to 10.05
     Distance 2: 9.69 to 9.87
     Distance 3: 9.73 to 9.91

The soil is significantly more acidic near the trunk of the tree (distance 1) than at the edge of the canopy (distance 2). At neither of these points does the soil acidity differ significantly from the soil acidity beyond the influence of the tree.

Exercise 10.3

```
ANALYSIS OF VARIANCE ON pH
SOURCE    DF  SS        MS        F     p
DISTANCE  2   0.08933   0.04467   4.96 0.027
ERROR     12  0.10800   0.00900
TOTAL     14  0.19733
LEVEL   N    MEAN    STDEV  --+---------+---------+---------+-----
  1     5   9.9600  0.0894                              (--------*--------)
  2     5   9.7800  0.1095         (--------*--------)
  3     5   9.8200  0.0837              (--------*--------)
                                 --+---------+---------+---------+-----
POOLED STDEV =  0.0949           9.70      9.80      9.90      10.00
```

Tukey's pairwise comparisons

	1	2
2	0.02005	
	0.33995	
3	−0.01995	−0.19995
	0.29995	0.11995

Conclusions as for Exercise 10.2.

Exercise 10.4

```
ANALYSIS OF VARIANCE ON nitrate
SOURCE  DF  SS       MS       F      p
year    2   20.316   10.158   12.17  0.001
ERROR   15  12.520   0.835
TOTAL   17  32.836
                      INDIVIDUAL 95% CI'S FOR MEAN
                      BASED ON POOLED STDEV
LEVEL  N  MEAN    STDEV   -------+---------+---------+---------
  1    8  3.8000  0.9087  (-----*----)
  2    5  3.7200  0.6611  (------*------)
  3    5  6.1400  1.1171                           (------*------)
                          -------+---------+---------+---------
POOLED STDEV = 0.9136     3.6       4.8       6.0
```

Clearly the nitrate concentration of the soil is significantly higher in the recently coppiced woodland.

Exercise 10.5

(a) F-ratio is 0.62, suggesting no significant differences in the mean yields between the three fertilizer formulae.
(b) The fertilizer treatment F-ratio is now significant at 21.0, suggesting that the mean yields do differ between the fertilizer treatments. In particular, formula 3 seems particularly effective.

(c) Because a great deal of variability exists between the two rice varieties, the varieties need to be taken as blocks. Otherwise the fertilizer effects are masked (as we saw in part a).

Exercise 10.6

Site F-ratio is 13.03. There appears to be a trend for the ammonia contamination to increase as the river runs downstream. In particular at site 3 (30 miles downstream of the source), the contamination is significantly higher than at site 1 (the source of the river).

Exercise 10.7

A two-way ANOVA using age as a blocking factor would not be safe. This is because interaction is seen to exist. Treatment 4 seems to be the best treatment for 3-year-old trees, but the worst for 4-year-old trees, whereas the other treatments do not show this effect.

Exercises 11

Exercise 11.1

(a) The expected counts would be as shown below:

| Cancer in child? | Radiation exposure of father | | | | |
	None	Low	Medium	High	Total
Yes	6	20	10	4	40
No	24	80	40	16	160
Total	30	100	50	20	200

(b) As the expected count for highly exposed fathers having children with cancer is small, categories must be merged as follows for a chi-squared test to be safe.

| Cancer in child? | Radiation exposure of father | | | | |
	None	Low	Medium	High	Total
Yes	6	20	10	4	40
No	24	80	40	16	160
Total	30	100	50	20	200

Exercise 11.2

(a) No, the chi-squared test should not be used on tables of percentages.

(b)

Wage	Male	Female	Total
10–15	24(24)	16(16)	40
15–20	60(72)	60(48)	120
Over 20	36(24)	4(16)	40
Total	120	80	200

(The main figures are observed counts; figures in parentheses are expected counts.)
Chi-squared test-statistic $= 20$, with 2 d.f. Therefore reject H_0 at 0.1% significance level.

Exercise 11.3

The chi-squared statistic (using Yates' correction) is 773.15, with 1 d.f. Therefore reject H_0 at a very high level of significance. Clearly the mortality rate was significantly lower in patients who had been vaccinated.

Exercise 11.4

(a) The mean number of incidents, $m = 0.8$. This produces the following table of observed and theoretical incidents

Number of incidents	Observed frequency	Theoretical Poisson frequency
0	55	53.9195
1	42	43.1356
2	16	17.2542
3 or more	7	5.6907

This results in a chi-squared test-statistic of 0.444 with 2 degrees of freedom. As the critical value for a 5% test is 5.99, we **do not reject H_0**, i.e. the number of incidents each year does appear to follow a Poisson distribution.

(b) If accidents are equally likely on any day of the week then we would expect $96/7 = 13.7143$ incidents for each day. Carrying out a chi-squared test on this basis a chi-squared test-statistic of 2.2917 is obtained with 6 degrees of freedom. So we **do not reject H_0 at the 5% significance level**.

Exercise 11.5

Chi-squared test-statistic is 100.63 with 6 degrees of freedom. This means there is very strong evidence to **reject H_0**, i.e. there **is** a relationship between the levels of lead and zinc in the soil samples. Usually high levels of one metal are found in conjunction with high levels of the other metal.

Exercise 11.6

Using the mean of 6.9479 and the standard deviation of 0.6805 provided, the following table of observed and expected values.

pH level	Observed number of lakes	Theoretical normal frequencies
Under 6.2	10	9.656
6.2 to under 6.6	9	11.999
6.6 to under 7.0	15	25.702
7.0 to under 7.4	21	15.336
7.4 to under 7.8	9	10.508
7.8 or over	7	7.455

The resulting chi-squared statistic is 7.5542, with 3 degrees of freedom. The critical value for a 5% significance test is 7.81. Therefore we **do not reject H_0 at the 5% level of significance**.

The conclusion here is that the distribution of pHs can be taken as being approximately normally distributed.

Exercise 11.7

The test-statistic is 46.197. There are 4 degrees of freedom. Reject H_0 at the 0.1% level of significance.

Exercise 11.8

The test-statistic (using Yates' correction) is 0.9956. The critical value for a test at the 5% level of significance is 3.84. Therefore we **do not reject H_0**.

Exercises 12

Exercise 12.1

Plot a: $r_S = -1$, $r =$ close to, but not exactly -1
Plot b: r_S and r both close to zero
Plot c: r_S and r both $+1$

Exercise 12.2

(a) $r_S = -0.8581$, so a strong negative relationship, the higher the GDP, the less reliant on wood as a fuel.
(b) r_S is significant at 0.1% significance level.

Exercise 12.3

(a) Plot as below. This shows a fairly strong linear relationship, although the spread of data seems to increase, as smoke levels, or SO_2 levels, increase.

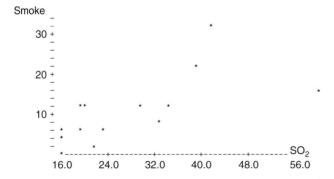

(b) $r = 0.594$, significant at 5% significance level.

Exercise 12.4

(a) Plot as below.

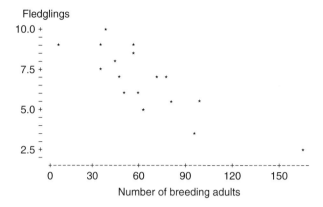

(b) The plot shows a strong negative relationship. That is, as the number of breeding pairs increases, the breeding success of each pair decreases. This is probably due to competition for food, nesting sites and shelter.

(c) $r = -0.801$, significant at 0.1% significance level.

(d) $r_S = -0.7996$, significant at 0.1% significance level.

Exercise 12.5

(a) When $x = 0$, $y = 10$

(b) When $x = 5$, $y = 30$

(c) Relationship as shown below.

Exercise 12.6

(a) Velocity $= 0.046 + 0.194$ cross-sectional area.

(b) a has no useful interpretation, a river with no cross-sectional area ceases to be a river! b means that for each extra m^2 cross-sectional area, the average velocity increases by 0.046 m/s.

(c) 0.2397 m/s

Exercise 12.7

(a) Wheat $= 3739 - 0.953$ barley

(b) Approx. 1.832 million acres

Exercise 12.8

(a) Wheat $= 3739 - 0.953$ barley

(b) If no barley was produced, 3.739 million acres would be used for wheat. For each extra acre of land used for barley, 0.953 acres less is used for wheat. The equation in fact suggests that the total wheat and barley acreage is constant.

(c) ANOVA p-value is 0.000, so the equation is extremely useful.

(d) $1.6723 - 1.9919$ million acres

(e) $r = \sqrt{0.922} = \pm 0.96$ (in fact -0.96 as relationship is inverse.)

Exercise 12.9

(a) 25 units
(b) 15 units
(c) $y = 325$ units

Exercise 12.10

(a) Volume $= -59.6 + 4.93$ height $+ 0.322$ diameter
(b) a of -59.6 has no sensible interpretation. b means that if diameter is fixed, each 1 foot increase in height leads to a $4.93\,\text{ft}^3$ increase in volume.   means that if height is fixed, each 1 inch increase in diameter leads to a $0.322\,\text{ft}^3$ increase in volume. (It could be argued that as changes in height and diameter go hand in hand, these interpretations are a little suspect.)
(c) ANOVA p-value is 0.000, so the equation is extremely useful.
(d) $23.122 - 40.606\,\text{ft}^3$

B

Appendix B:
Statistical tables

233

Table B1   Areas in the right-hand tail of the standard normal distribution

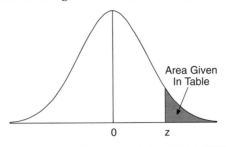

Area Given
In Table

Z	0.00	0.01	0.02	0.03	0.04	0.05	0.06	0.07	0.08	0.09
0.0	0.50000	0.49601	0.49202	0.48803	0.48405	0.48006	0.47608	0.47210	0.46812	0.46414
0.1	0.46017	0.45620	0.45224	0.44828	0.44433	0.44038	0.43644	0.43251	0.42858	0.42465
0.2	0.42074	0.41683	0.41294	0.40905	0.40517	0.40129	0.39743	0.39358	0.38974	0.38591
0.3	0.38209	0.37828	0.37448	0.37070	0.36693	0.36317	0.35942	0.35569	0.35197	0.34827
0.4	0.34458	0.34090	0.33724	0.33360	0.32997	0.32636	0.32276	0.31918	0.31561	0.31207
0.5	0.30854	0.30503	0.30153	0.29806	0.29460	0.29116	0.28774	0.28434	0.28096	0.27760
0.6	0.27425	0.27093	0.26763	0.26435	0.26109	0.25785	0.25463	0.25143	0.24825	0.24510
0.7	0.24196	0.23885	0.23576	0.23270	0.22965	0.22663	0.22363	0.22065	0.21770	0.21476
0.8	0.21186	0.20897	0.20611	0.20327	0.20045	0.19766	0.19489	0.19215	0.18943	0.18673
0.9	0.18406	0.18141	0.17879	0.17619	0.17361	0.17106	0.16853	0.16602	0.16354	0.16109
1.0	0.15866	0.15625	0.15386	0.15151	0.14917	0.14686	0.14457	0.14231	0.14007	0.13786
1.1	0.13567	0.13350	0.13136	0.12924	0.12714	0.12507	0.12302	0.12100	0.11900	0.11702
1.2	0.11507	0.11314	0.11123	0.10935	0.10749	0.10565	0.10383	0.10204	0.10027	0.09853
1.3	0.09680	0.09510	0.09342	0.09176	0.09012	0.08851	0.08692	0.08534	0.08379	0.08226
1.4	0.08076	0.07927	0.07780	0.07636	0.07493	0.07353	0.07215	0.07078	0.06944	0.06811
1.5	0.06681	0.06552	0.06426	0.06301	0.06178	0.06057	0.05938	0.05821	0.05705	0.05592
1.6	0.05480	0.05370	0.05262	0.05155	0.05050	0.04947	0.04846	0.04746	0.04648	0.04551
1.7	0.04457	0.04363	0.04272	0.04182	0.04093	0.04006	0.03920	0.03836	0.03754	0.03673
1.8	0.03593	0.03515	0.03438	0.03362	0.03288	0.03216	0.03144	0.03074	0.03005	0.02938
1.9	0.02872	0.02807	0.02743	0.02680	0.02619	0.02559	0.02500	0.02442	0.02385	0.02330
2.0	0.02275	0.02222	0.02169	0.02118	0.02068	0.02018	0.01970	0.01923	0.01876	0.01831
2.1	0.01786	0.01743	0.01700	0.01659	0.01618	0.01578	0.01539	0.01500	0.01463	0.01426
2.2	0.01390	0.01355	0.01321	0.01287	0.01255	0.01222	0.01191	0.01160	0.01130	0.01101
2.3	0.01072	0.01044	0.01017	0.00990	0.00964	0.00939	0.00914	0.00889	0.00866	0.00842
2.4	0.00820	0.00798	0.00776	0.00755	0.00734	0.00714	0.00695	0.00676	0.00657	0.00639
2.5	0.00621	0.00604	0.00587	0.00570	0.00554	0.00539	0.00523	0.00508	0.00494	0.00480
2.6	0.00466	0.00453	0.00440	0.00427	0.00415	0.00402	0.00391	0.00379	0.00368	0.00357
2.7	0.00347	0.00336	0.00326	0.00317	0.00307	0.00298	0.00289	0.00280	0.00272	0.00264
2.8	0.00256	0.00248	0.00240	0.00233	0.00226	0.00219	0.00212	0.00205	0.00199	0.00193
2.9	0.00187	0.00181	0.00175	0.00169	0.00164	0.00159	0.00154	0.00149	0.00144	0.00139
3.0	0.00135									
3.1	0.00097									
3.2	0.00069									
3.3	0.00048									
3.4	0.00034									
3.5	0.00023									
3.6	0.00016									
3.7	0.00011									
3.8	0.00007									
3.9	0.00005									
4.0	0.00003									

Table B2   Percentage points of the *t*-distribution

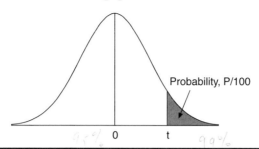

Probability, P/100

	1-tailed percentage, P						
	10%	5%	2.5%	1%	0.5%	0.1%	0.05%
				2-tailed percentage			
df	20%	10%	5%	2%	1%	0.2%	0.1%
1	3.0777	6.3137	12.7062	31.8210	63.6559	318.2888	636.5776
2	1.8856	2.9200	4.3027	6.9645	9.9250	22.3285	31.5998
3	1.6377	2.3534	3.1824	4.5407	5.8408	10.2143	12.9244
4	1.5332	2.1318	2.7765	3.7469	4.6041	7.1729	8.6101
5	1.4759	2.0150	2.5706	3.3649	4.0321	5.8935	6.8685
6	1.4398	1.9432	2.4469	3.1427	3.7074	5.2075	5.9587
7	1.4149	1.8946	2.3646	2.9979	3.4995	4.7853	5.4081
8	1.3968	1.8595	2.3060	2.8965	3.3554	4.5008	5.0414
9	1.3830	1.8331	2.2622	2.8214	3.2498	4.2969	4.7809
10	1.3722	1.8125	2.2281	2.7638	3.1693	4.1437	4.5868
11	1.3634	1.7959	2.2010	2.7181	3.1058	4.0248	4.4369
12	1.3562	1.7823	2.1788	2.6810	3.0545	3.9296	4.3178
13	1.3502	1.7709	2.1604	2.6503	3.0123	3.8520	4.2209
14	1.3450	1.7613	2.1448	2.6245	2.9768	3.7874	4.1403
15	1.3406	1.7531	2.1315	2.6025	2.9467	3.7329	4.0728
16	1.3368	1.7459	2.1199	2.5835	2.9208	3.6861	4.0149
17	1.3334	1.7396	2.1098	2.5669	2.8982	3.6458	3.9651
18	1.3304	1.7341	2.1009	2.5524	2.8784	3.6105	3.9217
19	1.3277	1.7291	2.0930	2.5395	2.8609	3.5793	3.8833
20	1.3253	1.7247	2.0860	2.5280	2.8453	3.5518	3.8496
21	1.3232	1.7207	2.0796	2.5176	2.8314	3.5271	3.8193
22	1.3212	1.7171	2.0739	2.5083	2.8188	3.5050	3.7922
23	1.3195	1.7139	2.0687	2.4999	2.8073	3.4850	3.7676
24	1.3178	1.7109	2.0639	2.4922	2.7970	3.4668	3.7454
25	1.3163	1.7081	2.0595	2.4851	2.7874	3.4502	3.7251
26	1.3150	1.7056	2.0555	2.4786	2.7787	3.4350	3.7067
27	1.3137	1.7033	2.0518	2.4727	2.7707	3.4210	3.6895
28	1.3125	1.7011	2.0484	2.4671	2.7633	3.4082	3.6739
29	1.3114	1.6991	2.0452	2.4620	2.7564	3.3963	3.6595
30	1.3104	1.6973	2.0423	2.4573	2.7500	3.3852	3.6460
35	1.3062	1.6896	2.0301	2.4377	2.7238	3.3400	3.5911
40	1.3031	1.6839	2.0211	2.4233	2.7045	3.3069	3.5510
45	1.3007	1.6794	2.0141	2.4121	2.6896	3.2815	3.5203

Table B2 Percentage points of the *t*-distribution (continued)

df	10%	5%	2.5%	1%	0.5%	0.1%	0.05%
			1-tailed percentage, *P*				
	20%	10%	5%	2%	1%	0.2%	0.1%
			2-tailed percentage				
50	1.2987	1.6759	2.0086	2.4033	2.6778	3.2614	3.4960
60	1.2958	1.6706	2.0003	2.3901	2.6603	3.2317	3.4602
70	1.2938	1.6669	1.9944	2.3808	2.6479	3.2108	3.4350
80	1.2922	1.6641	1.9901	2.3739	2.6387	3.1952	3.4164
100	1.2901	1.6602	1.9840	2.3642	2.6259	3.1738	3.3905
120	1.2886	1.6576	1.9799	2.3578	2.6174	3.1595	3.3734
150	1.2872	1.6551	1.9759	2.3515	2.6090	3.1455	3.3565
infinity	1.2816	1.6449	1.9600	2.3263	2.5758	3.0902	3.2905

Table B3 Percentage points of the F-distribution

df 2 (denominator df)	significance level, P	1	2	3	4	5	6	7	8	9	10	12	20	infinity
							df 1 (numerator df)							
2	5%	18.51	19.00	19.16	19.25	19.30	19.33	19.35	19.37	19.38	19.40	19.41	19.45	19.50
	1%	98.50	99.00	99.16	99.25	99.30	99.33	99.36	99.38	99.39	99.40	99.42	99.45	99.50
	0.1%	998.38	998.84	999.31	999.31	999.31	999.31	999.31	999.31	999.31	999.31	999.31	999.31	999.31
3	5%	10.13	9.55	9.28	9.12	9.01	8.94	8.89	8.85	8.81	8.79	8.74	8.66	8.53
	1%	34.12	30.82	29.46	28.71	28.24	27.91	27.67	27.49	27.34	27.23	27.05	26.69	26.13
	0.1%	167.06	148.49	141.10	137.08	134.58	132.83	131.61	130.62	129.86	129.22	128.32	126.43	123.46
4	5%	7.71	6.94	6.59	6.39	6.26	6.16	6.09	6.04	6.00	5.96	5.91	5.80	5.63
	1%	21.20	18.00	16.69	15.98	15.52	15.21	14.98	14.80	14.66	14.55	14.37	14.02	13.46
	0.1%	74.13	61.25	56.17	53.43	51.72	50.52	49.65	49.00	48.47	48.05	47.41	46.10	44.05
5	5%	6.61	5.79	5.41	5.19	5.05	4.95	4.88	4.82	4.77	4.74	4.68	4.56	4.37
	1%	16.26	13.27	12.06	11.39	10.97	10.67	10.46	10.29	10.16	10.05	9.89	9.55	9.02
	0.1%	47.18	37.12	33.20	31.08	29.75	28.83	28.17	27.65	27.24	26.91	26.42	25.39	23.79
6	5%	5.99	5.14	4.76	4.53	4.39	4.28	4.21	4.15	4.10	4.06	4.00	3.87	3.67
	1%	13.75	10.92	9.78	9.15	8.75	8.47	8.26	8.10	7.98	7.87	7.72	7.40	6.88
	0.10%	35.51	27.00	23.71	21.92	20.80	20.03	19.46	19.03	18.69	18.41	17.99	17.12	15.75
7	5%	5.59	4.74	4.35	4.12	3.97	3.87	3.79	3.73	3.68	3.64	3.57	3.44	3.23
	1%	12.25	9.55	8.45	7.85	7.46	7.19	6.99	6.84	6.72	6.62	6.47	6.16	5.65
	0.10%	29.25	21.69	18.77	17.20	16.21	15.52	15.02	14.63	14.33	14.08	13.71	12.93	11.70
8	5%	5.32	4.46	4.07	3.84	3.69	3.58	3.50	3.44	3.39	3.35	3.28	3.15	2.93
	1%	11.26	8.65	7.59	7.01	6.63	6.37	6.18	6.03	5.91	5.81	5.67	5.36	4.86
	0.10%	25.41	18.49	15.83	14.39	13.48	12.86	12.40	12.05	11.77	11.54	11.19	10.48	9.33
9	5%	5.12	4.26	3.86	3.63	3.48	3.37	3.29	3.23	3.18	3.14	3.07	2.94	2.71
	1%	10.56	8.02	6.99	6.42	6.06	5.80	5.61	5.47	5.35	5.26	5.11	4.81	4.31
	0.10%	22.86	16.39	13.90	12.56	11.71	11.13	10.70	10.37	10.11	9.89	9.57	8.90	7.81
10	5%	4.96	4.10	3.71	3.48	3.33	3.22	3.14	3.07	3.02	2.98	2.91	2.77	2.54
	1%	10.04	7.56	6.55	5.99	5.64	5.39	5.20	5.06	4.94	4.85	4.71	4.41	3.91
	0.10%	21.04	14.90	12.55	11.28	10.48	9.93	9.52	9.20	8.96	8.75	8.45	7.80	6.76

Table B3 Percentage points of the F-distribution (continued)

df 2 (denominator df)	significance level, P	df 1 (numerator df)												
		1	2	3	4	5	6	7	8	9	10	12	20	infinity
11	5%	4.84	3.98	3.59	3.36	3.20	3.09	3.01	2.95	2.90	2.85	2.79	2.65	2.40
	1%	9.65	7.21	6.22	5.67	5.32	5.07	4.89	4.74	4.63	4.54	4.40	4.10	3.60
	0.1%	19.69	13.81	11.56	10.35	9.58	9.05	8.65	8.35	8.12	7.92	7.63	7.01	6.00
12	5%	4.75	3.89	3.49	3.26	3.11	3.00	2.91	2.85	2.80	2.75	2.69	2.54	2.30
	1%	9.33	6.93	5.95	5.41	5.06	4.82	4.64	4.50	4.39	4.30	4.16	3.86	3.36
	0.1%	18.64	12.97	10.80	9.63	8.89	8.38	8.00	7.71	7.48	7.29	7.00	6.40	5.42
13	5%	4.67	3.81	3.41	3.18	3.03	2.92	2.83	2.77	2.71	2.67	2.60	2.46	2.21
	1%	9.07	6.70	5.74	5.21	4.86	4.62	4.44	4.30	4.19	4.10	3.96	3.66	3.17
	0.1%	17.82	12.31	10.21	9.07	8.35	7.86	7.49	7.21	6.98	6.80	6.52	5.93	4.97
14	5%	4.60	3.74	3.34	3.11	2.96	2.85	2.76	2.70	2.65	2.60	2.53	2.39	2.13
	1%	8.86	6.51	5.56	5.04	4.69	4.46	4.28	4.14	4.03	3.94	3.80	3.51	3.00
	0.1%	17.14	11.78	9.73	8.62	7.92	7.44	7.08	6.80	6.58	6.40	6.13	5.56	4.60
16	5%	4.49	3.63	3.24	3.01	2.85	2.74	2.66	2.59	2.54	2.49	2.42	2.28	2.01
	1%	8.53	6.23	5.29	4.77	4.44	4.20	4.03	3.89	3.78	3.69	3.55	3.26	2.75
	0.1%	16.12	10.97	9.01	7.94	7.27	6.80	6.46	6.20	5.98	5.81	5.55	4.99	4.06
18	5%	4.41	3.55	3.16	2.93	2.77	2.66	2.58	2.51	2.46	2.41	2.34	2.19	1.92
	1%	8.29	6.01	5.09	4.58	4.25	4.01	3.84	3.71	3.60	3.51	3.37	3.08	2.57
	0.1%	15.38	10.39	8.49	7.46	6.81	6.35	6.02	5.76	5.56	5.39	5.13	4.59	3.67
20	5%	4.35	3.49	3.10	2.87	2.71	2.60	2.51	2.45	2.39	2.35	2.28	2.12	1.84
	1%	8.10	5.85	4.94	4.43	4.10	3.87	3.70	3.56	3.46	3.37	3.23	2.94	2.42
	0.1%	14.82	9.95	8.10	7.10	6.46	6.02	5.69	5.44	5.24	5.08	4.82	4.29	3.38
25	5%	4.24	3.39	2.99	2.76	2.60	2.49	2.40	2.34	2.28	2.24	2.16	2.01	1.71
	1%	7.77	5.57	4.68	4.18	3.85	3.63	3.46	3.32	3.22	3.13	2.99	2.70	2.17
	0.1%	13.88	9.22	7.45	6.49	5.89	5.46	5.15	4.91	4.71	4.56	4.31	3.79	2.89
30	5%	4.17	3.32	2.92	2.69	2.53	2.42	2.33	2.27	2.21	2.16	2.09	1.93	1.62
	1%	7.56	5.39	4.51	4.02	3.70	3.47	3.30	3.17	3.07	2.98	2.84	2.55	2.01
	0.1%	13.29	8.77	7.05	6.12	5.53	5.12	4.82	4.58	4.39	4.24	4.00	3.49	2.59
40	5%	4.08	3.23	2.84	2.61	2.45	2.34	2.25	2.18	2.12	2.08	2.00	1.84	1.51
	1%	7.31	5.18	4.31	3.83	3.51	3.29	3.12	2.99	2.89	2.80	2.66	2.37	1.80
	0.1%	12.61	8.25	6.59	5.70	5.13	4.73	4.44	4.21	4.02	3.87	3.64	3.15	2.23

60	5%	4.00	3.15	2.76	2.53	2.37	2.25	2.17	2.10	2.04	1.99	1.92	1.75	1.39
	1%	7.08	4.98	4.13	3.65	3.34	3.12	2.95	2.82	2.72	2.63	2.50	2.20	1.60
	0.1%	11.97	7.77	6.17	5.31	4.76	4.37	4.09	3.86	3.69	3.54	3.32	2.83	1.89
100	5%	3.94	3.09	2.70	2.46	2.31	2.19	2.10	2.03	1.97	1.93	1.85	1.68	1.28
	1%	6.90	4.82	3.98	3.51	3.21	2.99	2.82	2.69	2.59	2.50	2.37	2.07	1.43
	0.1%	11.50	7.41	5.86	5.02	4.48	4.11	3.83	3.61	3.44	3.30	3.07	2.59	1.62
Infinity	5%	3.84	3.00	2.60	2.37	2.21	2.10	2.01	1.94	1.88	1.83	1.75	1.57	1.00
	1%	6.63	4.61	3.78	3.32	3.02	2.80	2.64	2.51	2.41	2.32	2.18	1.88	1.00
	0.1%	10.83	6.91	5.42	4.62	4.10	3.74	3.47	3.27	3.10	2.96	2.74	2.27	1.00

Table B4 Percentage points of the Mann–Whitney distribution

		1-tailed percentage						1-tailed percentage						1-tailed percentage			
		5%	2.5%	1%	0.5%			5%	2.5%	1%	0.5%			5%	2.5%	1%	0.5%
		2-tailed percentage						2-tailed percentage						2-tailed percentage			
n1	n2	10%	5%	2%	1%	n1	n2	10%	5%	2%	1%	n1	n2	10%	5%	2%	1%
4	4	1	0	–	–	7	13	24	20	16	13	12	12	42	37	31	27
	5	2	1	0	–		14	26	22	17	15		13	47	41	35	31
	6	3	2	1	0		15	28	24	19	16		14	51	45	38	34
	7	4	3	1	0		16	30	26	21	18		15	56	49	42	37
	8	5	4	2	1		17	33	28	23	19		16	60	53	46	41
	9	6	4	3	1		18	35	30	24	21		17	64	57	49	44
	10	7	5	3	2		19	37	32	26	22		18	68	61	53	47
	11	8	6	4	2		20	39	34	28	24		19	72	65	56	51
	12	9	7	5	3	8	8	15	13	9	7		20	77	69	60	54
4	13	10	8	5	3		9	18	15	11	9	13	13	51	45	39	34
	14	11	9	6	4		10	20	17	13	11		14	56	50	43	38
	15	12	10	7	5		11	23	19	15	13		15	61	54	47	42
	16	14	11	7	5		12	26	22	17	15		16	65	59	51	45
	17	15	11	8	6		13	28	24	20	17		17	70	63	55	49
	18	16	12	9	6		14	31	26	22	18		18	75	67	59	53
	19	17	13	9	7		15	33	29	24	20		19	80	72	63	57
	20	18	14	10	8		16	36	31	26	22		20	84	76	67	60
5	5	4	2	1	0		17	39	34	28	24	14	14	61	56	47	42
	6	5	3	2	1		18	41	36	30	26		15	66	59	51	46
	7	6	5	3	1		19	44	38	32	28		16	71	64	56	50
	8	8	6	4	2		20	47	41	34	30		17	77	69	60	54
	9	9	7	5	3	9	9	21	17	14	11		18	82	74	65	58
	10	11	8	6	4		10	24	20	16	13		19	87	78	69	63
	11	12	9	7	5		11	27	23	18	16		20	92	83	73	67
	12	13	11	8	6		12	30	26	21	18	15	15	72	64	56	51
5	13	15	12	9	7		13	33	28	23	20		16	77	70	61	55
	14	16	13	10	7		14	36	31	26	22		17	83	75	66	60
	15	18	14	11	8		15	39	34	28	24		18	88	80	70	64
	16	19	15	12	9		16	42	37	31	27		19	94	85	75	69
	17	20	17	13	10		17	45	39	33	29		20	100	90	80	73
	18	22	18	14	11		18	48	42	36	31	16	16	83	75	66	60
	19	23	19	15	12		19	51	45	38	33		17	89	81	71	65
	20	25	20	16	13		20	54	48	40	36		18	95	86	76	70
6	6	7	5	3	2	10	10	27	23	19	16		19	101	92	82	74
	7	8	6	4	3		11	31	26	22	18		20	107	98	87	79
	8	10	8	6	4		12	34	29	24	21	17	17	96	87	77	70
	9	12	10	7	5		13	37	33	27	24		18	102	93	82	75
	10	14	11	8	6		14	41	36	30	26		19	109	99	88	81
	11	16	13	9	7		15	44	39	33	29		20	115	105	93	86
	12	17	14	11	9		16	48	42	36	31	18	18	109	99	88	81
6	13	19	16	12	10		17	51	45	38	34		19	116	106	94	87
	14	21	17	13	11		18	55	48	41	37		20	123	112	100	92
	15	23	19	15	12		19	58	52	44	39	19	19	123	113	101	93
	16	25	21	16	13		20	62	55	47	42		20	130	119	107	99
	17	26	22	18	15	11	11	34	30	25	21	20	20	138	127	114	105
	18	28	24	19	16		12	38	33	28	24						
	19	30	25	20	17		13	42	37	31	27						
	20	32	27	22	18		14	46	40	34	30						
7	7	11	8	6	4		15	50	44	37	33						
	8	13	10	7	6		16	54	47	41	36						
	9	15	12	9	7		17	57	51	44	39						
	10	17	14	11	9		18	61	55	47	42						
	11	19	16	12	10		19	65	58	50	45						
	12	21	18	14	12		20	69	62	53	48						

Table B5   Percentage points of Wilcoxon's signed rank distribution

	1-tailed percentage			
	5%	2.5%	1%	0.5%
	2-tailed percentage			
Sample size, n	10%	5%	2%	1%
6	2	0	–	–
7	3	2	0	–
8	5	3	1	0
9	8	5	3	1
10	10	8	5	3
11	13	10	7	5
12	17	13	9	7
13	21	17	12	9
14	25	21	15	12
15	30	25	19	15
16	35	29	23	19
17	41	34	27	23
18	47	40	32	27
19	53	46	37	32
20	60	52	43	37
21	67	58	49	42
22	75	65	55	48
23	83	73	62	54
24	91	81	69	61
25	100	89	76	68
26	110	98	84	75
27	119	107	92	83
28	130	116	101	91
29	140	126	110	100
30	151	137	120	109
31	163	147	130	118
32	175	159	140	128
33	187	170	151	138
34	200	182	162	148
35	213	195	173	159
40	286	264	238	220
45	371	343	312	291
50	466	434	397	373

Table B6 Percentage points of the χ^2-distribution

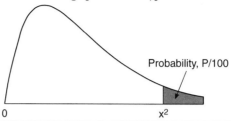

Probability, P/100

0   x^2

df	Significance level, P			
	10%	5%	1%	0.1%
1	2.706	3.841	6.635	10.827
2	4.605	5.991	9.210	13.815
3	6.251	7.815	11.345	16.266
4	7.779	9.488	13.277	18.466
5	9.236	11.070	15.086	20.515
6	10.645	12.592	16.812	22.457
7	12.017	14.067	18.475	24.321
8	13.362	15.507	20.090	26.124
9	14.684	16.919	21.666	27.877
10	15.987	18.307	23.209	29.588
11	17.275	19.675	24.725	31.264
12	18.549	21.026	26.217	32.909
13	19.812	22.362	27.688	34.527
14	21.064	23.685	29.141	36.124
15	22.307	24.996	30.578	37.698
16	23.542	26.296	32.000	39.252
17	24.769	27.587	33.409	40.791
18	25.989	28.869	34.805	42.312
19	27.204	30.144	36.191	43.819
20	28.412	31.410	37.566	45.314
21	29.615	32.671	38.932	46.796
22	30.813	33.924	40.289	48.268
23	32.007	35.172	41.638	49.728
24	33.196	36.415	42.980	51.179
25	34.382	37.652	44.314	52.619
26	35.563	38.885	45.642	54.051
27	36.741	40.113	46.963	55.475
28	37.916	41.337	48.278	56.892
29	39.087	42.557	49.588	58.301
30	40.256	43.773	50.892	59.702
35	46.059	49.802	57.342	66.619
40	51.805	55.758	63.691	73.403
45	57.505	61.656	69.957	80.078
50	63.167	67.505	76.154	86.660
55	68.796	73.311	82.292	93.167
60	74.397	79.082	88.379	99.608
70	85.527	90.531	100.425	112.317
80	96.578	101.879	112.329	124.839
90	107.565	113.145	124.116	137.208
100	118.498	124.342	135.807	149.449

Table B7 Percentage points of Pearson's correlation coefficient

Sample size, n	Significance level				Sample size, n	Significance level			
	10%	5%	2%	1%		10%	5%	2%	1%
3	0.9877	0.9969	0.9995	0.9999	30	0.3061	0.3610	0.4226	0.4629
4	0.9000	0.9500	0.9800	0.9900	32	0.2960	0.3494	0.4093	0.4487
5	0.8054	0.8783	0.9343	0.9587	34	0.2869	0.3388	0.3972	0.4357
6	0.7293	0.8114	0.8822	0.9172	36	0.2785	0.3291	0.3862	0.4238
7	0.6694	0.7545	0.8329	0.8745	38	0.2709	0.3202	0.3760	0.4128
8	0.6215	0.7067	0.7887	0.8343	40	0.2638	0.3120	0.3665	0.4026
9	0.5822	0.6664	0.7498	0.7977	42	0.2573	0.3044	0.3578	0.3932
10	0.5494	0.6319	0.7155	0.7646	44	0.2512	0.2973	0.3496	0.3843
11	0.5214	0.6021	0.6851	0.7348	46	0.2455	0.2907	0.3420	0.3761
12	0.4973	0.5760	0.6581	0.7079	48	0.2403	0.2845	0.3348	0.3683
13	0.4762	0.5529	0.6339	0.6835	50	0.2353	0.2787	0.3281	0.3610
14	0.4575	0.5324	0.6120	0.6614	52	0.2306	0.2732	0.3218	0.3542
15	0.4409	0.5140	0.5923	0.6411	54	0.2262	0.2681	0.3158	0.3477
16	0.4259	0.4973	0.5742	0.6226	56	0.2221	0.2632	0.3102	0.3415
17	0.4124	0.4821	0.5577	0.6055	58	0.2181	0.2586	0.3048	0.3357
18	0.4000	0.4683	0.5425	0.5897	60	0.2144	0.2542	0.2997	0.3301
19	0.3887	0.4555	0.5285	0.5751	62	0.2108	0.2500	0.2948	0.3248
20	0.3783	0.4438	0.5155	0.5614	64	0.2075	0.2461	0.2902	0.3198
21	0.3687	0.4329	0.5034	0.5487	66	0.2042	0.2423	0.2856	0.3150
22	0.3598	0.4227	0.4921	0.5368	68	0.2012	0.2387	0.2816	0.3104
23	0.3513	0.4132	0.4815	0.5256	70	0.1982	0.2352	0.2776	0.3060
24	0.3438	0.4044	0.4716	0.5151	80	0.1852	0.2199	0.2597	0.2864
25	0.3365	0.3961	0.4622	0.5052	90	0.1745	0.2072	0.2449	0.2702
26	0.3297	0.3882	0.4534	0.4958	100	0.1654	0.1966	0.2324	0.2565
27	0.3233	0.3809	0.4451	0.4869	110	0.1576	0.1874	0.2216	0.2446
28	0.3172	0.3739	0.4372	0.4785	120	0.1509	0.1793	0.2122	0.2343
29	0.3115	0.3673	0.4297	0.4705					

Table B8 Percentage points of Spearman's rank correlation coefficient

Sample size, n	Significance level			
	10%	5%	2%	1%
5	0.9000	1.0000	1.0000	1.0000
6	0.8286	0.8857	0.9429	1.0000
7	0.7143	0.7857	0.8929	0.9286
8	0.6429	0.7381	0.8333	0.8810
9	0.6000	0.7000	0.7833	0.8333
10	0.5636	0.6485	0.7455	0.7939
11	0.5364	0.6182	0.7091	0.7545
12	0.5035	0.5874	0.6783	0.7273
13	0.4835	0.5604	0.6484	0.7033
14	0.4637	0.5385	0.6264	0.6791
15	0.4464	0.5214	0.6036	0.6536
16	0.4294	0.5029	0.5824	0.6353
17	0.4142	0.4877	0.5662	0.6176
18	0.4014	0.4716	0.5501	0.5996
19	0.3912	0.4596	0.5351	0.5842
20	0.3805	0.4466	0.5218	0.5699
21	0.3701	0.4364	0.5091	0.5558
22	0.3608	0.4252	0.4975	0.5438
23	0.3528	0.4160	0.4862	0.5316
24	0.3443	0.4070	0.4757	0.5209
25	0.3369	0.3977	0.4662	0.5108
26	0.3306	0.3901	0.4571	0.5009
27	0.3242	0.3828	0.4487	0.4921
28	0.3180	0.3755	0.4406	0.4833
29	0.3118	0.3685	0.4325	0.4749
30	0.3063	0.3624	0.4251	0.4670

Table B9   Random number table

62825	65129	26998	79147	98041	45859	35875	39437	36770	52430
62675	59367	00666	19395	58029	76666	17275	04714	48995	03689
50859	94993	99651	56652	83407	05250	34710	96285	20678	44384
30641	41636	17200	45973	82886	90659	67383	17101	74055	98071
08978	08817	49118	87764	22031	64708	62452	07376	98970	57110
07987	13511	25608	71948	64235	10217	84298	14526	77344	86412
58117	01297	09315	09204	34221	08687	75164	00769	53893	07457
47855	77205	31723	67795	50794	99810	63464	21102	51064	09585
35474	91856	08255	23000	02994	63709	89914	86638	80049	09649
91150	37081	71349	47190	61463	93335	14609	14723	12788	46542
41791	55037	46587	38156	44284	20703	93687	98052	36888	97762
54737	34766	47685	95818	74705	40429	47675	12059	50249	34470
15142	69117	22284	68486	33382	88434	81445	14546	21138	52978
48715	90411	59543	21326	21861	23307	14072	84665	94406	66050
70863	41325	24083	99247	80142	68441	94272	96617	93909	07390
97738	57833	48319	77612	14312	20924	32899	62205	10115	45677
99137	18468	18338	43458	53693	11275	97616	98715	42264	88048
17256	03981	50910	57696	19197	99073	53068	53104	29033	38093
20947	79788	07368	95040	07909	61866	42495	80951	74164	31591
62785	76127	83653	27376	50321	70760	92358	20525	98279	33507
06294	60186	91003	72922	00127	51235	24298	13889	77059	83134
64012	09046	54973	79435	61751	00625	61448	12029	57783	53736
45925	26385	03422	98125	16075	69605	16235	43050	79923	05596
66193	13903	64738	95066	73014	14301	51410	22292	41788	34092
17718	88769	11095	44424	58611	80861	54522	66086	37414	31974
32747	90796	58178	39562	45079	84994	29942	22351	24539	88749
29851	94105	64991	99210	95467	79735	29504	63732	98375	16167
38061	69771	45591	65709	95473	99967	01260	49820	43919	80575
13335	74584	16063	41574	03586	94907	29058	21882	32308	68538
64907	45193	95909	03724	63240	37363	11019	80653	65661	00626
99743	38843	50384	46495	20825	27879	72967	71597	08243	26249
74188	54766	40946	48663	42137	77489	35674	29876	56859	89699
67485	39186	75738	44441	94382	71945	31580	05825	19284	53161
48583	63611	24075	56237	95982	36358	78313	44482	37962	91092
95048	39107	75697	85842	14089	84858	77056	76098	27925	97537
76079	99140	74909	61679	70893	28505	88138	04640	64136	35500
39468	05134	37398	43266	39856	24735	00102	00975	78809	79204
05810	61184	55233	80168	02531	49036	65098	08354	20781	86651
37304	73426	57189	68113	80485	50561	33452	09084	04723	56846
41598	63387	47219	48888	34113	48265	05420	06199	25016	94787

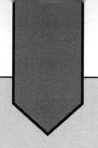

References

Department of the Environment (1992) *The UK Environment*. HMSO, London.

Foley, G. (1987) *The Energy Question*. 3rd edition, Penguin, London.

Gilbert, R.O. (1987) *Statistical Methods for Environmental Pollution Monitoring*. Van Nostrand Reinhold, New York.

Goodman, L.A. and Kruskal, V.H. (1954) Measures of association for cross classification. *J. Amer. Stat. Assoc.* **49**, 732–64.

Hampton, R.F. (1994) *Introductory Biological Statistics*. Wm C. Brown, Dubuque, Iowa.

Murphy, J. (1995) *Using Microsoft Excel 5.0 for Windows*. Houghton Mifflin, Boston, Mass., USA.

Nagari, N.K. and Brunenmeister, S.L. (1993) Estimation of trend in Chesapeake Bay water quality data, in *Multivariate Environmental Statistics* (eds G.P. Patil and C.R. Rao). North-Holland, Amsterdam, pp. 407–21.

Pelosi, M.R. (1995) *Doing Statistics with Minitab for Windows Release 10*. Wiley, New York.

Parish, H.J. (1968) *Victory with Vaccines*. Livingstone, Edinburgh.

Solomon, M.E. (1976) *Population Dynamics*, 2nd edition, Edward Arnold, London.

Sterling, E.M. *et al.* (1987) Field measurement for air quality in office buildings: a three-phased approach to diagnosing building performance problems, in *Sampling and Calibration for Atmospheric Measurements* (ed. J.K. Taylor). American Society for Testing and Materials.

Wonnacott, T.H. and Wonnacott, R.J. (1981) *Regression: A Second Course in Statistics*. Wiley, New York.

Index